Migrant Imaginaries

ITALIAN MODERNITIES

VOL. 18

Edited by
Pierpaolo Antonello and Robert Gordon,
University of Cambridge

PETER LANG
Oxford · Bern · Berlin · Bruxelles · Frankfurt am Main · New York · Wien

Migrant Imaginaries

Figures in Italian Migration Literature

Jennifer Burns

PETER LANG

Oxford · Bern · Berlin · Bruxelles · Frankfurt am Main · New York · Wien

Bibliographic information published by Die Deutsche Nationalbibliothek
Die Deutsche Nationalbibliothek lists this publication in the Deutsche
Nationalbibliografie; detailed bibliographic data is available on the Internet
at http://dnb.d-nb.de.

A catalogue record for this book is available from the British Library.

Library of Congress Control Number: 2013946003

Cover image: Donald Rodney, 'In the House of My Father, 1996-7'
© Tate, London 2013

ISSN 1662-9108
ISBN 978-3-0343-0986-8

© Peter Lang AG, International Academic Publishers, Bern 2013
Hochfeldstrasse 32, CH-3012 Bern, Switzerland
info@peterlang.com, www.peterlang.com, www.peterlang.net

All rights reserved.
All parts of this publication are protected by copyright.
Any utilisation outside the strict limits of the copyright law, without
the permission of the publisher, is forbidden and liable to prosecution.
This applies in particular to reproductions, translations, microfilming,
and storage and processing in electronic retrieval systems.

Contents

Acknowledgements — vii

Introduction — 1

CHAPTER 1
Identity — 21

CHAPTER 2
Memory — 65

CHAPTER 3
Home — 101

CHAPTER 4
Place and Space — 131

CHAPTER 5
Literature — 177

Afterword — 205

Bibliography — 209

Index — 219

Acknowledgements

The research which forms the basis of this study was facilitated by funding from the British Academy, through a Small Research Grant, and by the Arts and Humanities Research Council (AHRC), through a Study Leave Award. An AHRC Networks and Workshops Grant, awarded to Loredana Polezzi and myself within the 'Diasporas, Migration and Identities' theme, also allowed for a series of research seminars in 2006–7 which helped to feed this individual project. The University of Warwick, and particularly the Department of Italian, have generously supported this research through study leave, support to host and attend conferences and seminars, and funding for research trips. Grateful thanks are extended to all of these bodies, without whose support the development and completion of this book would not have been possible.

I offer very sincere thanks to the editors of the 'Italian Modernities' series, Pierpaolo Antonello and Robert Gordon at the University of Cambridge and Hannah Godfrey at Peter Lang, all of whom have supported and enabled publication of the volume with efficiency and warmth. I am particularly indebted to Robert Gordon for his encouragement from the outset, his prompt and attentive reading, and his astute advice. My thanks are also due to the estate of Donald Rodney for the kind permission to reproduce the cover image.

A long list of other individuals who have contributed to the fruition of this project could be included here, but, to avoid my own embarrassment at any unintended exclusions and the embarrassment of others at any unwanted inclusions, I simply extend general but profound thanks to all of the colleagues in my own department, and in Italian Studies and other disciplines in the UK and elsewhere, whose ideas and wisdom, shared often in relation to topics quite distant from migration cultures in Italy, have helped me to understand what I am looking for in this research and how best to look for it. To these must be added the writers who have generously collaborated in or accidentally re-orientated my research, and particularly Salah Methnani, Saidou Moussa Ba, Shirin Ramzanali Fazel, Ornela Vorpsi and Wu Ming 2. Credit for constantly pushing my research forwards, and often in unforeseen directions, lies also with the numerous students – from undergraduate to Master's to PhD, but particularly the latter – whose discussions with me of their own and of my research have pointed to perspectives which I had not seen. I thank warmly all of these important interlocutors.

Lastly, I give heartfelt thanks to those at home for accommodating with generosity and humour the high and low points of a major research project, and for reminding me of how important – and sometimes, how unimportant – stories are.

Introduction

> To speak means to come forward and to locate oneself in one's sphere of existence; it means to claim a modest quantum of agency.[1]

A novel published in Italy in 1980 indicates a wider cultural frame in which to view the literature of immigration which will be the focus of this study. *Nero di Puglia*, written by Antonio Campobasso, offers a first-person narrative of the experiences from childhood to around thirty years of age of a mixed-race boy in Italy.[2] Born on 2 June 1946, the day of inauguration of the Italian Republic, to an African American father serving briefly in the US armed forces in Italy, and a Puglian mother who subsequently married a British Italian man and moved to London, the narrator's life, after early years being cared for by his grandmother in a Puglian village, is told as a passage from an orphanage to numerous young offender institutions, to prisons, an asylum, and eventually drama school, each move contributing to the tracing of a map of Italy from Messina to Milan.[3] Physical abuse and hardship are a feature of all his stopping points. Acute anger and emotional

---

1   Michel de Certeau, *The Capture of Speech and Other Political Writings*, ed. by Luce Giard, trans. and afterword by Tom Conley (Minneapolis, MN: University of Minnesota Press, 1997), 98.
2   Antonio Campobasso, *Nero di Puglia* (Milan: Feltrinelli, 1980).
3   The early story of Campobasso carries echoes of Leonardo Sciascia's character, Candido Munafò, born in Sicily on a similarly significant date: the night of 9–10 July 1943, as Allied troops were landing on the island. He is born to Italian parents, but his mother subsequently leaves his father for an American officer. Most striking in this intertextual reference is perhaps the attention to colour in the context of narrating a history of nation: 'candido' and 'nero' are refracted also against the note Sciascia makes that the boy was intended to be named Bruno, after Mussolini's son. See Leonardo Sciascia, *Candido, ovvero un sogno fatto in Sicilia* (Turin: Einaudi, 1977).

violence characterize the narrator's responses to others and the delivery of his narrative. Permeated with depictions and metaphors of spitting, vomiting and ejaculating, the account generates a dominant sense of rejection. The narrator's spectacular ejections are his response to his 'sorella gemella', the Italian Republic, which has continually attempted to eject him, by means of confinement and marginalization, from its public space.[4] His movements around and across the national landscape seem to keep him perpetually on its surface, suggesting that an individual, albeit an Italian citizen, who has no familial network, nor any substantive knowledge of one, cannot find a home in this society. Furthermore, he is black, and thus bears the sign of a perceived error: as the novel's title suggests, a change in colour makes of something home-grown and 'national' something unpalatable, to be spat out.

My reason for positing Campobasso's narrative as a starting point for this discussion is absolutely not that I see a solid and seamless continuity between this novel and the literature of immigration to Italy which starts to emerge a decade later. *Nero di Puglia* is not inaugural and does not 'pave the way' for narratives which follow; in fact, it seems in many ways to be an isolated literary event.[5] Rather, I introduce the novel here in order to invite an adjusted perspective on questions of race and cultural representations of it in Italian culture, and specifically one which does not identify contemporary discussions about intercultural engagement in society and in literature in Italy directly and wholly with the rise in immigration in the 1980s. Campobasso's story is a reminder that other kinds of blackness and other kinds of difference insist in Italian society and culture throughout, indeed, the history of the Republic. Recent recovery of the memory of Italian colonialism has, of course, had a similar effect in telling the histories of Italian cultural intersections, or of Italian blackness, and some of these

---

4   Campobasso, *Nero di Puglia*, 16.
5   Campobasso is, however, identified (questionably) as a 'scrittore migrante' in a list compiled by the Biblioteca Salaborsa: see http://www.bibliotecasalaborsa.it/content/percorsi/scrittorimigrantifilm.html (accessed 30 April 2013).

histories will be discussed in the central chapters of this study.⁶ However, in between the national events of colonialism and immigration, the narrative of *Nero di Puglia* alerts attention to a relatively unseen and uninvestigated experience of being of mixed race and culture in Italy during the period of significant social change from the late 1940s to the end of the 1970s. Campobasso's 'microhistory' of sorts also opens a window upon a set of experiences of migration and mobility which tend to be associated with the contemporary period and with the 'phenomenon' of immigration to Italy, but are here revealed to have a longer history: his father was an African American from California serving in Italy, his mother moved from Puglia to London with a British Italian man. Lines of culture and identity can be traced from south to north, across the Atlantic and through Europe, through the apparently insignificant figure of an individual rendered psychologically and economically unstable by the perceived absence of stable roots. Echoed in this personal history are the multi-directional movements of a much longer history of migration and mobility in relation to Italy.

Against this background, this book addresses the corpus of narratives written in Italian by writers who are immigrants in Italy, published since 1990, and traces the figurative commonalities between what is in fact a highly diverse collection of literary materials, in order to identify the flashpoints which animate what might be termed the 'migrant imaginary'; or better, 'migrant imaginaries', signalling the plurality and diversity of the notion. In so doing, the aim of the study is to describe and discuss this literature in its own terms and to draw attention to the specific concepts, figures, and affects which it negotiates. Whilst significant and growing critical attention has been paid to migration literature in Italy in the last ten to fifteen years in particular, there has been a prevailing tendency to apprehend literary production as a form of expression of a social, political

---

6   On Italy's colonial memory, see Jacqueline Andall and Derek Duncan, eds, *National Belongings: Hybridity in Italian Colonial and Postcolonial Cultures* (Oxford: Peter Lang, 2010); Ruth Ben-Ghiat and Mia Fuller, eds, *Italian Colonialism* (New York: Palgrave Macmillan, 2005); Cristina Lombardi-Diop and Caterina Romeo, eds, *Postcolonial Italy: Challenging National Homogeneity* (New York: Palgrave Macmillan, 2012).

and economic condition – immigration – and as an instrument for addressing social and cultural challenges emerging from this condition. This it no doubt is – in part. It is a factor of reception as much as of production that a narrative in Italian, written by a writer whose first language is not Italian and who migrated to or through Italy from another country – and particularly another culture – of origin, inserts itself to some degree into discourses related to cultural difference which occupy significant space in the media and in public consciousness, in Italy and across Europe, in the contemporary moment.[7] This is one of the senses of Michel de Certeau's comment quoted above: to express oneself as a voice from elsewhere in the language and in the cultural space of Italy is itself a bid to be recognized, which cannot but signify entry into a discourse related to inclusion or exclusion and the response to difference. In short, it begs the question of what the writer is to be recognized *as*.

In this sense, to extract the analysis of Italian migration literature from its social and political context is impossible and, in any case, unproductive. My aim in this study is rather to adjust the critical economy within which these texts circulate in order to transfer value from the ethical towards the aesthetic and affective capital which they produce. In other words, I wish to privilege interpretation of the specifically literary strategies and figures which emerge and pass through these texts, apprehending them as samples and propositions of what contemporary literature (in Italy and beyond) might be as well as – rather than exclusively as – the manifestations of a complex cultural and social shift in Italy. In this, I follow Daniela Merolla and Sandra Ponzanesi, who assert that 'it is time to search for new paradigms of interpretation that can assess the value of a literature of migration

---

[7] My own early published work on Italian migration literature views it largely from this perspective, positing it as an instance of fragmented *impegno* in the context of postmodernity: see Chapter 8 of Jennifer Burns, *Fragments of impegno: Interpretations of Commitment in Contemporary Italian Narrative, 1980–2000* (Leeds: Northern Universities Press, 2001). See also Jennifer Burns, 'Recent Immigrant Writing in Italian: A Fragile Enterprise', *The Italianist*, 18 (1998), 213–44.

in its own terms'.⁸ Whilst not negating the importance of interpreting this literature in terms of – as has been common especially in critical production in Italy – a 'progetto interculturale', that position now established, this book aims to demonstrate that there are other analytical perspectives and methods which might be employed in order to move towards a more complex understanding of the significance of this literature.⁹

One element of this complexity is the frame of reference of 'Italian migration literature'. A view which apprehends narratives of migration as the cultural counterpart to a social and political process tends to place the focus on Italy.¹⁰ Again, this is an accurate and productive approach, arguably confirmed by the choice of Italian as the language of writing and, in earlier texts in particular, a narrative focus on the experience of living as a migrant in Italy. However, my analyses in the central chapters of this study

---

8   Daniela Merolla and Sandra Ponzanesi, 'Introduction', in Sandra Ponzanesi and Daniela Merolla, eds, *Migrant Cartographies: New Cultural and Literary Spaces in Post-Colonial Europe* (Oxford: Lexington Books, 2005), 1–52 (4).
9   For a comparable attempt to widen the perspectives from which to view migrant writings in Italy, see the collection of essays edited by Fulvio Pezzarossa and Ilaria Rossini, *Leggere il testo e il mondo: Vent'anni di scritture della migrazione in Italia* (Bologna: CLUEB, 2011).
10 This view is articulated clearly by Maria Cristina Mauceri and Maria Grazia Negro, in the conclusions to their *Nuovo immaginario italiano: italiani e stranieri a confronto nella letteratura italiana contemporanea* (Rome: Sinnos, 2009): 'Sono ormai passati quasi quarant'anni dai primi arrivi migratori in Italia e possiamo concludere dicendo che *in base ai testi analizzati* siamo appena all'alba di un'integrazione dinamica e dignitosa tra autoctoni e stranieri, che consiste in fruttuosi scambi reciproci e che comporti anche una trasformazione della società italiana in modo che nasca una nuova cultura basata sullo scambio e sulla valorizzazione reciproca' (315; italics added). Roberto Derobertis similarly positions literary self-expression in terms of impact upon Italian society and culture: 'L'insorgenza delle scritture migranti e l'invenzione di una nuova posizione autoriale nell'ambito del discorso letterario italiano non hanno semplicemente messo in forma di racconto esperienze di vita obliterate, ma *hanno inciso e incidono la realtà sociale e le politiche culturali in Italia*, reclamando a partire da sé anche una trasformazione della critica e dei processi formativi'; Roberto Derobertis, 'Insorgenze letterarie nella disseminazione delle migrazioni. Contesti, definizioni e politiche culturali delle scritture migranti', in *Scritture migranti*, 1 (2007), 27–52 (50).

aim to demonstrate that these narratives are about many other places and many other forms of experience as well. In part, this is indeed an 'intercultural' process, through which the cultural and political reality of countries perhaps unfamiliar to Italian readers is brought into their consciousness, and, in fact, their imaginary. Blind-spots can occur in this view, though, and this study will attempt to illuminate them by promoting a critical practice which also sees references to and accounts of the country of departure as an expression of experience there in its own terms. Put crudely, many of these narratives are about Algeria, Somalia, Tunisia, etc., and the figuration of what it feels like to inhabit those places may be read as simply that, rather than a more teleological initiative to communicate across a cultural divide. In this sense, de Certeau's assertion that the act of voicing oneself means 'to locate oneself in one's sphere of existence' could be read according to a different logic: a writer voices herself in Italian in order (also) to locate herself in a sphere of existence established and experienced elsewhere.

Outlining what these texts are looking at is a tangential step towards the problem of identifying what they are. Since critical work related to narratives written by migrants began to emerge in the 1990s, the question of definitions has been crucial and contested, and, needless to say, has remained unresolved. The perceptions and anxieties which underline definitions in fact indicate quite helpfully the different critical positions assumed or developed in response to these texts. In Italy, early critical response was led by Armando Gnisci, who, in a huge number of texts and critical interventions, has proposed a number of definitions and some neologisms, generally moving away from notions of migration towards a more global view of 'letteratura dei mondi'.[11] A statement which broadly characterizes his position over almost thirty years, is that 'la letteratura lavora, oggi come non mai, a tenere in comunicazione gli umani e le culture attraverso la traduzione continua di tutto l'antico e il possibile dei vari

---

11   See Armando Gnisci, *Il rovescio del gioco* (Rome: Sovera, 1993), as probably the first published critical essay on migration literature, focusing on notions of hospitality and hospitability. The term 'letteratura dei mondi' is coined in Armando Gnisci, *Una storia diversa* (Rome: Meltemi, 2001), 14.

mondi in tutte le lingue'.¹² Privileging a globally comparative approach which has produced some important insights and methods, Gnisci has tended to reject a critical approach which places Italian migration literature in the framework of postcolonialism. Others, especially outside Italy and more recently within, have linked migration to Italy to the broader frame of reference of postcoloniality, in line with a significant effort to embed postcolonial theory and a postcolonial temperament in Italian scholarly discourse, albeit this migration is not overwhelmingly from former *Italian* colonies.¹³ The very mismatch indicated here points to the issue – actually, a very productive one, as this study will aim in places to demonstrate – that the key questions and methods of postcolonial theory are highly appropriate to interpretation of migrant cultural production in Italy to a point, but that to subsume all experiences and expressions into this framework would be to erase some important differences. Merolla and Ponzanesi articulate this problem when they expose their own debates about the definition of the 'migrant writer and artist': 'The major thorny question was whether such a notion would not be ethnocentric, by assuming that the migrant is not just a traveler, a wanderer, but implicitly the person who reproduces the colonial divide in new global terms'.¹⁴

To talk of postcolonial Italian literature is, then, to talk of something which overlaps with and has distinct thematic and political commonalities with the texts I am discussing here, but is in no way coterminous with them. To talk of migrant writers and migration literature encompasses more accurately the range of material which is my focus, although, by the same token, to describe some texts as migration narratives when their context is clearly postcolonial is also to force an elision. However, the notion of

12 Gnisci, *Una storia diversa*, 12.
13 See, in particular, Daniele Comberiati, *Scrivere nella lingua dell'altro: La letteratura degli immigrati in Italia (1989–2007)* (Brussels: Peter Lang, 2010), and *La quarta sponda: Scrittrici in viaggio dall'Africa coloniale all'Italia di oggi* (Rome: Edizioni Pigreco, 2007); and Sandra Ponzanesi, *Paradoxes of Postcolonial Culture: Contemporary Women Writers of the Indian and Afro-Italian Diaspora* (Albany, NY: State University of New York Press, 2004).
14 Merolla and Ponzanesi, 'Introduction', 4.

migration is the one which best articulates both the lived experience of the writers concerned and the figures which animate their writing, and it encompasses diverse contexts of, motivations for, and directions of travel. Arguably, it encompasses too much, in the sense that Italian 'migration literature' could include narratives (in Italian, English, Spanish, Portuguese, German, or a range of languages) by emigrants to the USA, Australia, South America, northern Europe, and so on. The more specific label of 'immigration literature' sharpens the focus neatly on contemporary Italy and on incoming migrants, but the focus is uncomfortably sharp since the term 'immigration' recalls governmental or inter-governmental policy, border controls, alarmist public discourse, and, most importantly, suggests a single movement in one direction from 'origin' to 'destination'. Migration, in this sense, affords a perception of a much broader pattern of travel and settlement which avoids the romanticism of 'nomadism' by retaining reference to a mobility forced or precipitated by economic or political privation and by reaffirming, gently, the connection with a contemporary social, economic, and cultural condition.[15] I share Graziella Parati's view that 'privileging the word "migrant" allows for a more articulated, multidirectional translation into disparate geographical and cultural contexts'.[16] Indeed, her discussion of terminology in the introduction to her study of migration culture in Italy offers a lucid and insightful assessment of alternative positions which need not be reproduced here.[17]

More controversial is perhaps my use of the term 'literature' in association with migration, rather than 'writings' or 'textual renditions', as

---

15 The concept of nomadism has been revised and updated by Rosi Braidotti in *Nomadic Subjects: Embodiment and Sexual Difference in Contemporary Feminist Theory* (New York: Columbia University Press, 1994). Whilst it usefully releases mobility from notions of attachment to specific origins and destinations, in doing so, it risks suggesting a freedom of movement which is not realized for migrants seeking access to many nation states in the contemporary world.

16 Graziella Parati, *Migration Italy: The Art of Talking Back in a Destination Culture* (Toronto: University of Toronto Press, 2005), 14.

17 See Parati, *Migration Italy*, 14–16.

have been favoured elsewhere.[18] Critics and writers alike have rejected the term, literature, inasmuch as it is seen to posit access to a high-cultural arena of production, associated with the nation-state, with heritage, and with notions of the canon. It also seems to beg interpretation of these texts according to conventionally 'literary' practices and values. There is certainly evidence to support this objection, very often within the very mechanism of cultural hospitality intended to include migrant writers within the sphere of Italian literary production and reception; namely, the prefaces written by Italian writers and journalists to texts – especially early ones – written by migrants.[19] Campobasso's novel, interestingly, offers a foretaste of this, in that the preface by Alfonso di Nola addresses its 'naif' style and hybridity of genres, as if these were literary faults which need to be justified.[20] The preface to Mohsen Melliti's novel, *Pantanella*, similarly foregrounds, and attempts to explain, its unsettling mixing of voices and narrative modes; a preface, in this instance, written by an Algerian (migrant) writer, Rachid Boudjedra.[21] However, such anxieties seem to refer to a somewhat rigid and outdated notion of literature which perhaps holds faster in Italy than in other cultural traditions, but has been displaced by an inclusive conception of literature which functions simply as a description of a written text which envisages a readership and not as a vehicle for the conferral of artistic or cultural merit.

18   The University of Bologna-based journal, *Scritture migranti: Rivista di scambi interculturali*, published by CLUEB (Bologna) since 2007, privileges the term 'writings'. The notion of 'textual renditions' is used by Anne-Marie Fortier, in *Migrant Belongings: Memory, Space, Identity* (Oxford: Berg, 2000) to distinguish between written and other forms of representation, and also to avoid establishing or perpetuating hierarchies between different forms of text.
19   On collaborations between Italian-born and migrant writers, see Jennifer Burns, 'Borders Within the Text: Authorship, Collaboration and Mediation in Writing in Italian by Immigrants', in Jennifer Burns and Loredana Polezzi, eds, *Borderlines: Migrant Writing and Italian Identities (1870–2000) / Borderlines: Migrazioni e identità nel Novecento* (Isernia: Iannone, 2003), 387–94.
20   See Alfonso M. di Nola, 'Prefazione', in Campobasso, *Nero di Puglia*, 9–11.
21   See Rachid Boudjedra, 'Presentazione', in Mohsen Melliti, *Pantanella: Canto lungo la strada*, trans. by Monica Ruocco (Rome: Edizioni Lavoro, 1992), 7–9.

The term 'migrant writers', which I use throughout my discussion, may seem relatively transparent, given that I have already explained by choice of 'migrant' rather than 'immigrant', and indeed it is less discussed and contested than others. I would draw attention, however, to two connotations of the term, which I intend to exploit in my analysis of migration literature. Firstly, the term refers to migrants who write; secondly, to writers who migrate. To identify and retain this tension in the term, albeit minimal, is important in avoiding some of the clichés which pertain to migration literature and which are indicated in some of the debate around terminology outlined above. The perception that migrants come to writing because they have a story to tell about Italy, and to tell specifically to Italians about Italy, is a powerful one which is borne out by some texts, particularly early ones (Pap Khouma's *Io, venditore di elefanti* is an example).[22] It is sufficiently powerful to cement the connection between migration literature and the empirical socio-economic event of migration which I attempt in this study to loosen. A large number of migrant writers make it clear through their own comments, through their publication history, and through the expressional fabric and frame of reference of their narratives that they were writers, or had the ambition or inclination to write, before they were migrants. In a very few cases, arguably, they came to migration because they wanted a story to write (Salah Methnani might be an example).[23] Whilst not wishing to overstate this case, I think an important measure in calibrating critical

22 Pap Khouma, *Io, venditore di elefanti: Una vita per forza fra Dakar, Parigi e Milano*, ed. by Oreste Pivetta (Milan: Garzanti, 1990). The preface in particular frames the production of the text as the meeting of a migrant seeking political voice and representation with a journalist seeking to represent 'authentically' the condition of migrants in Italy.

23 Salah Methnani, who co-authored with Mario Fortunato the novel, *Immigrato* (Rome: Theoria, 1990), tells the story of this collaboration as the meeting of a migrant seeking an alternative representation of the Maghreb countries as the home of a strong literary culture with a literary journalist also seeking a cultural 'angle' on the issue of immigration (comments made in an unpublished interview with myself, 13 November 2001). Fortunato articulates a similar background in his preface to the third edition of the novel: see Mario Fortunato, 'Introduzione: Sedici anni dopo', in Mario Fortunato and Salah Methnani, *Immigrato* (Milan: Bompiani, 2006), I–IX.

response to migration literature in Italy is a consciousness that literature in the widest sense, including reading, writing, and a broad literary sensibility, is, like culture, something which migrants inhabit and possess in and across two or more locations, and whilst migration might allow access to different forms or articulations of it, this is not an entry into a new world.

My commitment to investigating the figures which populate migrant imaginaries stems from a sense that these narratives often privilege, systematically, an imaginative perception of experience and tell the stories of highly charged emotional itineraries, much of which tends to be left unquestioned where the socio-political story which they suggest is the primary object of analysis. By shifting attention from the socio-economic and political reasons for and implications of migration towards the personal investment involved in such a decision and process, it becomes clear that migration calls upon and generates a significant range of emotions and operations of the imagination: fear, hope, anger, projection, idealization, nostalgia, abjection, self-satisfaction, love, hatred. The exploration of how these emotions and imaginings regulate the empirical experience and process of migration, how they impinge upon or determine decisions, choices, and responses as the individual leaves one culture and enters another or others, is an important factor of any attempt to develop a cultural understanding of migration itself, and of why migration literature has a specific identity.[24]

Deleuze and Guattari identify as the second of three key characteristics of minor literature that 'in it everything takes on a collective value', and they are probably right: when an individual identified with a minority enters, through literary production, the field of the majority, it is almost impossible that the experience he articulates will not be received as representative

---

24   Derobertis echoes this point, albeit whilst focussing attention still specifically on the point of arrival: 'La scrittura letteraria si sottrae alla mera funzionalità e eccede la trascrizione, sfuggendo a un discorso critico orientato unicamente alla (ri)costruzione di un canone o di una tradizione per divenire pratica di significazione che attraversa obliquamente il campo sociale. Essa rappresenta un potente strumento di costruzione e re-invenzione dell'immaginario ed è centrale nella elaborazione dell'autonomia del migrante nella società di arrivo: una resistenza che i corpi migranti oppongono a tutti quei processi e dispositivi che si producono sulle soggettività'; Derobertis, 'Insorgenze letterarie nella disseminazione delle migrazioni', 41.

of the minority as a collective.[25] To return to the quotation of de Certeau which opens this introduction, to speak in the dominant language and thus 'claim a modest quantum of agency' might imply that one claims that agency on behalf of a collective. This is a burden, in many senses, and one which, arguably, many migrant writers attempt to shake off precisely by foregrounding intensely in their narratives the experience of the individual, as distinct from the collective of migrants in Italy, of citizens in their home country, of citizens of their home country in Italy, of Muslim men or women in Italy, etc. The telling of a narrative of interior experience alongside or over one of public presence and action calls for a recognition of the emotional and imaginative specificity of any one individual's experience of what is seen as a social 'phenomenon'. By probing the interiority of migrants, as expressed in migration narratives, and by reading their work as the stories of individuals, a connection of affect and imagination can be forged, which is as powerful as a political commitment, or indeed, by Deleuze and Guattari's definition, is itself 'political'. Wayne Booth notes that figurative language requires an engagement of energies and therefore 'figurative language will always figure the mind more incisively than plain language'.[26] He continues:

> The energy I expend in reconstructing the figure is somehow transferred to retaining the figure itself and bonding with its maker. In short, since 'energy expended = ethical power', every deviation from the conventional way of speaking, every special demand on the listener's powers of reconstruction, will add to the effect. A figure used not only calls for the recognition that a figure has been used but for a special kind of re-creative engagement with the figurer.[27]

---

25 Gilles Deleuze and Félix Guattari, *Kafka: Toward a Minor Literature*, trans. by Dana Polan (Minneapolis, MN: University of Minnesota Press, 1986), 17. The two other characteristics identified are 'that in it language is affected with a high coefficient of deterritorialization' (16), as will be discussed in Chapter 5 of this book, and 'that everything in them is political' (17), as discussed in the present introduction.
26 Wayne Booth, *The Company We Keep: An Ethics of Fiction* (Berkeley, CA: University of California Press, 1988), 298.
27 Booth, *The Company We Keep*, 299.

The work the reader does, across cultures, in reimagining the sometimes challenging images and figures of migration literature, performs an ethics of imagination and affect.

Emphasizing interior experience, as I have above, runs the risk of implying that it is distinct and distinguishable from the 'exterior' experience of the body in the world. Prompted by the texts themselves that I am examining, a principle which I hope to establish through this study is precisely the opposite: bodily presence and bodily experience form the interface between the interiority of the individual and the public, populated space. Several factors make this a particularly important and interpretatively productive principle in the context of migration literature. Physical struggle is the subject matter of many narratives, whether of clandestine subsistence in Italy, of postcolonial oppression in Somalia, of sectarian violence in Algeria or Iraq, or of the migration journey itself. Here, the skin is not a smooth container for the interiority of an individual, but rather is precisely the permeable surface through which external experiences, and the marks or wounds they leave, impact upon the emotions and imagination of the individual. Geneviève Makaping describes vividly the challenge of recounting 'in prima persona le cose che ho visto, inteso, vissuto, sperimentato, anche dolorosamente, sulla mia pelle. Sono delle piccole frustate, piccole violenze che, messe tutte insieme, possono diventare una gogna.'[28] Equally, the affects with which external experiences are identified can be expelled through bodily reactions such as – as in Campobasso's case – spitting, vomiting, ejaculating. The body and the skin are also the carriers of markers of culture, ethnicity, and socio-economic status – be they modes of dress, skin decoration, jewellery, beards and hairstyles, or simply colour of the skin. In this way, the body functions as the regulator of the individual's visibility as a migrant, as a practitioner of a particular faith, as a member of a particular culture, or citizen of a particular nation. Responses of others to such visibility, and the sense of inhabiting such a model or mask, make impressions upon the individual's experience of self. Again, Campobasso's narrative makes this point eloquently.

---

28   Geneviève Makaping, *Traiettorie di sguardi: E se gli altri foste voi?* (Soveria Mannelli: Rubbettino, 2001), 109.

In positing the importance of the body as the site of engagement between subject and world, as a border that feels, touches and is touched, I am following much recent work in feminist cultural theory, and principally the work of Sara Ahmed.[29] In particular, Ahmed argues persuasively that emotions are central to the individual's sense of self and other. Emotions are not simply the property of an individual then played out in public, nor are they stimulated by the effect of external sources on the individual's interiority. Rather, they produce the distinction between the two: 'emotions create the very effect of the surfaces and boundaries that allow us to distinguish an inside and an outside in the first place. So emotions are not simply something "I" or "we" have. Rather, it is through emotions, or how we respond to objects and others, that surfaces or boundaries are made: the "I" and the "we" are shaped by, and even take the shape of, contact with others.'[30] Since the experience of migration, as the journey itself or as a broader condition of belonging and un-belonging in plural places and times, is played out in textual representations overwhelmingly as one of encounter (with people, places, practices, images, beliefs), this model of the production of boundaries through emotion is particularly suggestive for my enquiry. It is, in turn, emotions and affects which crystallize and colour the figures which I seek to explore and identify, and which the process of figuration seeks in some way to manage or make interpretable and communicable. Ahmed posits the interchange between the empirical and the figural in the circulation of emotion in a way which points very directly towards my analyses in the central chapters of this book: 'Affect does not reside in an object or sign, but is an effect of the circulation between objects and signs (= the accumulation of affective value). Signs increase in affective value as an effect of the movement between signs: the

---

29   See Sara Ahmed, *Strange Encounters: Embodied Others in Post-Coloniality* (London and New York: Routledge, 2000), especially 'Embodying Strangers', 38–54. In addition to Ahmed's works, cited below, see Braidotti, *Nomadic Subjects*, Judith Butler, *Gender Trouble: Feminism and the Subversion of Identity* (London: Routledge, 1990), and Fortier, *Migrant Belongings*, 171–5.

30   Sara Ahmed, *The Cultural Politics of Emotion* (Edinburgh: Edinburgh University Press, 2004), 10.

more signs circulate, the more affective they become'.³¹ As signs – or, in my terms, figures – circulate within and across migrant imaginaries and populate migrant narratives, so their affective charge becomes increasingly potent and present in the text.

My map of the space of Italian migration literature uses the commonly agreed boundaries, according to which this literature began to appear in 1990 and continues to grow and to shift to this day. There has been a tendency to cordon off certain areas, specifically the early texts and especially co-authored or edited ones which narrate in the first person the individual migration story (those already referred to by Fortunato and Methnani, and Khouma, for instance).³² These have been regarded as a preliminary phase before narratives fully 'authored' by migrants emerge. This distinction has some validity, but for the purposes of my enquiry in particular, I think it is important to recognize the foundational quality of these early examples.³³ This is not to claim that they determine the practice and form, or reception, of migration literature in Italy, but a study of the figures which animate migrant imaginaries demonstrates that tropes and images of the early texts, used to express emotional experiences related to migration, recur frequently and are reformulated in later texts. This is by no means a linear connection or progression: my individual chapters aim to show that particular themes and figures are differently inflected and expressed according to different experiences associated with migration. Nevertheless, there is a critical value in placing the earlier texts in relation to later ones across multiple axes of connection, in that this reveals the intricacy and the specificity of how certain, perhaps common, tropes are refigured to express the affects or the

---

31 Ahmed, *The Cultural Politics of Emotion*, 45.
32 This view is expressed succinctly by Daniele Comberiati: 'La fase testimoniale è da tempo finita' (*Scrivere nella lingua dell'altro*, 255). More broadly, Comberiati's conclusion offers a useful overview (255–60).
33 An interesting analysis of how Fortunato and Methnani's narrative moves beyond the autobiographical is Franca Sinopoli, 'Poetiche della migrazione nella letteratura italiana contemporanea: il discorso autobiografico', in Armando Gnisci, ed., *Miscellanea comparatistica; Studi (e testi) italiani: Semestrale del Dipartimento di italianistica e spettacolo dell'Università di Roma 'La Sapienza'*, 7 (2001), 189–206.

imagination of an experience specific to a particular moment, location, or human subject. Similarly, though I recognize a passage from 'testimonial' narratives of the migration journey to fictions which figure migration in terms only of a mobile or intercultural sensibility, I resist any critical narrative of Italian migration literature which traces an evolution from autobiographical accounts to novels. Such a view resonates with a highly culturally specific notion of what fully formed literature is which, as noted above, has little currency. Moreover, it applies a rigid interpretative framework, and probably a 'western' one, to texts of which the analytical richness lies to a large extent in the different traditions, forms, and imaginaries which they stitch together within the frame of 'Italian' literature.

Certain exclusions from my map of Italian migration apply, however, for practical as well as intellectual reasons. This study addresses prose narratives of migration – novels and short stories – and does not include the vast production in poetry, and, to a lesser extent, theatre, by migrant artists. Though migrant imaginaries might arguably be more vividly expressed in lyric poetry than in narrative prose, it is in many ways the expression of a poetic sensibility within, or a poetic vision of, the 'realist' migration story which I am interested to explore. Whilst, as indicated above, I include postcolonial writers alongside migrant writers precisely because of productive continuities and discontinuities between their imaginary repertoires, I have taken the decision to exclude the so-called 'second generation', largely Somali Italian writers, because a study of this scope cannot adequately accommodate the different experiences and positions which they articulate – albeit there are, of course, intersections of imaginaries – and their work calls on a rather different set of theoretical reference points.[34] Their recent visibility and success, and their more distinctly postcolonial experience, also mean that they are receiving significant critical attention, whereas my

---

34 The most prominent examples are Cristina Ubax Ali Farah, Gabriella Ghermandi and Igiaba Scego. For comments on the appropriateness to these writers of the term, 'second generation', see Comberiati, *Scrivere nella lingua dell'altro*, 257. See also the short story collection by Gabriella Kuruvilla, Ingy Mubiayi, Igiaba Scego, and Laila Wadia, *Pecore nere: Racconti*, ed. by Flavia Capitani and Emanuele Coen (Rome: Laterza, 2005), which identifies these four women writers as 'second generation'.

interest in this study is directed in part towards understanding the context in which certain migrant writers succeed or disappear over the twenty years or more of migrant literary production in Italy. Lastly, and for reasons of coherence, I have included almost exclusively migrant writers from Africa and the Middle East, with some reference to Albanian writers.[35] A common – but often very differently inflected – cultural background (Arab Islamic and Islamic) allows for imaginaries of migration, which are also, intrinsically, imaginaries corresponding between at least two cultures, to be examined and interpreted using a reasonably cohesive set of analytical tools. These tools are not redundant in the analysis of, say, the work of Chinese, Indian or Pakistani migrant writers in Italy, but to use them would entail adjustments and justifications. My aim in this study is, in any case, not to be exhaustive or to offer a comprehensive taxonomy of figures which occur in Italian migration literature, but rather to sketch a collection of images and to suggest modes of reading them, both of which can be richly illustrated using the texts I have selected and subsequently tested with other writers and other cultural trajectories. These others might well include 'native' Italian writers whose work figures notions of mobility, belonging, habitation in spaces, contested identity, passages and connections across space and time. The current book does not intend to circumscribe Italian migration literature as a discrete body of texts existing in parallel to 'Italian literature'. Rather, it seeks to indicate the particular nodal points of literary enquiry and expression to which migrant writers have recurrent recourse, and which mark the distinctiveness of the condition of migration and of its expression, but which also speak directly to concerns about contemporary experience which reside in the work of contemporary (Italian) writers in their broadest definition.

The corpus of writers whose texts are analysed in the study is identifiable as such simply by virtue of the writers' status as migrants in Italy at

---

35 For more comprehensive information on migrant writers publishing in Italy since 1990, see Comberiati, *Scrivere nella lingua dell'altro* (particularly the 'Schede bio-bibliografiche degli autori migranti e postcoloniali di espressione italiana citati', 261–82), and BASILI (Banca Dati sugli Scrittori Immigrati in Lingua Italiana), http://www.disp.let.uniroma1.it/basili2001/ (accessed 1 May 2013).

some point, and the term in itself incorporates multiple histories and routes of migration, with multiple motivations and outcomes. The selection of primary texts for close analysis in the volume is steered by the five key terms identified, rather than by the nationality or ethnicity of the writers, their gender, their mode or moment of migration, their permanence or not in Italy, their experience or inexperience as a writer, or the period in which their works were published. As such, the volume engages at its broadest with the work of around fifteen writers, but returns to key works by eight core authors (Amor Dekhis, Shirin Ramzanali Fazel, Mario Fortunato and Salah Methnani, Amara Lakhous, Mohsen Melliti, Abdel Malek Smari, Younis Tawfik), in order both to indicate the indefinite confines of the corpus and to suggest the prominence of certain authors and works, whether this be owed to their distinctive or influential literary strategies, their commercial success, their critical reception, the conditions of their works being published, or their particular gender, ethnicity, or experience of migration. As noted above, the study underscores the importance of early texts in positing and delineating the contours of the 'migrant imaginaries' analysed in it, but also draws attention in specific chapters to a non-chronological development of thematics which tends to highlight the singularity of authors rather than their representative function.

The five chapters of the book are each dedicated to one of the key figures or concepts which have emerged from my readings of Italian migration literature as prominent: identity, memory, home, place and space, literature. Each of these five terms is complex, overlain with theoretical speculation and long-standing figurative currency in literature. Each is used as a title with no explanatory subtitle precisely in order to afford the scope to enquire into the range of theoretical positions from which each notion has been approached, into the commonplaces and stereotypes which have on occasion been attached to each, and, primarily, into the diverse articulations of the notion which individual migrant writers offer. As is obvious from the very density and range of each of these terms, each overlaps significantly with others: there are aspects which I will discuss in terms of 'memory' which have much to do with 'home', for example, and certain constructions of 'identity' are predicated upon 'place and space'. Language might be identified as a salient theme missing from my scheme, but, as the very means of expression which these texts rely upon, and as one of the very reasons for identifying migrant writers as such (in that they write in a language other than their first), questions of language surface in every theme or chapter, and are discussed most directly in the final one on literature. Just as the concepts and figures are horizontally layered and meet at various points, so are the texts which I analyse: no one text is used as an exhaustive example of any one figure, and instead, the interdependency of the figures is demonstrated by the revisiting of single texts in two or more chapters. This overlapping between figures and texts itself articulates eloquently the notion of 'imaginaries'. It is not, in my view, a system of signs which is at work in Italian migration literature, whereby who one is, who one was, where one has come from, where one might be now or in the future, and by which modes of expression one might express this experience, are each articulated by discrete figures or images. Rather, figures, powered by affects, circulate with and through one another, as Ahmed suggests. From this perspective, the imaginary might be viewed as an economy, in which figures, images, visions, projections, signs, icons, motifs exist and accrue meaning only through exchange. My key figures and chapter titles are therefore leaky containers, through which others circulate productively.

The approaches which I adopt to each figure will be explored in the chapters themselves, but some preliminary comments here will help to indicate general orientations. As suggested above, my focus is primarily in all cases on the individual's investment in these figures, though where notions of the collective are implicated, these will be discussed. 'Identity' is taken to refer to constructions of the subject and negotiations of sameness and otherness. 'Memory' covers the recollection in the present of past events, and particularly the processes of assembly of that memory, in the terms of the present. My discussions of 'Home' are focused upon the country or culture of departure, and on the construction of a sense of 'origin'. 'Place and Space', on the other hand, turns the view towards the landscape of Italy, and the playing out of notions of habitation and belonging on the surface of Italian cities. The final chapter, 'Literature', merits further introduction. Whilst it begins by considering, in line with earlier chapters, the notions of reading, writing and inhabiting a literary perception of experience as a figure of the imaginaries expressed in the texts analysed, the chapter then moves towards the conclusions of the book by widening the scope to a discussion of what migration literature is and how it operates, and where it might be sited – if it must be sited at all – in relation to other forms of cultural production. It is in this chapter that many of the questions rehearsed in this introduction, and especially those concerning the visiting of various notions of ethical significance upon migration literature, are reviewed and expanded. To some degree, this final chapter situates my analysis of literary figuration back into the social, economic, historical and political context to which, ultimately, it has to belong. The figures analysed in each chapter necessarily develop in large part from material conditions of migrants' experience, and refer to questions of language, religion, employment, health, social exclusion, racism, rights, law and order, political representation. Each act of literary representation functions, in some part, within a process of cultural mediation which is the less conspicuous adjunct of the contested process of legislative and political management of large-scale immigration in Italy since the 1980s, and/or of the, likewise, contested process of recuperation of Italy's colonial memory. My concluding chapter therefore takes account of the inevitable cultural instrumentalization of Italian migration literature by viewing it through the lens of cultural production, circulation and reception in Italy. The Afterword then extends this context into the global literary market and asks if Italian migration literature has a place there.

If I may return one final time to de Certeau's comment quoted in the opening of this introduction, the question which I perhaps arrive at in conclusion to this study of migrant imaginaries is whether, for migrant writers in Italian, 'to speak means to come forward and to locate oneself in one's sphere of existence', where that sphere of existence is construed of as global literature. Might these writers 'claim a modest quantum of agency' as transnational Italian writers?

CHAPTER I

Identity

One of the principal concerns of Italian migrant writing is, indisputably, identity. In the process of migration, identity is at stake because identity is customarily understood to be structured according to context: it is, arguably, impossible to formulate an individual identity without recourse to the physical, human, social and cultural features which surround the individual and serve as tools and markers of association or disassociation.[1] If identity is thus dependent on 'location', then migration from one location to another involves a pronounced dislocation of the identity established in the place of departure and a renegotiation of it within the context of the place of destination. Sara Ahmed foregrounds the notion of encounter between people, 'strangers' to each other, and notes its disruptive effects: 'The term encounter suggests a meeting, but a meeting which involves surprise and conflict'. She articulates a question which subtends my discussion in this chapter: 'We can ask: how does identity itself become instituted through encounters with others that surprise, that shift the boundaries of the familiar, of what we assume that we know? Identity itself is constituted in the "more than one" of the encounter: the designation of an "I" or "we" requires an encounter with others'.[2]

---

1   See Judith Butler, *Gender Trouble: Feminism and the Subversion of Identity* (London: Routledge, 1990) and, in terms particularly of representing oneself as a subject in the social sphere, her *Giving an Account of Oneself* (New York: Fordham University Press, 2005); Stuart Hall, 'Cultural Identity and Diaspora', in Jonathan Rutherford, ed., *Identity, Community, Culture, Difference* (London: Lawrence and Wishart, 1990), 222–37; Stuart Hall and Paul du Gay, eds, *Questions of Cultural Identity* (London: Sage, 1996), especially the essay included by Zygmunt Bauman, 'From Pilgrim to Tourist – or a Short History of Identity', 18–36.
2   Sara Ahmed, *Strange Encounters: Embodied Others in Post-Coloniality* (London: Routledge, 2000), 6–7.

Before examining such encounters, it is helpful to look at the factors which the human figures in any one encounter bring to bear upon it. Family, kinship, and immediate community are often regarded by the individual as formative influences and as primary indicators of identity, though it is interesting (as will be discussed in Chapter 3, see pages 108–12 and 114–16), that disassociation from family and local community and all that mark them is often a key motivation for migration, demonstrating that family is a reference point in terms of differentiation as much as of recognition. Education, knowledge and values, including political position, are powerful markers which the narrator or protagonist of migrant narratives often uses as a tool to differentiate himself from those in the immediate community in the place of departure, and which contribute to the motivation for departure. There tends to be an assumption that this knowledge or mentality will serve as a passport for entry into a community of like-minded individuals in the place of destination, and the debunking of this assumption often features as a major drama of identity.

In a broader context, where individual and collective interact, nationality and ethnicity are clearly major factors in the transition of identity from one location to another. This is best discussed as represented in specific texts, but an interesting general observation is that national affiliations tend rapidly to give way to regional or ethnic ones – Senegalese becomes African, Tunisian becomes Arabic – articulating much broader global lines drawn between areas identified by political, economic, and cultural commonality. This transition towards a broader cultural identification also draws attention to the fact that identity relies to a great extent on recognition: one is what one is recognized as being by those in the surrounding environment. Ethnicity, similarly, may in some instances be expressed in terms of singular categorizations, but is more often a complex of figures or notions. Michael Fischer notes that narratives of ethnicity reveal:

> the paradoxical sense that ethnicity is something reinvented and reinterpreted in each generation by each individual and that it is often something quite puzzling to the individual, something over which he or she lacks control. Ethnicity is not something that is simply passed on from generation to generation, taught and learned; it is something dynamic, often unsuccessfully repressed or avoided. [...] Insofar as ethnicity is a deeply rooted emotional component of identity, it is often transmitted

less through cognitive language or learning (to which sociology has almost entirely restricted itself) than through processes analogous to the dreaming and transference of psychoanalytic encounters.³

As this observation indicates, the negotiation between, on the one hand, the performance and reception of public-facing markers of identity, and on the other, the interior experience of their significance to the individual subject, is often not a straightforward one.

Religious faith similarly generates strongly felt associations and disassociations. Religion is, in many migration narratives, characterized as one of the formative elements of identity established (even imposed) in the home environment, and as one to be shaken off in the process of renegotiation which takes place in the location/s of migration. It can also serve, however, as a powerful personal and cultural support, reinforcing identity by means of reaffirming certain values and practices when identity is undermined in the process of re-negotiation. One of the very early narratives published by a migrant, Mohamed Bouchane's *Chiamatemi Alì*, figures the careful reproduction in his life in Italy of Islamic practices of worship and eating as a key element in combating a sense of loss of identity. The diary format of the text allows the everyday rhythms of Islamic culture to be overlain upon daily experience in Italy.⁴ Michel de Certeau articulates aptly the detachment that insists in such a mechanism:

> These fragments of rites and practices no longer organize everyday life, but only 'punctuate' it. [...] Certain gestures, certain objects, expressions, birthdays, and perfumes, in fact retain in the text of daily activities and work the capital function that punctuation has in a written text. As signs that have nothing to do with the letters

3   Michael M.J. Fischer, 'Ethnicity and the Post-Modern Arts of Memory', in James Clifford and George E. Marcus, eds, *Writing Culture: The Poetics and Politics of Ethnography* (Berkeley, CA: University of California Press, 1986), 194–233 (195–6).
4   Mohamed Bouchane, *Chiamatemi Alì*, ed. by Carla De Girolamo and Daniele Miccione (Milan: Leonardo, 1990). Graziella Parati also notes that the use of a name still identifiable with Islamic culture, as foregrounded in the novel's title, rather than one adopted from Italian, has a similar effect. See Graziella Parati, ed., *Mediterranean Crossroads: Migration Literature in Italy* (Cranbury, NJ: Associated University Presses, 1999), 27.

organizing the meaning of the text, they punctuate the practice of the lexical and syntactic order imposed by the dominant society. These are 'signifiers', but we can no longer be sure what they signify.[5]

A more public perspective on similar influences is offered by Anne-Marie Fortier, who describes the unsettling effect, as a French Canadian of Catholic upbringing, but not a practicing believer, of attending a service at St Peter's Church, historical hub of the London Italian community: 'As I sat there in the pews, it seemed as if I was watching a re-run of part of my identity *in the making*'.[6] She cites in this context Judith Butler's claim that identity is constructed through 'the stylized repetition of acts'[7] and notes that 'the rituals cultivated a sense of belonging'.[8] Fortier's position as a migrant studying migrant cultures within her destination culture draws attention very productively to the central role which organized religion can play in the reconstruction of identity – particularly a collective identity – in a new environment. Such a choral and often public-orientated re-enactment of cultural identity achieves a visibility which, however, can create tensions both within the migrant community and between communities. Abdel Malek Smari's novel, *Fiamme in paradiso*, locates the source of some of his own sense of hostile unbelonging in Italy in what he regards as an absurd simulacrum of Islamic faith and community which other Algerian migrants in Milan construct around their mosque.[9]

Gender and sexuality are the primary context of Butler's notion of the performative in identity, and of the power of repetitive acts to reproduce models which reinforce identities by making them appear 'natural'. Much of this chapter will explore these mechanisms, considering also the role of the body in the negotiation of identity. The constitutive function in identity of acts and of forms of embodiment places a sharp emphasis

---

[5] Michel de Certeau, *The Capture of Speech and Other Political Writings*, ed. by Luce Giard, trans. and afterword by Tom Conley (Minneapolis, MN: University of Minnesota Press, 1997), 172.
[6] Anne-Marie Fortier, *Migrant Belongings: Memory, Space, Identity* (Oxford: Berg, 2000), 133 (italics in original).
[7] Butler, *Gender Trouble*, 140.
[8] Fortier, *Migrant Belongings*, 133.
[9] Abdel Malek Smari, *Fiamme in paradiso* (Milan: Il Saggiatore, 2000).

on questions of visibility. Migration narratives often figure the migrant as constantly under surveillance. She monitors herself, and she is monitored by the society into which she has migrated. There is an acute sensitivity in narratives of migration to Italy to the exterior markers of identity, and to their reception and interpretation by Italian observers. As Homi Bhabha notes, '[T]he question of identification is never the affirmation of a pre-given identity, never a *self*-fulfilling prophecy – it is always the production of an image of identity and the transformation of the subject in assuming that image. The demand of identification – that is, to be *for* an Other – entails the representation of the subject in the differentiating order of otherness'.[10]

I have so far referred to 'identity', in the singular, for reasons of simplicity. The discussion itself indicates, however, the central and important consideration that identity is always, inevitably, plural, in process, modelled upon and in various contexts. Even the point made above about visibility and recognition highlights the fact that an identity which signifies one thing to its bearer might signify quite another to its observer, so identities are multiplied and contested from the very instant they are displayed as such. It is not a case of the migrant carrying a single, constant, and identifiable identity into a new context and adapting it there, but rather of a package of more or less fluid identities formulated according to one set of circumstances being shifted into different circumstances in which they are reinvestigated and reworked. My discussion of specific texts will look at how identity is deferred through a process of testing and adaptation, ever provisional: Fortier refers evocatively to 'the quivery character of identity'.[11] It is perhaps, therefore, more useful to address, rather than identity or even identities, the process or acts of identification. Ahmed notes that these acts are in fact constitutive 'encounters' between human subjects: 'identity does not simply happen in the privatised realm of the subject's relation to itself. Rather, in daily meetings with others, subjects are perpetually reconstituted: the work of identity formation is never over, but can be understood as the sliding across of subjects in their meetings with others'.[12]

---

10   Homi K. Bhabha, *The Location of Culture* (London: Routledge, 1994), 45 (italics in original).
11   Fortier, *Migrant Belongings*, 2.
12   Ahmed, *Strange Encounters*, 7.

My exploration in this chapter of the processes of identification narrated in Italian migration literature will privilege four main examples. *Immigrato*, by Mario Fortunato and Salah Methnani, is an explicitly autobiographical narrative of becoming a migrant in Italy, and in terms of the processes it foregrounds and the focal points of identification which it indicates, offers, in my view, a foundational story of the negotiation of individual identities through migration.[13] Younis Tawfik's novel, *La straniera*, on the other hand, posits a solidly constructed identity as a 'straniero integrato' which is progressively dismantled through dialogue with an 'other', raising the question of agency, and gender, in constructing identities.[14] Analysis of two novels by Amara Lakhous, *Scontro di civiltà per un ascensore a piazza Vittorio* and *Divorzio all'islamica a viale Marconi*, then allows the notion of the construction and performance of identity, and indeed its performative quality, to be discussed.[15] The second of these novels affords further insight into the particularities of the identification process for female migrant subjects, which are finally explored in the context of a female-authored novel, *Nuvole sull'equatore*, by Shirin Ramzanali Fazel.[16]

In *Immigrato*, co-written by Italian journalist and novelist Mario Fortunato and Tunisian writer Salah Methnani, and generally identified as the first published narrative in Italian of migration from a non-European country into Italy, migration emerges as both an accident in and a cause of a complex process of identification. The first-person narrative of the protagonist, Salah's, adolescence in Tunisia makes clear that he has struggled with the notion of who he is and wants to be from an early age, and migration to Italy simply accentuates this struggle. In fact, in the first chapter, 'A Tunisi', which recounts his adolescence at home, he identifies himself in many ways as already elsewhere. Italy, and the Italian language, serve him as a point of differentiation from his friends and peers: he learns some first

---

13   Mario Fortunato and Salah Methnani, *Immigrato* (Rome: Theoria, 1990).
14   Younis Tawfik, *La straniera* (Milan: Bompiani, 1999).
15   Amara Lakhous, *Scontro di civiltà per un ascensore a piazza Vittorio* (Rome: e/o, 2006) and *Divorzio all'islamica a viale Marconi* (Rome: e/o, 2010).
16   Shirin Ramzanali Fazel, *Nuvole sull'equatore. Gli italiani dimenticati. Una storia* (Cuneo: Nerosubianco, 2010).

words in Italian (with his father's help), watches black and white Italian films broadcast by RAI, studies languages and literatures at university and develops there relationships with Italian girls, and eventually makes a short visit to Sicily. In other words, Italy allows Salah gradually to construct an identity different from that which seems a 'given' in his home environment, and to fashion himself as a cosmopolitan individual whose identity is not determined by national, regional, or ethnic boundaries. A trip to Sicily allows him to articulate this distinction:

> Molti miei amici avevano già fatto quel viaggio: venivano in Italia per acquistare jeans Carrera o Levi's e qualche maglietta. Noi non comprammo niente. A Palermo, visitammo chiese e musei e, una sera, andammo al cinema, a vedere *C'era una volta in America*.
>
> Quando tornammo a Tunisi, i nostri amici si scandalizzarono. Dicevano: 'Siete andati in Italia e non avete comprato niente'. Anche mia madre era piuttosto delusa. Io non capivo perché un ragazzo tunisino non poteva andare in giro, in un Paese straniero, e comportarsi come voleva. Non capivo perché dovevo essere costretto a spendere i miei soldi solo per mostrarmi, sull'Avenue Burghiba, vestito come un fighetto occidentale.[17]

The resistance expressed here to a certain model of the relationship between Europe and the southern shore of the Mediterranean is insistent, articulated in the repetition of 'non capivo'. In place of a relationship expressed through dumb mimicry, as the narrator represents it, and through 'dressing up' as affluent Italians, Salah stakes a claim to be himself, but in a different place. The performance of the 'fighetto occidentale' is one he rejects, denoting for him a commodification of identity which annuls individual agency and appears to make of the subject simply a product for the consumption and pleasure of others. Interestingly, the adjective 'occidentale' in this term has, I think, a double value. On the one hand, it refers straightforwardly to the western male, dressed up to have sexual appeal (and whether to men or women or both is ambiguous). On the other, the notion of performing for the gaze of another which the phrase highlights suggests that the gaze

---

17   Fortunato and Methnani, *Immigrato*, 11–12.

itself may be 'occidentale', whilst the object of the gaze could be 'occidentale' or 'orientale' or, crucially, as the narrator's emphasis on dressing up and mimicry indicates, neither and both at once. Instead, the figure of the 'fighetto occidentale' might offer a construct of 'queered' national, ethnic and sexual identity, where codes of interpretation of conventionally marked behaviours are disrupted.

In this reading of the central importance of sexuality in the process of identification narrated in this novel, and the reference to queer theory, I am responding to and extending Derek Duncan's analysis of the novel as one which 'accent[s] the crisis in heterosexual masculinity that the phenomenon of immigration instigates and/or at least through which it is figured'.[18] In naming the 'fighetto occidentale' as an anti-model for Salah so early in the novel, the authors name a taboo which will in many ways govern the processes of identity formation and deformation which the novel recounts through Salah's Italian journey. It bespeaks an urgent anxiety in the subject that what he is depends almost entirely on what he is seen to be, and that this places his ambition of 'integration into Italian society through reproductive heterosexuality' in jeopardy if he falls under the gaze of the 'western' homosexual male.[19] On departure, he poses himself the question, '"Sto partendo come un emigrante nordafricano o come un qualsiasi ragazzo che vuole conoscere il mondo?". Quel giorno, non sapevo rispondermi'.[20] Again, as he projects himself into a new environment his concern is with how others will identify him; in other words, in his performance of his identity as a traveller in Italy his subjecthood is at stake.

---

18 Derek Duncan, 'Cultural Assimilation and Heterosexual Entitlement in Fortunato and Methnani's *Immigrato*', in Jennifer Burns and Loredana Polezzi, eds, *Borderlines: Migrant Writing and Italian Identities (1870–2000) / Borderlines: Migrazioni e identità nel Novecento* (Isernia: Iannone, 2003), 379–85 (380).
19 Duncan, 'Cultural Assimilation and Heterosexual Entitlement', 379.
20 Fortunato and Methnani, *Immigrato*, 14. As Duncan points out, the question is a rhetorical one, and 'the prescient reader probably thinks he knows which' (Duncan, 'Cultural Assimilation and Heterosexual Entitlement', 380).

Identity

Taking stock at the end of his brief stay in his first destination in Italy, Mazara del Vallo in Sicily, the narrator tacitly responds to the question he posed himself on departure from Tunis:

> Appena arrivato, pensavo che la vicinanza non solo geografico mi avrebbe aiutato un poco a inserirmi, a trovare una qualche definizione di me stesso. Pensavo che qui le cose sarebbero state, per così dire, a una giusta distanza. Ora invece, ancora senza un lavoro sia pure minimo, e con i soldi che diminuiscono pericolosamente, mi sento di colpo restituito a una realtà che non riesco, che non voglio accettare. Sono costretto a non vedermi più, in così poco tempo, come un giovane laureato all'estero. Non sono già più un ragazzo che vuole viaggiare e conoscere. No: di colpo, mi scopro a essere in tutto e per tutto un immigrato nordafricano, senza lavoro, senza casa, clandestino. Un individuo di ventisette anni venuto qui alla ricerca di qualcosa di confuso: il mito dell'Occidente, del benessere, di una specie di libertà. Tutte parole che già stanno cominciando a sfaldarsi nella mia testa.[21]

The sense that his identity is determined by the recognition of others is articulated clearly here in the use of an almost passive voice: 'mi sento [...] restituito', 'sono costretto a non vedermi', 'mi scopro a essere'. He appears to have no agency in the matter of his identification in the Italian context: he is seen rather than being able to present himself. He appears, indeed, to have nothing: all the positive values he had seen himself as possessing ('un giovane laureato all'estero') are replaced by a sense of absence and worthlessness ('senza lavoro, senza casa, clandestino'). The last adjective suggests even that he has, forcibly, become invisible. He no longer possesses the cultural credentials he enjoyed because they appear to have no value in this culture when attached to an 'immigrato nordafricano', so instead of being a 'laureato', he is simply 'un individuo', identifiable only by the basic marker of age. Even his well-defined and long-established cultural and intellectual motivations for migration are replaced by 'qualcosa di confuso' and by words which have become meaningless to him. This passage voices, then, a powerful sense of degradation and of loss: the experience of migration has stripped him of the attributes he possessed and left him meaningless, undifferentiated.

---

21 Fortunato and Methnani, *Immigrato*, 25–6.

Salah's encounters with other migrants in the novel similarly offer a range of identifications of himself which he struggles to resist. A Moroccan migrant named Jabari, in particular, whom he encounters on repeated occasions in his earliest days in Sicily, interprets and names the narrator in ways which Salah refuses but which he also accepts have such credibility as to make certain identities stick. These are 'encounters' in Ahmed's sense of the term, in that the everyday brushing against an 'other' forces a reconstitution of identity. The first such meeting with Jabari takes place in a shop in Trapani, shortly after disembarkation in Italy. Salah tries initially to establish contact with him simply by smiling, but this is met with hostility. He then notices that Jabari is putting items from the shelves into his pockets, and, curious to see whether he is genuinely stealing, and to what extent, Salah lingers and watches him for a while, as does the shop assistant. Jabari, anxious that Salah's attention will draw unwanted further attention to himself, leaves the shop: 'Con la mano destra, fa un gesto minaccioso. Bisbiglia in arabo: "Vaffanculo"'.[22]

This incident is interesting, and influential, for three main reasons. The first is that Jabari offers immediately a negative model of a migrant in Italy: his shoplifting is an act of disaffection and resentment, which Salah associates with social marginalization, and as such is 'proof', before he has properly arrived in Italy, that access to the 'mito dell'Occidente' is not guaranteed to outsiders. The second is that he articulates an absence of solidarity amongst migrants from similar cultures who are trying to find an identification in Italy. Whilst Salah makes quite clear and deliberate moves to establish contact with him in the shop, Jabari counters these with covert aggression. Identification is thus denied on two important levels. The third striking aspect of this incident is its impact on Salah. He is fascinated by Jabari, and fascinated by his hostility. Whilst contact of any kind is forcefully rejected on this occasion by Jabari, he nevertheless re-emerges in the narrative as an unsettling but compelling image of the individual Salah might become in Italy, or the flip-side of the 'giovane laureato all'estero'.

---

22   Fortunato and Methnani, *Immigrato*, 16.

The story which Jabari recounts when he and Salah later meet, by chance, in a bar illustrates that Jabari has travelled all over Italy and that he has breached every taboo that his culture holds: 'Spiega di aver fatto tutto: ha rubato, ha spacciato eroina, ha fatto il protettore di puttane'. After a short pause, Jabari continues, and this time what he says is recorded as direct speech: '"Solo una cosa non ho mai fatto: andare con i froci. Troppo vecchio. A quelli gli piacciono i ragazzini, quelli che hanno il cazzo giovane. Tu quanti anni hai?". Dico, con un brivido di paura: "Ventisette". Lui: "Allora vai bene. Il cazzo te lo puoi ancora vendere"'.[23] Jabari thus names the taboo which Salah feels most anxiety about, and furthermore, he dissociates himself from it and attaches it firmly to Salah, with the air of setting down a challenge to him to take this step which he has never taken. This, he indicates, is the identification which will bring Salah success in Italy. It is the absolute realization of the identification Salah had so emphatically rejected at home, embodied by the 'fighetto occidentale' which other Tunisian men of his age aimed to impersonate; those who, as he noted then in a brief reference to European male homosexual tourism in North Africa, earned some extra spending money by casually prostituting themselves to tourists. The fear acknowledged by Salah in the quotation above underscores that this image of the migrant male prostitute is his absolute taboo, the identification which most threatens to de-stabilize his carefully constructed sense of subjecthood in the world.

The effect of the encounter with Jabari in reorientating Salah's identity towards that of a homosexual prostitute remains a point of reference in the discussion of identity in this text, recharged in encounters with others in cities across Italy. A migrant friend and room-mate in Palermo, Jamel, discusses with him his ambition, and efforts, to find himself an Italian male lover to provide for him. Still in Palermo, when spending the evening with another young friend of a friend, Rached, the two of them are approached by an Italian man who is attracted to Rached. They go to his flat and Rached has sex with the man whilst the narrator waits, uneasily, in an adjacent room: 'Ogni tanto, sento dei gemiti, e poi Rached che mi

---

23 Fortunato and Methnani, *Immigrato*, 19.

parla in arabo: "Vedi un po' se riesci a fregare qualcosa". Per non ascoltarlo, riaccendo il televisore. Volume alto. Non voglio sentire. Non voglio pensare. Conto fino a dieci. Non sono qui'.[24] The counting to ten is an established tic, explained in the opening chapter of the novel. When his father first teaches him Italian, he learns to count to ten, but continually slips on the number ten, pronouncing 'dieci' as 'diaci'.[25] The repetition of the sequence here draws attention to a profound anxiety about any kind of slippage: a transgression in pronunciation is equated with the transgression of a personal code, and the voicing of the correct word serves again as a sort of litany to ward off danger and keep to the 'straight' path of the identification of himself that he seeks.[26] This absolute distancing from his surroundings and all they imply is undermined, however, by an attraction to the situation which recalls Salahs' attraction to Jabari (the link Rached voices between prostitution and theft seals the association). The sexual act behind closed doors is preceded by a fairly elaborate seduction on the streets of Palermo and then at Sandro's flat, which Salah observes and narrates with fascination: he notes Sandro's gestures and expressions, Rached's gestures and expressions, the room, its contents, the rapid financial transaction between the two men. The text suggests strongly that he is, hypothetically, placing himself in Rached's position.

This projection is ultimately realized when, in Rome, Salah is engaged to do some decorating work for a scenographer named Emilio, who seduces him into a sexual encounter in which Emilio asks Salah to abuse him. As he does so, Salah examines his own interior responses to this situation: 'Non so perché lo faccio. È come se tutta la mia rabbia si scaricasse. Una parte di me si domanda: "Ma che cazzo stai facendo?". Ma è una piccola parte remota. È lontana, in fondo al mio corpo. La bocca e il cervello sono pieni di odio e di saliva. Mentre sputo, ripeto fra i denti: "Mibun". In arabo, vuol

---

24 Fortunato and Methnani, *Immigrato*, 36–7.
25 Fortunato and Methnani, *Immigrato*, 10.
26 Duncan also comments on this mechanism: 'The hybrid form "diaci" is invoked to re-establish an imperilled identity and linguistically to echo his ailing heterosexual ambition' (Duncan, 'Cultural Assimilation and Heterosexual Entitlement', 382).

Identity

dire finocchio'.[27] This interior dialogue articulates finally a confrontation between two contrasting identifications of himself, in which anger surfaces, and is exteriorized through physical action (spitting and slapping), but also through verbal aggression expressed in Arabic. His recourse to his first language in order to express his rejection of the identity he is performing here indicates the motivation for this rejection in a different, and differently cultured, part of his subjecthood. That he uses Arabic suggests he is abusing himself as much as Emilio, for having realized the model he so powerfully rejected of the 'fighetto occidentale'.

Ahmed's foregrounding of 'encounters with others that surprise, that shift the boundaries of the familiar, of what we assume that we know'[28] is vividly justified in this encounter between Salah and Emilio, which produces in the narrator a sense of self-estrangement:

> È come se, all'improvviso, si fosse aperta una finestra che affaccia su una parte di me, prima totalmente sconosciuta. Nel buio di quell'angolo della mia coscienza, è filtrata una luce livida, bianca. Non sono offeso moralmente. Sono stupito. Mi osservo come se, da un momento all'altro, dovessi sorprendermi abitato da una seconda identità molto più sfuggente, obliqua. Qualche volta, fra me e me, mi chiamo per nome, per appurare di essere sempre io.[29]

The self-naming recalls the use of Arabic commented upon above, and draws attention to a sense of detachment from the 'mother-tongue' and the identity it established, presumed fixed but now revealed to be mobile. Salah also attempts to contact Mariella, a young Roman woman with whom he had had a relationship as a student in Tunis, which seems to be a bid to retrieve or perhaps simply to test an identity defined by 'normal' heterosexual relationships. It is a failed attempt: he speaks to Mariella on the telephone, but she has no recollection of his name and shows no recognition of him as a figure in her past. The brief verbal exchange between them is dominated by enunciation of his name, which he proposes and she questions with incomprehension. As Duncan notes, 'This is the only time in the text in which he

---

27 Fortunato and Methnani, *Immigrato*, 67.
28 Ahmed, *Strange Encounters*, 7.
29 Fortunato and Methnani, *Immigrato*, 67–8.

is named, yet in naming himself, he passes unrecognised'.[30] Corroborating the absence which his own self-naming indicated, the suggestion as Salah moves on from Rome is that the identity with which he left Tunis, that of the 'giovane laureato', presumed heterosexual, has been erased.

It is worth noting that the discourse on sexuality as a framework for identity construction has, in *Immigrato*, a counterpart in the narrator's engagement with drug culture in Italy. This manifests itself in casual use of 'soft' drugs (significantly, in the episode with Emilio discussed above), and, in the chapter recounting his time in Florence, as a brief experiment in using heroin as a prelude to becoming a dealer. As a taboo which somewhat parallels that of (commercialized) homosexuality in the narrative, to use and deal in drugs seems to offer Salah an identity, and one which he both resists and feels attracted to. It provides him with a role and with recognition, and one which is strikingly visualized as a somewhat grotesque embodiment, recalling that of the 'fighetto occidentale': 'Mi muovo con l'andatura tipica dei tossici: a piccoli passi, nervosi e saltellanti. Anch'io sono un tossico, adesso. Un tossico clandestino. Finalmente, ho un'identità.'[31]

Duncan notes that the narrative in *Immigrato* is one of a number which trace the course of a 'migrant ambition whose chief characteristic seems to be its failure'.[32] The migration to Italy which was intended to establish and consolidate the narrator's identity comes to nothing. As demonstrated in my analysis of this novel, the series of Salah's 'strange encounters' (to use Ahmed's term) in Italy produces a significant reconstitution of his identity, erasing his positive identifications of himself and installing in their place temporary identifications which he experiences as negative, and rejects as far as possible. The return to Tunisia at the end of the novel may seem structurally to signal a return to his roots in an attempt to retrieve the identity with which he ambitiously departed. The fact that he returns there to visit his father seems to confirm this. However, the encounter with his father is characterized by understatement, and by words and sentiments left

---

30   Duncan, 'Cultural Assimilation and Heterosexual Entitlement', 383.
31   Fortunato and Methnani, *Immigrato*, 80.
32   Duncan, 'Cultural Assimilation and Heterosexual Entitlement', 379.

Identity 35

unsaid: there is no redemptive re-building of a 'lost' identity. Salah recounts his stories of Italy to his father, and receives almost nothing in response. Significantly, even if his father were to be regarded as a primary reference point (something about which the narrator is somewhat diffident), this reference point has shifted, in the sense that his father is now not in Tunis, where Methnani grew up, but in the more southern city of Kairouan, which, as the narrator notes, is a city associated with mobility.³³ The suggestion is that there is nothing to be regained, in terms of identity, but rather that the process of identification, of piecing together and testing identities through multiple encounters, must of necessity continue. Indeed, Salah at the end of the novel anticipates his return to Italy, to start all over again, to some degree, but from a reconfigured starting point.

The discourse regarding identity in *Immigrato* is, then, very much an individual and relatively introspective one, concerned predominantly with distinguishing the individual from any sort of collective identity and with establishing a distinct and recognizable identification which is valid and significant in itself, irrespective of the cultural context (home or the destination culture) in which it is posited. Migration, in these circumstances, can be interpreted as in part a bid to release a sense of selfhood and of self-esteem from paradigms established by a specific culture, society or religion, and instead to forge an identification which is genuinely individual, informed but not dictated by context. The element of struggle which this implies is discernible in *Immigrato*, as illustrated above, but is played out also in other narratives of immigration to Italy, particularly Younis Tawfik's *La straniera*. The underlying premiss of this novel is – as will be discussed in Chapter 3 – that the encounter with the 'straniera' of the title provokes a reassessment of the male protagonist's positions with regard to his relations with Italy and with home, and this involves a re-evaluation of the identifications he has established as a successful Turinese architect of Middle

---

33 The narrator notes that the word means 'encampment' in Arabic, and describes the mobility connoted in the very architectural fabric of the city: 'Le sue case, la Medina, le strade, le piazze paiono, da un momento all'altro, dover riprendere il loro cammino' (Fortunato and Methnani, *Immigrato*, 127). He happens to arrive there on market day, which underscores the sense of a community in motion.

Eastern origin. Since the novel will be discussed in other chapters of this study, I will limit my comments here to those which pertain specifically to the elaboration of a dialogic negotiation of identity, and to the calibration of the self against a starkly differentiated 'other' – 'la straniera' – in which degrees of sameness and otherness are instrumental.

The entry of the 'foreign woman', a Moroccan female migrant named Amina, into the architect's life provokes a mixture of identification (or reidentification) with migrants in Italy and dismissive distancing from them. On the first evening that they meet, the architect takes Amina to a bar and notes as they enter: 'Lei si guarda intorno perplessa, come per chiedere se noi stranieri, o, come ci chiamano, "extracomunitari", possiamo entrare oppure no'.[34] The use of the first person plural, and the explicit application to himself as well as to Amina of labels attached by Italians to migrants, establishes a clear solidarity between them and a recognition, or recollection, on the architect's part, of the feelings which certain encounters produced in himself as a new arrival in Italy. However, as this second observation suggests, there is also an implicit distancing of himself from Amina, despite the apparent declaration of solidarity, in that she is marked as the one who displays a lack of experience that differentiates him as authoritative. This gap between them is articulated starkly by the architect only moments later, when a comment made by Amina about aspects of his personal life gleaned from being in his flat (where she has had sex with his friend) provokes an angry (interior) response: 'Vattene! Non potevi restare al tuo paese, invece di fare questa fine, in terra straniera? Che cosa te lo fa fare?'.[35] She is now an other to be addressed with hostility, and it is clear that she has transgressed a boundary of gender and class in enquiring into and commenting on his personal life. This reaction also reveals that Amina embodies for the architect a taboo, and – as is the case in *Immigrato* – one associated with sexuality and particularly its commodification across cultures. The architect goes on to articulate this in his narrative, exposing as he does a highly patriarchal notion of the policing of female sexuality as an issue of male integrity and

---

34   Tawfik, *La straniera*, 10.
35   Tawfik, *La straniera*, 11.

Identity 37

identity: 'Forse per orgoglio, o per falso pudore, mi sento ferito, umiliato. Mi sento geloso delle nostre donne. "Nostre", ecco dove sta il problema. Non perché fa quella vita, ma perché la fa qui, lei danneggia un'immagine che vogliamo conservare, per sembrare "stranieri brava gente"'.³⁶ Amina's sudden presence and visibility in his experience in Italy brings to life for him the identifications of a migrant that he has worked to deny – she is an illegal migrant, a sex worker, and a woman operating outside of a domestic role and of the jurisdiction of a man. Again, to assert his inclusion and her outlandish exclusion, he deploys and re-works the notion of 'italiani brava gente' to stress his command of Italian language and culture.³⁷

Encounters with the wider community of migrants in Turin reveal the full complexity of the architect's ambiguous identifications with Arabic and European cultures. Again, the peripheral presence of Amina in his life causes him to see and reflect upon this community, to which it seems he has so far been almost oblivious: in itself a sign of his non-identification of himself as a migrant. An episode of the novel, which I shall return to in Chapter 4 (see pages 154–5), merits discussion here in terms of its function as a tool for 'live' analysis of the architect's identifications. Returning home alone from a dinner party with Italian friends, where immigration and Middle Eastern affairs have been prominent topics of conversation, he sees, as if for the first time, the invisible night-time population of the city:

---

36 Tawfik, *La straniera*, 12.
37 See Sandra Ponzanesi, 'Outlandish Cinema: Screening the Other in Italy', in Sandra Ponzanesi and Daniela Merolla, eds, *Migrant Cartographies: New Cultural and Literary Spaces in Post-colonial Europe* (Oxford: Lexington Books, 2005), 267–80. She identifies the adjective, 'outlandish' as one which denotes the deterritorializing effect – following Gilles Deleuze and Félix Guattari, in *Kafka: Toward a Minor Literature*, trans. by Dana Polan (Minneapolis, MN: University of Minnesota Press, 1986) – of migrants' otherness in Italy: 'It literally but also metaphorically refers to the deterritorialization that characters impersonate, and to the way they are perceived – as weird and exotic – within the Italian society' (270). This effect is manifest here, and, interestingly, is visited upon an individual who is himself a migrant, claiming ownership of the positions of a 'major' culture.

> Per la prima volta, noto delle figure sbandate. Persone, spesso sole o in piccoli gruppi, che popolano le strade della notte. Stranieri caratterizzati dai loro modi di camminare e di vestire. [...] Li guardo con occhi diversi: forse li vedo per la prima volta con una mente più chiara. Sono soli come me. Vivono in un mondo loro, un mondo di ricordi e di sofferenze, un mondo di emarginazione e senza domani. Sono fantasmi della coscienza collettiva. Ripudiati dall'indifferenza. Come al solito, e soprattutto quando rientro a mezzanotte passata, mi prende una grande voglia di sostare davanti a uno di quei chioschi ambulanti, improvvisati nelle piazze, per prendere un panino caldo e parlare con le persone radunate intorno. Poco dopo, mi rendo conto di aver paura. Non capisco perché vederli tutti lì, abbracciati tra di loro, o impegnati in accese conversazioni, mi faccia sentire un estraneo. Fanno parte della categoria degli emarginati, mentre io appartengo a quella degli integrati. Sento di non essere uno di loro. Spingo l'acceleratore e mi avvio verso casa. Forse sto scappando.[38]

It is interesting that his first response is to take the position of an Italian insider, identifying the migrants as 'stranieri', and responding visually to their external characteristics – clothes, gait, etc. - as 'outlandish'. He remains in the comfortable seclusion of his car and observes them with almost scientific intensity, as an anthropological curiosity, so articulating a position of detached superiority and also attraction which is markedly, almost stereotypically, 'orientalist'.[39] He defines his own position of successful Italian-ness by measuring and categorizing their otherness. However, reiterating that he is now seeing them anew or afresh ('per la prima volta'), he then shifts to imagining their interior experience – their solitude, nostalgia, anxiety – and thus recognizes himself as one of them, shifting to the position of an outsider with respect to Italian society. This produces the impulse to join the group of migrants and share stories with them, but the prospect of such an encounter suddenly estranges him again from this group, not, this time, because he rejects them from the position of an Italian insider, but rather because their solidarity and contiguity of experience makes their identification with each other seem exclusive: he cannot identify

---

38   Tawfik, *La straniera*, 121–2.
39   I refer to Edward Said, *Orientalism* (London: Routledge & Kegan Paul, 1978), in which he establishes the mechanism, central to postcolonial thought, of constructing the 'Orient', by means of the western gaze, as a set of essential characteristics which, through binary opposition, confirm the superiority of western culture.

Identity

with them. They share a warmth ('panino caldo', 'accese conversazioni') of which he, as cold observer, seemingly cannot partake. The fear attached to this realization is an indicator of the anxiety which the subsequent statement of 'belonging' attempts to hide. He marks 'them' as different because marginalized, whereas he is part of an integrated group, and yet the reader knows from the position of distance and isolation articulated during the social event with Italians that he has just attended that he is not entirely part of any group. His very recourse to categories is itself a signal of his anxiety about belonging, in that they refer to externally applied definitions of type, which fit awkwardly with the complex interior senses of association and disassociation he expresses here. His isolation is stressed by the rapid acceleration away at the end of the above passage.

This mediated perspective on migrants in Turin – mediated by the 'safe' and status-confirming viewing enclosure provided by his car – is repeated in a further encounter with migrants on the night-time streets, despite the significant difference that on this second occasion the architect is on foot, and accompanied by Amina. The mediation on this second occasion derives from a substantial difference of experience between the architect and the migrants on the street. Though the use again of terms carrying a heavy emotional charge – 'emarginati', 'esclusi', 'sofferenza', 'solitudine' – exposes a level of empathy between the narrator and those he observes, the distance he ultimately feels is clearly marked by his position precisely as an observer and by the tone he adopts. He permits himself to perform an almost Lombrosian exercise in behavioural analysis, categorizing and dehumanizing the objects (emphatically 'loro') of his apparently expert gaze:[40]

> Si sentono accenti come echi di un *hammam* surreale. Arabi, africani e albanesi s'incontrano con tensione e diffidenza, e presto si scontrano. Sembrano cani abbandonati e pieni di rabbia. Non si sopportano a vicenda, e danno l'idea di avercela con il mondo intero. Forse perché si sentono emarginati ed esclusi, sfogano la loro ira in quel modo. Hanno sui volti i tratti della solitudine quando diventa sofferenza. Si

---

40 I refer to the work of nineteenth-century Italian criminologist Cesare Lombroso, whose positivist and anthropological view of criminality identified the propensity to commit crime as innate and manifested in physical features and behaviours.

atteggiano in mille modi diversi. Il modo di camminare ha un significato. Il modo di guardare e di sputare per terra. Anche il modo di fumare una sigaretta ha un significato per loro. Ogni gesto cerca di dire o sottolineare la loro esistenza, di cui forse sono al corrente soltanto loro.[41]

The otherness of the people observed, and of their behaviour, is underscored by the suggestion that it is beyond reality: 'surreale'. Interestingly, a very similar motif is used by Fortunato and Methnani in *Immigrato*, in an incident in which Salah and two other migrants, Majid and Mohamed, drink alcohol as a form of escape from their desperation, after which the other two start to fight. Salah comments: 'Guardo Majid e Mohamed che continuano ad azzuffarsi come fossi davanti allo schermo di un cinema.'[42] Again, there is an unreal quality to the scene and a powerful sense, albeit here in part alcohol-induced, that the observer is totally detached from it. In both cases, the narrator's sense of distance articulates a differentiation of himself from the 'mass' of migrants. As well as creating a sense of protected detachment, however, the simile used by Fortunato and Methnani – the cinema screen – draws attention to the powerful element of performance in the scenes observed in both *Immigrato* and *La straniera*. In all cases, the reader's attention is drawn to – as the passage quoted immediately above stresses – 'modi'. We look at the manners, fashions, self-presentations which the migrants offer; or in short, how they act. In emphasizing migrant identity as performance, Tawfik, by means of the mechanism of his narrator's observation of the 'strangers' and their strange behaviours, reveals the self-reflexive critique enacted by the architect's gaze. His acute sensitivity to their performance of their identity bespeaks a critical awareness of his own self-fashioning as a middle-class Italian.

Tawfik's novel, in many ways, articulates a dialogue about the notion of 'passing', which is at the centre also of Amara Lakhous's novels set in Rome: *Scontro di civiltà per un ascensore a piazza Vittorio* and *Divorzio all'islamica*

---

41 Tawfik, *La straniera*, 128.
42 Fortunato and Methnani, *Immigrato*, 24.

a viale Marconi. Both, again, dialogical or polyphonic novels,[43] the central male protagonist in each occupies an equivocal position between being identified as, or indeed being, either Italian or North African. In *Scontro di civiltà per un ascensore a piazza Vittorio*, the protagonist's name is the fulcrum of this discussion: he is Ahmed, an Algerian migrant, but is identified by almost all of the 'witnesses' whose individual accounts of him make up the body of the text as Amedeo, an Italian, and specifically a Roman. The interplay in the structure of the novel between these accounts of the protagonist and his own reflections and comments, recorded in eleven 'ululati' interspersed between the witness statements, serves to illuminate the gap that exists between the individual subject's identifications of himself and the identifications constructed of him by others.

The interplay of perspectives or gazes on 'Amedeo', as an identity constructed within and by the public life of the community, also illustrates the mechanisms of passing: Amedeo appears to have no strategy or will to appear to be someone other than he is, and yet, a number of visible or performable attributes and behaviours ('modi', recalling Tawfik's novel) which he displays challenge the construction of a migrant harboured by his neighbours and associates, and thus render him effectively unrecognizable as a migrant. For instance, the statement of bar owner Sandro Dandini opens with a rapid taxonomy of migrants' linguistic tics, aimed at establishing Sandro's expertise in identifying and placing the migrants who form the majority of his clientele. It is this 'expertise' which permits Sandro to deny unequivocally Amedeo's foreign-ness:

> Ricordo ancora il nostro primo incontro: ha chiesto un cappuccino e un cornetto, si è seduto e ha cominciato a leggere la rubrica di Montanelli sul *Corriere della Sera*. Non ho mai visto nella mia vita un cinese, un marocchino, un rumeno o uno zingaro o un egiziano leggere *Il Corriere della Sera* o *La Repubblica*. Gli immigrati leggono solamente *Porta Portese* per vedere gli annunci di lavoro.[44]

---

43 The structure of *Divorzio all'islamica a viale Marconi* is in fact similar to that of Tawfik's *La straniera*, with male and female protagonists narrating their experiences in the first person in alternating chapters. See Chapter 5 of this book, 'Literature', for further comment on this structure.

44 Lakhous, *Scontro di civiltà per un ascensore a piazza Vittorio*, 130.

Amedeo's performance of Italian-ness here, structured around the three pivotal points of cappuccino, cornetto, *Corriere* (which together function as something of a totem repeated elsewhere in the novel),[45] is demonstrated to possess literally performative power, in the sense that by reproducing this set of behaviours, he instantiates himself in that place and in that moment as Italian (indeed, Roman).[46] By being like an Italian (and unlike a migrant), in Sandro's eyes, Amedeo becomes Italian.

Amedeo's capacity to pass also has much to do with place.[47] Just as, in calibrating nationality according to reading habits in the quotation above, Sandro defines migrants as those who read for immediate necessity rather than for pleasure or broad enquiry, the fact that Amedeo knows Rome much better than he needs to is, for many of the witnesses (both Italian and non-Italian), evidence that he is a native to the capital. Sandro himself comments on this, asserting knowledge as the possession of Italians and so implying that migrants somehow do not 'know' (and here, use of the Italian 'conoscere', with its notions of familiarity and acquaintance, is germane): 'Voi non conoscete Amedeo come lo conosco io. Conosce la storia di Roma e le sue strade meglio di me, anzi meglio di Riccardo Nardi, fierissimo delle sue origini che risalgono agli antichi romani. Riccardo il tassista, che attraversa le strade di Roma su e giù ogni giorno da vent'anni.'[48] Only the permanence and the roots with which being a 'native' is endowed can produce, he suggests, the depth and thickness of intimacy and understanding of the city which Amedeo displays, whilst for a migrant to have anything but the most literally superficial and instrumental 'knowledge' of place would be, in this view, preposterous. Interestingly, another non-Italian

---

45 In a diary entry within the 'ottavo ululato' (139–43) which follows Sandro's testimony, Ahmad notes, 'Sono diventato un credente estremista della triade cappuccino, cornetto, e *Corriere della Sera*!' (Lakhous, *Scontro di civiltà per un ascensore a piazza Vittorio*, 139).

46 My notions of the performative and of ritualized production of an identity here are informed by Butler's *Gender Trouble* and her *Bodies That Matter: On the Discursive Limits of 'Sex'* (London: Routledge, 1993).

47 There is fuller discussion of this aspect in Chapter 4, pages 166–8.

48 Lakhous, *Scontro di civiltà per un ascensore a piazza Vittorio*, 134.

Identity 43

in the novel articulates in his statement a similar association of Amedeo with place. Iranian refugee, Parviz Mansoor Samadi, comments: 'non posso immaginare Roma senza Amedeo'.[49] In this instance, and from the perspective of another migrant, Amedeo constitutes the city not because he knows its history and topography intimately, but because he constitutes a form of mutual sociality for migrants trying to make a life in the city: he permits an inclusive community to be 'imagined', as the choice of lexis signals.[50] The justification Parviz offers for his statement that Rome would not be Rome without Amedeo is the story of how Amedeo in effect rehabilitated him to life in the capital after, as a desperate articulation of his protest at being denied refugee status, he literally sewed up his own mouth. For Parviz, Amedeo is Rome because he endows the city with humanity.

Lakhous's novel challenges very directly the notion of identity as sameness, in terms of the relation any object or person bears to itself, and as such develops the enquiry into self-estrangement established in *Immigrato* and *La straniera* into new territories. The statements which make up the text of the novel, interchanging with Amedeo's accounts of himself in diaristic mode, repeatedly draw attention to the gap between his own identification of himself and of his presence in the world and the constructs of Amedeo which others have assembled, and to the impossibility of him genuinely seeing his own sense of his subjecthood reflected in the responses of others around him, even while he acquiesces willingly in these constructs as part of his everyday life. The effect of this, and of the tension between the Amedeo recognized by his neighbours and the Ahmed of the past, is to produce the almost schizophrenic anguish which speaks in the final three 'ululati', and which is, of course, articulated powerfully in the very unspeakability, the failure of language (and of naming) which the howl expresses. In one of the excerpts, dated 16th March, within the final 'ululato', Amedeo himself questions whether he fits the identity constructed for him by his fellow Romans: 'Ogni tanto mi prende il dubbio quando penso che passo per

---

49 Lakhous, *Scontro di civiltà per un ascensore a piazza Vittorio*, 24.
50 I draw for this notion on Benedict Anderson, *Imagined Communities: Reflections on the Origin and Spread of Nationalisms* (London: Verso, 2006).

buono agli occhi di tutti. Ma che ne sanno? Amedeo potrebbe essere una semplice maschera! Io sono un selvaggio animale che non può abbandonare la sua natura d'origine'.[51]

In expressing his own estrangement from the model of the Roman citizen which has been established around his person or persona, Amedeo here also highlights the mechanisms of identification which the reader has just witnessed in action within the police inspector's summing up of the murder investigation. The conclusion of Mauro Bettarini in fact consists of two narratives of the case, in which Amedeo is first guilty then innocent of the crime. What the first account relies upon in identifying Amedeo's culpability is not any specific and reliable evidence related to the crime itself, but rather Bettarini's uncovering of the fact that Amedeo was a migrant: 'abbiamo scoperto che è un immigrato e che il suo vero nome è Ahmed Salmi. Come vi ho già detto, i criminali e i delinquenti sono abituati a falsificare i dati personali'.[52] The slippage between his being a migrant and being a murderer is achieved without obstacle here, with the assumption of a shared propensity for using multiple identities being sufficient to overcome any divide between migrant and criminal. In this way, Bettarini's deduction illustrates perfectly the irony of the logic of Amedeo's statement, in the 'ululato' cited above, of his incapacity to overcome what is his 'nature'. Bettarini's identification of this 'truth' exposes a powerful principle that a migrant must absolutely be visible in society as a migrant: to be seen to pass as Italian or Roman is simply a deceit which can entirely be equated with any other, however morally or legally unacceptable (Lombroso is again called to mind).

This 'truth' is, however, the first of two which Bettarini recounts in his statement, and the second concludes in Amedeo's innocence. In this version, Amedeo was involved in a road accident on the morning of the murder (hours before the murder was estimated to have taken place) and has been unconscious since. Proof of the culpability of another resident of the apartment block, Elisabetta Fabiani, has been found. Bettarini states

---

51   Lakhous, *Scontro di civiltà per un ascensore a piazza Vittorio*, 186.
52   Lakhous, *Scontro di civiltà per un ascensore a piazza Vittorio*, 180.

Identity

before offering his two conclusions to the investigation that: 'Ho imparato dal mio lavoro di commissario di polizia che la verità è come una moneta, ha due facce. La prima completa sempre la seconda.'[53] In this way, despite offering two accounts of the case, one of which based on supposition and the other on evidence, he asserts the co-dependency of the two accounts: the fact that Amedeo was a migrant passing as a Roman cannot be overlooked, even in the second outcome, where it has no bearing on the events whatsoever. In explicitly offering two sides to his truth in this statement, Bettarini concludes the discourse on 'truths' which the structure of the text assembles through its chapter headings, each of which (Amedeo's 'ululati' aside) is entitled 'La verità di', followed by the name of each witness. These chapters or statements, delivered using the first person singular, serve to underscore that the 'truth' is something which each individual possesses, and which belongs uniquely to him. In this sense, it is not something empirically verifiable nor fully shared, but rather it is constructed according to the unique perspective of each individual, albeit sharing common ground (literally, in this novel) and some common experience.

Amedeo's story itself – in the form of the 'ululati' – has structural primacy in that it is expressed in eleven episodes which punctuate the novel regularly from beginning to end. Also, since it is made of diary entries sharing impressions and ideas, rather than being a statement self-consciously performed as part of a police investigation, it appears to confide in the reader closely and consistently and so to bear a different level of truth, in terms of the expression of individual subjecthood. That this confessional – at places, almost psychoanalytical – account is itself punctured, uncertain, disturbed, and destructively self-questioning seals the novel with a sense that the 'truth' even of intimate individual identity is as contested and contingent as the reified truth of judicial processes. Drawing self-reflexively upon the framework story of the *Thousand and One Nights*, in the final excerpts of his final 'ululato' (bearing dates which correspond, presumably, to the period in which he remains in a coma in hospital), Amedeo calls to Shahrazad to help him to narrate a story in order to survive, and

---

53 Lakhous, *Scontro di civiltà per un ascensore a piazza Vittorio*, 177.

to Shahrayar (sister and accomplice of Shahrazad, against the authority of the Sultan).[54] He thus suggests that the construction of stories, the elaboration of multiple, fragmented 'truths' to fit the place and the moment, is a mode of survival which shields the teller from the single gaping truth, which is death. Creating identities is thus a way of creating a framework for existence in society around a central void.

It is interesting that the structural principle of an exchange of voices, narrating in the first person, defines the novels discussed here by Tawfik and by Lakhous (both novels), articulating a sense intimated in novels as early as *Immigrato* that a fundamental intercultural mechanism might be identified in the capacity to see and experience subjecthood through the eyes of another. First-person accounts, especially in these later, multi-voiced novels, facilitate the direct and intimate expression to the reader of the migrant's position – emotional, political, ethical, religious, economic, cultural – in relation to the society into which s/he has moved. Distinctive in Tawfik's *La straniera* and in Lakhous's *Divorzio all'islamica a viale Marconi* is the attempt to articulate specifically the position of a woman migrant via this same narrative means. The characterization of Amina in *La straniera* will be discussed in Chapter 3 ('Home'), so I will not discuss her expression of her identity here. Safia/Sofia, in Lakhous's more recent novel, is discussed briefly there and in Chapter 4 ('Place and Space'), but the expression through her of a migrant female identity is striking in this novel, and merits further exploration here, alongside – to a lesser degree – that of her male counterpart.

In *Divorzio all'islamica a viale Marconi*, the male protagonist, Christian, is the Sicilian grandson of a man born in Tunis to Italian parents who had migrated there from Trapani. Raised in Mazara del Vallo (Methnani's first stop in Italy as narrated in *Immigrato*), he describes the fishing port as a

---

54 Adriana Cavarero, in *Tu che mi guardi, tu che mi racconti: Filosofia della narrazione* (Milan: Feltrinelli, 1997), analyses the function of Shahriyar in relation to Sheherazade (her spellings) in terms of the resistance to closure which characterizes also Lakhous's novel: 'È infatti tipico di ogni storia esigere un racconto che si fermi solo alla fine, quando la storia stessa è finita e può parlare il silenzio.[…] La storia, sempre, è sospesa *sulla* sua fine' (159; italics in original).

community accommodating a fluid intercultural mix, where the shared activity of fishing is the primary mode of recognition and community, and nationality – be it Italian or Tunisian – is a secondary factor. Language, similarly, passes fluidly between Tunisian Arabic and Italian. Building on this open sense of identity, better described, perhaps, as Mediterranean rather than Italian, Christian has reconstructed a North African identity by studying Arabic language and culture at university. The novel begins as he is assigned the task, as a police officer, of going undercover amongst the North African migrant community of Rome in order to investigate a possible terrorist plot (which ultimately turns out to be a 'messa in scena'[55] designed to test his capacity to work undercover and to pass as a North African Muslim). As such, he becomes Issa, a Tunisian migrant in the capital. The question of passing is thus central again to this novel, though reversed: an Italian national seeks to pass as a migrant (and succeeds).

Revealing though the process of Issa's 'becoming' a North African migrant is in this novel, it is the insight into the construction of female migrant identities offered by his co-protagonist and co-narrator, an Egyptian woman named Safia, who calls herself Sofia in Italy, which is of particular interest. The question of agency in the construction of identity, which was explored in Lakhous's earlier novel in terms of whose formulation of Amedeo might prevail, is here played out in terms of gender as well as ethnicity. Whilst Issa's story to some extent tests the limits of his agency and freedom – his playing of the role of Issa is at once a realization of identifications he has long prized and nurtured and an expression of his subordination to his immediate boss and to the broader law enforcement structures of a sovereign state – Sofia's is a complex and protracted exploration of her capacity to pursue the construction of her own projected subjecthood within the quite stark strictures of a 'protected' and heavily surveyed cultural construction of adult femininity. By means of the spirited and confessional tone which the first-person narrative facilitates, the reader is able to participate in Sofia's responses to and articulations of major issues related to her identity and her view of the societies she knows

---

[55] Lakhous, *Divorzio all'islamica a viale Marconi*, 185.

or encounters. This participation taking the form of sharing Sofia's rigorous and largely non-ideological questioning of practices and behaviours which she witnesses within the domestic space and within public space in Italy, and those which she recognizes from her home culture. Sofia also shares her ambitions and desires – expressed vividly through her recounting of her dreams and nightmares in some instances –, elaborating a future for herself as a sought-after hairstylist in Italy, running her own business and transforming the lives of women by realizing for them the untapped potential which their hair holds for them to be someone different. Whilst inhabiting Rome in a way which may, from the outside, accord with a stereotype of the cloistered Muslim wife and mother whose engagements with the world are limited to the demands of her domestic work, Sofia demonstrates compellingly through the expression of her interiority that such spatial and cultural confinement need not necessarily equate with lack of agency. The prominent presence of Sofia's voice in the novel is a powerful illustration of a principle established by Sara Ahmed, Claudia Castañeda, Anne-Marie Fortier and Mimi Sheller in the introduction to their co-edited volume, *Uprootings/Regroundings*, that '*Being grounded is not necessarily about being fixed; being mobile is not necessarily about being detached*'.[56]

The ways in which Sofia asserts a capacity to act, move, and change despite being, relatively, 'grounded' in the viale Marconi zone where she lives, and in which she articulates the attachments to principles established in her home culture which persist despite having moved into a different cultural environment, centre on her attitude to wearing a veil. She recounts in her second chapter that her husband – a trained architect named Said who, when they agreed to marry, had already migrated to Rome to work there as a chef, taking the name Felice – instructed her shortly before their marriage to wear the veil when she joined him in Italy, and she refused. She recalls the conversation, in which she offered a robust and reasoned defence of her manifest respect for her faith, and argued that wearing the

---

56   Sara Ahmed, Claudia Castañeda, Anne-Marie Fortier and Mimi Sheller, eds, *Uprootings/Regroundings: Questions of Home and Migration* (Oxford: Berg, 2003), 1 (italics in original).

veil would make neither her faith itself nor her demonstration of it more powerful. She also recalls that she capitulated when she realized that to call off the marriage at this point would inevitably be interpreted in her community as evidence that she was no longer a virgin, and that this would have consequences not only for her, but for her whole family, including female relatives who hoped to marry and would be rejected because of the shame attached to the family as a result of her presumed behaviour. This episode, recalled from a different environment prior to migration, offers an illustration, following from Lakhous's earlier novel, of the capacity of communities to construct individual histories and identities with recourse predominantly to the assumptions and projections they harbour and minimally to the self-expression and behaviour of the individual concerned. More strikingly, it offers a rich confirmation of a stereotype related to the status of women – and of women's sexuality – in a Muslim society (recalling the anxiety Tawfik's architect expresses about the control of female sexuality). Sofia represents herself as having severely limited agency in this situation, but interestingly, she represents herself as asserting all agency she possesses within the specific, one-to-one relationship between herself and her future husband: she argues powerfully against him. It is his capacity to invoke and to stand for broader cultural practices which annuls her agency: she cannot challenge his will without challenging the marriage itself, and she cannot challenge the marriage without exposing her challenge to the embedded responses which will inform its interpretation by the wider community. Sofia expresses this using the analogy of boxing, describing Felice's instruction to her to adopt the veil as 'Un vero colpo basso. Un pugno sotta la cintura'. She then reflects that 'Se fossimo stati sul ring l'arbitro l'avrebbe subito ammonito e io avrei guadagnato dei punti', only to conclude that 'Il vero problema è che viviamo in una società nella quale il maschio fa contemporaneamente l'avversario e l'arbitro. Noi donne che dobbiamo fare?'.[57] Her sense of being cornered, of having no recourse to natural justice because her perspective and her reasoning hold no authority, is expressed all the more powerfully precisely because of the

---

57 Lakhous, *Divorzio all'islamica a viale Marconi*, 39.

illusion of a fair contest which is created both by the boxing metaphor and by her rigorous attempt to make her case individually to her husband and to persuade him to negotiate.

Once in Italy, the veil continues to hold symbolic value as the regulator and measure of Sofia's identity. She notes its function, in fact, as a metonym for an entire system of anxieties and prejudices about Islam in the west:

> Il mio velo era come un semaforo davanti al quale la gente deve fermarsi. Quella sosta obbligata era il momento ideale per scaricare tensioni, paure, inquietudini, ansia eccetera eccetera. [...] In realtà, quando camminavo per le strade di viale Marconi non ero mai sola. Ero sempre a braccetto con tanti accompagnatori fantasma: i loro nomi? Jihad, guerra santa, kamikaze, undici settembre, terrorismo, attentati, Iraq, Afghanistan, Torri Gemelle, bombe, undici marzo, al-Qaeda, talebani. E chi più ne ha più ne metta.[58]

In analysing this reaction, or indeed, cultural phenomenon, Sofia effectively dismantles the construct of an identity which has been assembled around her by dint of the associations triggered by her dress. She then takes the decision to deconstruct it by challenging directly the associative mechanisms upon which it depends, and does so again through the device of the veil. She chooses brightly coloured veils instead of black, combining these strikingly with clothing in contrasting colours, and commits also to transmitting an exaggeratedly positive image ('Cerco di essere sempre sorridente').[59] In this way, she seeks to expose the absurdity of the reflex association of Islam with terrorism by hyperbolically making a spectacle of its opposite, forcing a recognition of an Islamic identity manifested through colour, vitality, and human warmth. She notes that this requires a massive effort of will and of 'fiducia in me stessa,'[60] and this in itself offers an interesting example of the assertion of a very specific, and in some ways limited, form of individual agency against the weight of deeply rooted cultural constructs of identity. From a position in which she apparently has very little room to act, to gain a purchase on cultural habits and practices

---

58   Lakhous, *Divorzio all'islamica a viale Marconi*, 62.
59   Lakhous, *Divorzio all'islamica a viale Marconi*, 63.
60   Lakhous, *Divorzio all'islamica a viale Marconi*, 63.

in the wider world, she articulates her own identity with studied eloquence against an identification of her which – perhaps even more than in the case of male migrant characters such as Amedeo – is almost unassailably solid and fortified by prejudice: that of the veiled and silent, invisible, presumed therefore almost non-existent, Muslim woman.

The identification made of this figure of the veiled female migrant is spoken very directly by an Italian man whom she encounters in the market, and who assaults her verbally and physically for no reason other than his racism. It is striking that he identifies her first as lacking speech: he gives her a hostile look and then asks if she understands Italian, and when he hears her respond in fluent Italian, names her as 'Una mummia che parla!' (interestingly, exposing her rhetorically to the crowd around them as such, rather than addressing her as an individual subject). He then associates her with extremism and terrorism, before drawing attention to her invisibility, 'Ma vattene in Afghanistan con il tuo burqa'. It is at this moment that he pushes her so that she falls, confirming that she is, in his identification, an object to be removed, rather than a human subject to be engaged with. Sofia herself is attuned in this moment to the spectacle she creates for the crowd around her: 'La gente si dispone in cerchio intorno a noi per godersi lo spettacolo dal titolo "La Maya velata e il cretino razzista".'[61] In recounting the moment in this way, and noting that she does not or cannot respond to the aggressor (rather Issa, as a passer-by, steps in to protest against the man's behaviour), Sofia draws attention to the performative force of the racist's identification of her. Staged, as it is, in public, and with the conviction of the right-ness of his own, albeit nonsensical, description of her and of the crowd's acquiescence in that identification, his naming of her has the effect of producing her, in this situation, as a speechless, invisible object. The incident fits so perfectly the construction of the encounter between racist Italian and female migrant which Sofia identifies the onlookers – whether Italian or non-Italian – as willing to recognize, that it performs the stereotype in action. Her sense of her own subjecthood and her agency are glimpsed briefly here in her initial speech and in her comments to the

---

61   Lakhous, *Divorzio all'islamica a viale Marconi*, 105.

reader or listener, but in effect, in the public place, her agency and her humanity are annulled in this performative transaction.

The impact of this incident, in terms of Sofia's sense of her identity and her self-expression, is twofold. On the one hand, the policing of the way in which she acts out her own identity in the public sphere escalates, and from multiple directions. Her husband, when he eventually hears of the incident (Sofia does not tell him herself), suggests that he accompany her now on all excursions from their apartment, in a move which will deny her any identification other than that of his wife, and deny her the opportunities for free expression offered by conversations in the park with women (of a number of ethnicities) whom she has come to know, by visits to the market, visits to friends, etc. Her response is a refusal to him, and a comment in her narrative that 'Questa è una trappola vera e propria, però io non ci casco'.[62] An Italian woman known well in the migrant community, converted to Islam and married to a Muslim who styles himself as an *imam* in order to propagate extremist interpretations of the scriptures, visits her and in effect issues a *fatwa* against her veil ('Il velo colorato crea disordine e tentazione'),[63] threatening her with reprisals if she insists on wearing it. The fear and humiliation which the incident itself necessarily engenders also threaten to press her back into the relative safety of the domestic space, realizing an outcome to which she alludes earlier in the novel, when discussing the metonymic function of her veil, commenting that she should resist the pressure on her of the effect of the fear of others (Italian), 'per non isolarmi fra le quattro mura domestiche'.[64] In other words, from within, between, and beyond her own ethnic community in Rome, judgments of her behaviour are conveyed to her which rely upon different criteria and different models of acceptable public performance of her identity as a Muslim woman in Italy, but which accord in attempting to restrict her movement and her already veiled self-expression.

---

62   Lakhous, *Divorzio all'islamica a viale Marconi*, 145.
63   Lakhous, *Divorzio all'islamica a viale Marconi*, 107.
64   Lakhous, *Divorzio all'islamica a viale Marconi*, 62.

On the other hand, and as predicated earlier in the text, Sofia does resist this pressure to retreat from the public space and the instrument of resistance is again the veil. She now adopts this as part of her presentation of herself and thus as an essential property of her exterior identity and almost a prosthetic organ: 'Con il passare del tempo divento solidale con il mio velo. Sì, è proprio così. È vero che all'inizio non l'ho scelto, però adesso è il simbolo della mia identità, anzi è la mia seconda pelle'.[65] Not only does she accept it into her own person and her own body, but she actively defends it and so wields it as a political instrument as well: 'Non è più una questione di velo, di vestito, di tessuto, ma di dignità. Se non accettano il mio velo vuol dire che rifiutano la mia religione, la mia cultura, il mio paese di origine, la mia lingua, la mia famiglia, in breve la mia intera esistenza'.[66] Her act of resistance is also here an appropriation of the metonymic value of the veil itself: no longer will she let onlookers interpret what it means to them, and thus allow them to determine who she is, but instead, she will invest in it all that she understands of her own identity, and will insist on displaying this within the gaze of the others. Her response here to the evidence that she is always, in public, under scrutiny is to challenge those who survey her by attempting to re-set the terms of her performance of identity from her own perspective.

One might read this reaction to the veil itself, and to reactions to the veil, as a process of Sofia in fact adapting herself to the dual force of ideologies dominating in the domestic sphere and in the public space of Italy in order to appear in public ultimately as others expect to see her: a veiled Muslim woman. According to this view, in asserting her own decision to wear and to defend the veil, she is in fact demonstrating her own complicity with patriarchal and racist authority, rather than representing herself as an individual in the face of it. Indeed, Lakhous offers his reader no narrative of female emancipation in this novel, and at the typically inconclusive end of the narrative, Sofia's position is uncertain: she faces the anxiety of being a divorced Muslim migrant woman in Italy, and/or the possibility

---

65   Lakhous, *Divorzio all'islamica a viale Marconi*, 105.
66   Lakhous, *Divorzio all'islamica a viale Marconi*, 105–6.

of a new life with Issa, whose double identity she knows nothing of. In many ways, she is as dependent, compromised, and confined as she was at any point in her narrative.

What is important to recognize within Sofia's story in this novel is, however, the force of her agency in constantly reviewing and negotiating her position as a wife, mother, Muslim, migrant, daughter, Italian citizen, linguist, businesswoman, etc. Though moving within a restricted area in Rome, identified by viale Marconi and mapped by the coordinates of her apartment block, the market, the park where she meets friends, her daughter's school, and the 'Little Cairo' call centre from where she telephones her family in Egypt, she is constantly active within and between these places, observing others, observing their responses to and expectations of her, reflecting upon these, and calibrating her representations of herself accordingly. She is, arguably, complicit in her identity remaining in many respects as her husband and others would wish it, but this is not a static or passive complicity, but rather a restless process of negotiation. The account of a migrant woman's processes of identification which Lakhous offers in Sofia is one which thus bears out the assertion of Ahmed, Castañeda, Fortier and Sheller, cited above, that to be grounded (in the domestic space) is not to be fixed. It also illustrates quite powerfully the analysis offered in the same volume by Irene Gedalof, challenging again the notion that migrant women who occupy predominantly the domestic sphere in their destination location somehow do not change, act, move, or exert agency. Gedalof argues:

> The notion of citizen as a public individual negotiating civil society needs to be de-linked from its conceptual association with, and opposition to, a private sphere in which the work of kinship, affective ties and belonging continues to be done. It is this conceptualization of the opposition between public citizen and private senses of belonging that also is at work in binding women to a particular version of 'home' and 'place', which in turn makes their access to the status of citizen problematic. The problem, therefore, is not only the association of women with fixed notions of community belonging, but also the definition of community belonging in terms of fixity. There is a binary logic at work here which defines fixed notions of belonging,

Identity

together with 'woman', 'home' and the reproductive sphere – as the realm of 'being' – in opposition to the mobile, fluid space of citizenship, rights, justice and political 'desire' or becoming. That underlying binary logic also needs to be refused.[67]

In the persistent, purposeful negotiation which Sofia's accounts of herself bespeak in this novel, the reader is able to witness a process of becoming which is as active, assertive, and public-orientated as is the very differently engendered negotiation of citizenship and desire which is recounted in Issa's chapters. Sofia is as much (or as little) a citizen of Italy as is Issa.

The piecemeal assembly and flexing of an outward-orientated female identity, apparently within the confinement of conventional domestic roles, is traced in comparable ways, though in a radically different political and geographical context, in Shirin Ramzanali Fazel's second novel, *Nuvole sull'equatore*.[68] Here, the story of two women is told: that of Amina, a Somali woman, and her daughter, Giulia, whose father is an Italian who travelled as part of the Italian colonial enterprise to Eritrea, and then after World War II, moved to Somalia under the A.F.I.S., and later to Kenya.[69] The story of Amina is in part one of enterprise and of travel, and indeed the dimension which this novel extends over the story of female agency told through Lakhous's novel is that of space. Amina moves repeatedly as her life progresses, and though this is almost invariably because she is taken or sent somewhere by authority figures in her life (her family or husbands), each re-location, however restricted the economic or emotional circumstances, becomes through her agency an opportunity in which she constructs a further element of her identity, often by acquiring knowledge. Her father, in a rural Somali community, having died when she was a very

---

67 Irene Gedalof, 'Taking (a) Place: Female Embodiment and the Re-grounding of Community', in Ahmed, Castañeda, Fortier and Sheller, 91–112 (96).
68 Shirin Ramzanali Fazel, *Nuvole sull'equatore. Gli italiani dimenticati. Una storia* (Cuneo: Nerosubianco, 2010).
69 A.F.I.S. was the 'Amministrazione fiduciaria italiana della Somalia', under the terms of which the area of Somalia which was formerly an Italian colony was placed by the UN under Italian administration from 1949 to 1960, when the country gained independence. See Antonio Maria Morone, *L'ultima colonia: come l'Italia è ritornata in Somalia, 1950–1960* (Rome: Laterza, 2011).

young age, Amina lives with her mother, who re-marries, and subsequently dies in childbirth. Sent then to Mogadishu and to the care of a relative of her stepfather, Amina is in this environment simply a labourer, and learns to work and to endure physical abuse as a result. Married to a relative of this family as an expedient when she is approaching adulthood and therefore proving a greater and riskier responsibility, she passes into another form of emotional and physical slavery under her mother-in-law.

It is notable that out of this situation of extreme confinement, with almost no opportunity for engagement with a world outside a very tightly constructed domestic space, possibilities are created or seized by the female subject which open up new perspectives on life in society and establish principles for dealing with them. Fazel recounts quite rapidly the collapse of Amina's first marriage, and establishes its context economically in the following description: 'La notte, Amina sentiva il corpo che le doleva. Le luci della lampada a petrolio proiettavano sul muro l'ombra del corpo pingue del marito che copriva il suo. Nelle orecchie le ronzavano gli abusi verbali della suocera accumulate durante la giornata'.[70] She feels pain emanating from inside her body in response to injuries inflicted upon her skin, she sees the shape of her husband weighing on her in such a way as to obliterate her own body from sight, and she hears the repetitive and endless denigration of her person filling her ears. Grammatical choices ('La notte', the imperfect tense) confirm, moreover, that this is habitual, routine. The sense of oppression, of being nothing other than that which serves a purpose for others, is almost overpowering here. However, three important elements of Amina's identity and singularity are established out of this particular context.

Firstly, she discovers female solidarity and friendship independent of kinship, amongst the local young women of her age who 'sapevano la vita che doveva patire' and encourage her to resist it in whatever way possible.[71] That these women share an understanding of the emotional and physical confinement in which Amina exists and seek ways to combat it

---

70   Fazel, *Nuvole sull'equatore*, 26.
71   Fazel, *Nuvole sull'equatore*, 26.

within those very confines signals a capacity to negotiate and to achieve movement in a fixed location which echoes my comments on Lakhous's character, Sofia, above. Accordingly, this minimal experience of a form of sociality beyond the family affords Amina the opportunity to build an identity as an individual woman, active in forming and conducting her own relationships, alongside her given roles as daughter-in-law and wife. Secondly, and through the agency of her female friends, she discovers cinema, and this allows her to feed and expand an imaginary which again affords her the capacity to fashion different worlds and experiences and so to fashion herself as someone independent of the function she performs for others, and someone who has the possibility to become (again, like Sofia). Interestingly, given the emphasis I noted above on spatial constructions of identity in this novel, it is the distance of the screen world from the one she experiences everyday which captures her most powerfully: 'Scoprì una dimensione così lontana dal suo mondo! Tigri, elefanti addobbati. Ragazze bellissime, vestite con i sari luccicanti'.[72] Thirdly, these opportunities to enter as an individual into a society and into a culture (or cultures) beyond the abusive home enable Amina to act on her own behalf and to assert her subjecthood back in the domestic space. Returning from this first visit to the cinema, she is abused verbally by her mother-in-law and then physically, at his mother's instruction, by her husband himself. His incapacity to assert himself against the will of his mother, and thus his capitulation to and slavish reproduction of the regime of domestic oppression, is a shock to her, and she resists succinctly and definitively when she goes to bed, in pain: 'Quando lui si coricò accanto per cullarla tra le braccia, gli morsicò la mano fino a farla sanguinare. L'uomo rimase zitto continuando a stringerla. Quella fu l'ultima notte che Amina lo volle vicino'.[73]

The story of Amina after the end of her first marriage is in many ways one of her construction of a particular kind of citizenship (recalling Gedalof's comments), alongside the somewhat distinct story of her relationship with her daughter, Giulia. The entry into the world which the

---

72   Fazel, *Nuvole sull'equatore*, 26.
73   Fazel, *Nuvole sull'equatore*, 26.

experiences outlined above propel her towards is an assertion of a kind of agency and independence which her early experiences seemed to disavow. Importantly, it is also an entry into particular spaces, as articulated very clearly when she comments on her adjustment to being a young – and sought-after – divorced woman in Mogadishu: 'Amina doveva difendere la sua rispettabilità e non si lasciava incantare. Inoltre voleva essere padrona del suo spazio. La città, oltre al cinema, le faceva scoprire negozi di stoffe, oreficerie, quartieri residenziali e gente nuova'.[74] It is interesting that this description inscribes an expansion of the domestic space into and through the public arena, since the localities identified are all those of 'respectable', as is emphasized above, female presence and exchange, and yet they open channels into a wider and less gender-regulated *polis*. In many ways, Amina can be seen to be deploying the protection and respectability of the domestic and gendered space in which she was previously confined in order to gain entry into full citizenship and full presence in the city.

Amina in fact becomes, as the novel proceeds, a successful businesswoman and a political activist, and it is striking that this success, whilst independent and entirely 'self-made', is anchored to the coordinates of the spaces and principles of approved female action that she outlines above: her trade is in fabrics for clothing and she sells the jewellery which constitutes her only culturally sanctioned independent property in order to support her political cause, the *Lega dei Giovani Somali*, in the campaign for independence. The preparations she and her close friend, Faduma, make before they attend a party meeting, seen through the eyes of Giulia, offer a vignette of adult female identity which illustrates the ways in which an unconventional mode of female citizenship can not only co-exist with, but is in fact expertly packaged within, a more conventional performance of femininity in public. Giulia watches her mother dress and admire herself in the mirror, whilst Amina and Faduma discuss first, choice of perfume, and then, their husbands' reactions to their political activities and to their donation of their gold to the party's funds. The politics of their nationalist commitment and action pre-date and are a given in the conversation,

---

74   Fazel, *Nuvole sull'equatore*, 27.

which centres instead on the domestic politics of how they negotiate their freedom to act with partners who implicitly or explicitly would prefer they did not. They then leave for the meeting, and 'Le due amiche uscendo si lasciarono dietro una scia di profumo'.[75] The scene enacts a bodily realization of the phenomenon of citizenship through domesticity, or becoming through being, which Gedalof describes in the citation above: whilst performing a female identity crafted to meet the expectations of the male public gaze, the two women are also enacting a form of ungendered, active citizenship which places them in the thick of the nation's bid for independence. Strikingly, this is not viewed in the novel as a subterfuge or even a contradiction: Fazel celebrates Amina's achievement of a conventionally glamorous femininity which draws consciously on exoticizing notions of the (black) feminine mystique within one and the same body and consciousness as the achievement of success in the commercial, political, and social spheres. Giulia is the vehicle of this celebration of a particular model of adult female agency: 'Anche se la madre presa dai suoi vari impegni, aveva poco tempo da dedicarle, Giulia era felice. La vedeva sprizzante allegria e buonumore'.[76]

For Giulia, then, Amina provides one model of female identity, but her relationship with her mother is somewhat distanced and estranged at times, and there are other models of adult identity – both female and male – which are prominent in her life, and particularly her carer as a child and Amina's housekeeper, Dada, her stepfather, Yusuf, and her predominantly absent Italian father, Guido. Just as her identifications are mobile, so is she, moving with her parents to Nairobi as a child, then back to Somalia to join her mother (leaving Guido behind), then to a remote *Collegio* in Somalia, then back to Mogadishu, and finally to Rome. Fazel stresses in this way that the identity of this *meticcio* girl, already divided from birth in the eyes of almost all who apprehend her, is constructed around a much richer multiplicity than simply Somali Italian. The novel begins and ends with Giulia and as such is in many ways her story, a *Bildungsroman* de-centred

---

75 Fazel, *Nuvole sull'equatore*, 36.
76 Fazel, *Nuvole sull'equatore*, 36.

from masculinity and from Europe. Amina and others dominate, however, in certain chapters, and in this sense, the drifting focalization of the novel serves to underscore the drifting focalization of Giulia's identity, which remains at play, open to multiple potentialities, throughout the novel.

This by no means indicates that Giulia is unequivocally privileged, however: much of her movement is owed to the fundamental obstacle of her mixed race which creates such intense anxiety about how and where and whether she might 'fit', especially from her mother who seeks to protect her from prejudice and denigration, that Giulia spends much of her time estranged in various ways from her surroundings and from her mother. Her years in the *Collegio* are the prime example of this, where she is the object of an intensely repressive regime aimed at cleansing mixed-race children ('le figlie del peccato'),[77] as best possible, of the sin of miscegenation which they are seen to embody. As such, she is stripped of any identity with which she is familiar, in the sense that the clothes, hair, possessions, language, eating habits, pastimes, and even the mother, which she considered her own are all removed and substituted with other, strictly uniform and controlled, objects, practices, and reference points. The model of a subservient, Italian-speaking and Italian-schooled, Catholic girl is the one into which the regime of the *Collegio* aims to straitjacket her, with some success. The reduction of Giulia to a barely existing human life, without any identity of which she can genuinely feel possession, is countered somewhat, as in the story of her mother's first marriage, by the discovery of female friendship and mutual support, which establishes a framework for survival and for growth. This, along with the somewhat difficult sustenance of her mother's love (which the regime attempts to deprive her of as far as possible), enables her to construct a sense of her subjecthood despite efforts to erase or re-form it.

Giulia's rehabilitation to adolescent and then adult female identity is realized by means of very different kinds of education which she receives when she returns to Mogadishu and to the family home, having completed her primary education. The family home, as fixed reference point, has itself shifted in the interim, in the sense that Amina, having long lost

---

[77] Fazel, *Nuvole sull'equatore*, 148.

contact with Guido after leaving him in Kenya to return to Somalia, has married a Somali businessman (Yusuf) and had a son with him. Her identifications, as an adolescent, are negotiated between the models offered by family, adult friends, school friends, classmates, and cinema (recalling her mother's capacity to project her identity into different worlds, and that of Lakhous's Sofia), engendering conflicts which are perhaps typical of adolescence (around dress, for example, with her mother)[78] or which continue to arise from her mixed-race identity (she is involved in a fight at school after a classmate calls her a 'bastarda').[79] Her education, in its broadest sense, as a mixed-race young woman, is a particularly striking example of the multiplicity of reference points between which Giulia is able to move (and, again, she also travels physically between geographical locations in order to do so). Her continuing 'Italian' education, albeit now taking place within the city, is the formal site of her schooling, but a visit soon after her return to the capital to see Dada, her carer as a child, in a rural area just outside the city, proves to be the space of a different kind of education. Giulia is exposed, through sharing her living space with Dada for an extended period, to the rituals, practices, and beliefs of rural life in Somalia. Additionally, her engagement with the religious practices and principles played out in everyday life prompts her to attend Koranic school there in order better to understand an alternative to the Catholicism drilled into her in everyday life at her *Collegio*.

The sense this excursion to rural Somalia brings Giulia of belonging responds on the one hand to the presence of Dada, who was a point of constancy and unconditional care in her early years, but on the other, to the alternative education she experiences, through practice, in what it is to be human – and particularly female – in a rural community. The exposure to models of adolescent and young adult femininity different from those she encounters at school and through family connections in the city in many ways compounds the 'mystique' of femininity associated with her mother in

---

[78] Yusuf buys Giulia a pair of jeans, to which Amina objects strongly, though Yusuf negotiates for Giulia to be allowed to wear them within the home. See Fazel, *Nuvole sull'equatore*, 159–61.

[79] See Fazel, *Nuvole sull'equatore*, 145–8.

the example I discussed above. Amongst the group of lively young women she sees visit the well each day to bring water for the community, she identifies Gigia as embodying the vitality and physical attractiveness of young female sexuality. Gigia and her friends include Giulia in their group, inviting her to the well with them and then to a dance. Giulia's remains, however, a partial initiation into their female micro-community, and as such, she gains a partial understanding of them: 'avevano i loro segreti e perciò parlavano senza completare le frasi, usando molti sottintesi, sguardi, allusioni e anche timbri di voce differenti'.[80] As this illustrates, the young women in effect have a language of their own, which Giulia can only partly de-code. Similarly, when news suddenly spreads in the community that Gigia has been found dead, it is clear from piecemeal references that a pregnancy was the underlying cause, but unclear whether she tried to abort the foetus herself, suffered a miscarriage, or was the victim of another's violence.

In this way, the intimations of practices and events such as infibulation, intercourse, pregnancy, abortion, and miscarriage, which Giulia pieces together from her experience in this community, provide her with a certain kind of sexual education, rooted not at all in knowledge of biological facts, but rather in the gauging of responses within the community to the models of behaviour which others play out, in order to acquire an understanding of what is acceptable and what is not. Though a fundamental ignorance of reproductive biology and of reproductive health is demonstrated in the novel – through the story of Gigia – to be potentially fatal, Fazel reveals to the reader through this episode the ways in which young women in a traditional, rural community effectively self-educate in what it is to be an adult woman in society through observation, mimicry, reproduction of existing models and behaviours, the astute interpretation of 'allusioni' and 'sguardi', and the judicious completion of half-finished sentences. Gedalof's argument is again borne out in this model of female adolescence locked fast in a particular kind of ignorance and incapacity to act, and yet, nevertheless, working constantly to generate understanding and agency from the bits of intelligence available.

80 Fazel, *Nuvole sull'equatore*, 115.

Identity

Amina, who is herself mobile, and still more so, Giulia, because of her hybrid identity, posit processes of identification which have no single, fixed framework, and therefore function as a constant movement and negotiation between models offered in different places and moments and by different interlocutors, connected either by kinship, friendship, community, formal education, or authority. As noted above, to forge subjecthood in and through mobility is no privilege in itself, and lack of fixity does not necessarily denote freedom. Rather, the absence of a visible, single ethnic identity plays out for Giulia almost exclusively as exclusion from particular communities or practices, or the confinement to an in-between territory which is restrictive and isolating, rather than liberating (the *Collegio* is a geographical and institutional realization of this space). This is articulated very powerfully when Giulia's feet first touch Italian soil on her arrival at Rome's Fiumicino airport: 'Lei, italiana di pelle scura, non si sente per niente a casa sua.'[81] Immigration procedures at a national border of course accentuate this emotion of anxiety and exclusion, and as Giulia moves through Rome itself, to Ostia temporarily, and then back to Rome, mechanisms of recognition, such as the familiarity to her of Rome's architecture from films she has watched, trigger a sense of cultural and imaginative inclusion and even possession which enable her to become a citizen of Rome. She discovers the pleasure of being in Rome, but a Rome which is also Mogadishu. Fazel underscores this connection powerfully, referring to the joy Giulia derives from going to Termini station to meet the Somalis who gather or pass through there:

> Questi incontri portavano sprazzi di energia nella mente di Giulia. Era il pentolone da cui attingere i sapori mai dimenticati di una terra che si stava lentamente sgretolando. Come le onde del mare corrodono la spiaggia lentamente e ti mostrano le radici nude di una pianta un tempo sana e forte, prosciugata della sua linfa, così la diaspora somala aveva iniziato il suo corso, un fiume che trasportava le vite delle persone attraverso terre nuove, dando forma a un individuo diverso: 'il nomade metropolitano'.
>
> Non si studiano più i pianeti e le stelle, ma s'individuano nuove rotte. Cambiano le mappe, il mondo intorno può essere più confortevole se hai la nazionalità giusta e il colore adatto. A questi nuovi soggetti non manca la grinta per farsi strada in questi

---

81   Fazel, *Nuvole sull'equatore*, 194.

insoliti paesaggi; frontiere protette da uomini in divisa, visti, permessi, passaporti, e sguardi freddi e sospettosi.[82]

Whilst Fazel is explicitly here referring to the future (and past) of Somalia specifically, the principle she describes of a form of knowledge derived from tracing routes, and the figure of the 'nomade metropolitano', have wider import in the analysis of identity-formations in migration literature. The movement in *Nuvole sull'equatore*, which is not linear between an 'origin' and a 'destination', but rather itinerant, sketches a notion of identity, subjecthood, and belonging, which undermines conventional conceptions of race and nationality by mapping the becoming of individual subjects (and indeed, collectives of various kinds) across geographical and cultural space. There is nothing triumphalist, romantic or idealistic about this notion: as Fazel notes, it is facilitated for those of particular colours and nationalities, and others will encounter significant obstacles. However, the analogy of astronomy points very compellingly to the construction of a form of knowledge about a world beyond that which has been mapped by established human expertise and experience. The routes of migration are, as Fazel's novel as well as others discussed in this chapter have evidenced, also the routes of identity formation, which operates as a form of travel between reference points, encountering various 'strangers', and is also profoundly influenced by geographical and cultural spaces. Fazel's comment suggests that by identifying connections between points in the life stories of migrants, which might be geographical, political, historical, or cultural, and so tracing the itinerary by which each individual or community comes to be what it is in any one space or moment, the reader or observer might succeed in overturning conventional notions of identity as uniquely plotted according to particular features of nationality, ethnicity, gender, class, age, etc. This somewhat bureaucratic form of understanding of human subjecthood might be replaced with a knowledge informed by reference to space and movement. The narratives of identity formation which I have traced in this chapter might contribute to such a knowledge.

82 Fazel, *Nuvole sull'equatore*, 201.

CHAPTER 2

Memory

Paul Connerton, in his analysis of *How Modernity Forgets*, states that 'The history of mass migration is part of the history of modern forgetting', justifying this powerful claim in terms of the dissociation of national cultures from their home experiences and practices, and thus the progressive 'forgetting of local roots'.[1] I cite this claim not to refute it – in the terms of social anthropology, Connerton is presumably right – but rather to call attention to its counterweight, in the form of the acts of resistance to such forgetting which are visible at the level of individuals or of specific migrant collectives, and manifest themselves as acts of narrative memory. Indeed, Connerton himself goes on to recall V.S. Naipaul's search, in 1950s London, for material with which to establish a career as a writer, and his late realization that in the west London boarding house in which he stayed with a mix of economic and political migrants, he had arrayed before him all the subject matter he could wish for in the form of the stories those individuals could tell: 'the people he saw were full of their memories', Connerton notes.[2] This chapter will explore the ways in which migration literature in Italian negotiates, through telling in a number of ways, which include *not* telling, the desire to remember and also to forget. I will discuss experiences and operations of the mind which are encompassed under the broad heading of memory, but incorporate a range of interior movements and levels of consciousness which operate in the gap between present and past and/or between one location and another, in the context of the experience of migration and the expression of it in migration literature in Italian.

1   Paul Connerton, *How Modernity Forgets* (Cambridge: Cambridge University Press, 2009), 135.
2   Connerton, *How Modernity Forgets*, 136. He refers to V.S. Naipaul, *The Enigma of Arrival* (London: Viking, 1987).

As outlined in different ways in all the chapters of this book, the imaginary of a migrant, whilst notionally projected forwards in time, is also heavily imbricated with her past, and as expectations and images are disrupted and personal principles challenged by the reality of being a migrant in Italy, this past comes to figure as an index of interpretation of the present. Memory itself, of course, is an amorphous concept, studied and theorized widely across disciplines in the sciences, social sciences, and humanities. I draw in this chapter on a number of theorists in the area of memory studies, but the instances of memory or the levels of relationship with the past with which I am most concerned, because they figure so significantly in the texts I am discussing, can be brought together around a number of specific mechanisms. Habitual memory is often dismissed as the least critically fertile mode of memory, since it refers to long-established practices learned so well and repeated so widely and frequently that they offer little scope for examination of specific mechanisms of remembering or of telling instances of variation: Mieke Bal uses the example of learning to avoid stepping in puddles.[3] However, there is some value in my particular context of enquiry, I think, in looking at moments in which habitual memory is, in a sense, disabled. The practice so embedded as to have become a 'behavioral tic'[4] rather than a memory may be recalled precisely as a sequence of events or instructions in the past if the personal or cultural conditions in which it was gradually habitualized change, for example, through migration. New 'habits' may need to be acquired, in such a way as to recall the processes or experiences in the past through which an action once memorable became negligible.

Most prominent in the texts I shall discuss, and simplest, in many ways, is memory as the cognitive recalling of experiences, events, people, sounds, smells, tastes, etc. from the past. As my list suggests, though, these recollections involve sense as well as cognition, and at this point the 'simple'

---

3   Mieke Bal, 'Introduction', in Mieke Bal, Jonathan Crewe and Leo Spitzer, eds, *Acts of Memory: Cultural Recall in the Present* (Hanover, NH: Dartmouth College and University Press of New England, 1999), vii–xvii (viii).
4   Bal, *Acts of Memory*, viii.

recalling to the present of aspects of the past overlaps with a further type of memory, embedded in the emotions of the individual. Personal memory, infused with psychological traits and conditions, tends to be associative and to weave together discrete strands of feelings evoked by recollections of the past to form a blanket of emotion which appears to enfold all experiences in the past and lend them a collective significance for the individual. Bal draws attention to this process in her identification of specifically narrative memories: 'Narrative memories, even of unimportant events, differ from routine or habitual memories in that they are affectively colored, surrounded by an emotional aura that, precisely, makes them memorable'.[5] Since I am concerned in this chapter with the modes of telling of the past in migration literature, then these narrative memories, emerging from and, in a sense, organizing, personal memory, will be my central concern.

In themselves, though, narrative memories demonstrate different tendencies or operations of memory. In the first instance, there is inevitably a distortional element to the 'blanketing' of past experience, with every aspect of the past associated with a sense of loss and of desire, in which negative elements might be obfuscated. In this instance, memory comes close to nostalgia: a term which has come often to be used dismissively to denote a form of memory constructed through selective reification of elements of the past and associated with the kitsch (memory as souvenir). Nostalgia as, literally, the pain of loss, remains, however, a powerful emotional condition in some of the narratives I shall discuss, and the interplay between this form of nostalgia and the more neatly packaged motif of an idealized past is a productive one to examine. In a second instance, the 'emotional aura' which Bal refers to may be a profoundly negative one which brings back to current experience the pain of a violent loss, wound, or injury suffered in the past: traumatic recall, and the ways in which it is narrativized explicitly or not, will be a significant strand of enquiry in this chapter. In a third instance, out of both of these differently inflected experiences of the past in the present emerges, specifically in textual accounts of the memory of the past, a move towards memorialization of the past. The inscription of

---

5   Bal, *Acts of Memory*, viii.

the past as personal history, as something fixed in a certain context and time-scale, constructs it both as a reference point for the individual and as a message to others bearing a lapidary quality. In this performative function of memory, whereby the telling of an individual memory acquires in its very narrativization an active function in bearing witness to or communicating the experience of an individual for an audience, lies a key element of cultural memory. Clearly, in literature which seeks, in part at least, to communicate across or between linguistic and national cultures, these acts of narrative memory which themselves work to create a certain kind of cultural identity and experience for the reader or audience are crucial. Much of this chapter will examine moments in which individual memory is performed for a presumed audience in the interests of animating a particular kind of cultural experience for interlocutors perceived to be unfamiliar with that culture.

A further form in which cultural memory takes shape in some of the literature I shall discuss is the textual reconstruction – often using direct speech – of the sharing of memories orally. Opportunities for the open sharing of interior experiences and feelings are often demonstrated to be limited for the migrant in Italy, but nevertheless, casual and temporary meetings between migrants are often marked by the exchange of individual versions of the story of migration and of home. Where circumstances allow friendship to develop further, it tends to be nurtured by the telling of more detailed, intimate stories of the same experiences. Here, the performance is directed at others who share, to differing degrees, similar cultural formations and experiences, and has less the function of bearing witness and performing a cultural identity than of tracing a collective experience and a collective memory. The oral sharing of memory – albeit transcribed in written texts – is distinct from the telling of individual memories in its fluidity. The response of the listener can be incorporated into the narrative more readily and influentially than the response of a reader who may be distant in time, space and experience, and 'ownership' of the story is less defined than when it appears in a written volume with a name or names on its cover. Told rather than written, the story becomes part of a general currency of similar stories, to be exchanged, amassed, spent again in different circumstances. Here, one can perhaps talk of a collective memory being voiced and developed, and, as my reference above to 'the story' of migration, in the singular, suggests, it is reasonable to argue that, whilst the written and published texts which are my focus in this book inscribe distinct and individual experiences of migration and of the past in which each experience is embedded, they also give voice to a collective expression of the relationship between then and now, and to a shared imaginary less of a specific past than of past-ness.

Access to memory often takes forms, in the narratives which I will discuss, which are themselves an aspect of the interior life of an individual, and as such specific memories are powered by broader desires, anxieties and emotions. Dreams, and also semi-conscious reveries and fantasies, are privileged textual events in many narratives, during which memory can be expressed and enjoyed freely, and can be re-told within an alternative narrative structure, informed not by the history of events, but by desire. Dreams figure prominently as escape in Italian migration literature (as will be discussed in Chapter 4; see pages 158–62 and 170–1), or even as some sort of haven of individual consciousness where the anxieties and humiliations which trouble the conscious mind in the present are erased. They can provide the opportunity for something which has been lost to be – at least provisionally – replaced and enjoyed. They can also, of course, provide the forum for a traumatic recalling of an injury in the past.

In order to explore in this chapter the range of figures which emerge from engagements with memory in Italian migration literature, and to map out their connections and functions, I will start by looking at personal memory, and the sharing of it, in an early novel, *Pantanella*, by Tunisian writer and film-maker, Mohsen Melliti.[6] I will then move to consideration of the performance of cultural memory in two later novels, *Il profugo*, by Younis Tawfik, and *I lupi della notte*, by Algerian writer, Amor Dekhis.[7] Each offers powerful modes and figures for creating the connection between personal and cultural memory, using the inscription of individual experience as a way to construct the memory of a nation. These novels engage closely

---

6   Mohsen Melliti, *Pantanella*, trans. by Monica Ruocco (Rome: Edizioni Lavoro, 1993).
7   Younis Tawfik, *Il profugo* (Milan: Bompiani, 2006); Amor Dekhis, *I lupi della notte* (Naples: L'ancora, 2008).

with the theme of the past as damage and figure the activity of narrating the past as an element of the recovery process, functioning at the levels both of the individual and the cultural. In this context of the past as trauma and of telling it as therapy, I shall also briefly re-visit Amara Lakhous's *Scontro di civiltà per un ascensore a piazza Vittorio*.[8]

Melliti's first novel, as suggested by its date of publication, is one of the earliest narratives of migration and, like Fortunato and Methnani's *Immigrato* (discussed in the previous chapter), it deals with the problems of being a clandestine migrant (and a clandestine community of migrants) in Italy in that period: the struggle for housing, labour, money, legitimacy, presence, is a major concern of the day-to-day life recounted. The Pantanella of the title is the name of a disused factory and warehouse complex near the centre of Rome, which became the temporary home of a community of migrants of multiple nationalities, almost exclusively non-European, from around 1989 to 1991. Melliti tells the story of this community in a polyphonic narrative in which the dominant consciousness, whose interiority the reader engages with in a sustained way, is that of a young migrant named Ahmad, though multiple other voices intervene in the narrative. In this novel, the narrative of the present, in Italy, is only the pretext, in some ways, to the narrative of other places, markedly distant and remote in both space (as will be discussed in detail in Chapter 4) and time. The migrant consciousness, if it is possible to talk coherently of such a thing, is revealed in this novel to be so heavily imbued with past experience, and particularly past attitudes and feelings, that it appears to be impossible to think the present without thinking the past: indeed, the processes of thought, and also imagination and sense, are revealed to be complex and multi-referential, drawing energies from several different levels of experience and feeding back to them at any one time. As such, *Pantanella* is an important 'case study' for the examination of memory in italophone migrant writing. Arguably, I think it also establishes a vocabulary and a grammar of narrating memory, to be outlined below, which are by no means unique to Italian migration literature but which are used and modified repeatedly in other and later narratives.

8   Amara Lakhous, *Scontro di civiltà per un ascensore a piazza Vittorio* (Rome: e/o, 2006).

An example of such a vocabulary is the term, *ghurba*, introduced as a culturally specific phenomenon (and therefore untranslatable), by means of a footnote at the beginning of the novel: 'indica, per gli arabi costretti a emigrare in occidente, la vita all'estero e il sentimento di esilio e di nostalgia per il proprio paese'.[9] It is a concept spoken of in other migration narratives, and significantly, it refers not simply, as the above definition suggests, to a bundle of emotions evoked by memories of the home left behind, but signifies also a condition of existence in the destination country.[10] It is interesting, in terms of my comments above about nostalgia, that the definition links nostalgia with exile, which Edward Said defines 'a condition of terminal loss', drawing attention to the sense of a severance at the centre of individual being: 'It is the unhealable rift forced between a human being and a native place, between the self and its true home: its essential sadness can never be surmounted'.[11] This helps, I think, to articulate one of the ways in which Melliti's novel suggests a specific understanding of memory in the context of migration, in that memory is represented as being not simply a recollection, indeed re-collection, in the present of images, thoughts and feelings from a past clearly demarcated in space and time, but rather is part of a much broader condition of systematically recalling and referring to principles constructed as being of a past which is experienced as absence and loss. It is a condition of experiencing past-ness in every context, in the sense that everything important to individual being appears to have been and gone, retrievable through memory but only with the impression enforced by memory that these are salvaged fragments of a coherent whole which may never again be one.

9 Melliti, *Pantanella*, 12.
10 Furthermore, it is cited in one instance in this novel as a condition experienced prior to migration, pertaining to being physically 'at home' in a society from which one feels already estranged for political reasons and in which one cannot sustain plans for a future. Ahmad recalls his feelings – and those of fellow students – whilst at university in his home country: 'L'oscurità cominciò a scendere sulla città dove soffrivano della *ghurba* malgrado fossero ancora nel proprio paese' (Melliti, *Pantanella*, 26).
11 Edward Said, *Reflections on Exile and Other Essays* (Cambridge, MA: Harvard University Press, 2000), 173.

As noted above, a young migrant named Ahmad (nationality unspecified) forms the principal narrative filter for the events and emotions recounted in *Pantanella*, and the narrative scans his interiority so closely as almost to emulate the effect of proximity and inclusion generated by free indirect speech. The flux of Ahmad's stream of consciousness (albeit dislocated somewhat by the persistence of the third-person narrative) is often prompted and directed by his experience of the urban space of Rome, and for this reason, it is in Chapter 4, 'Place and Space', that I will examine this interaction in detail. However, in order to establish the territory in which memory emerges, it is helpful here to examine an example of the passage from Rome to elsewhere – with the emphasis on time here rather than space – and the cognitive and affective shifts it produces in Ahmad. A contemplation of the city skyline in the early evening prompts thoughts of ancient Rome, and then the following account:

> Il tempo faceva scorrere nella sua mente una storia fatta di ricordi dolorosi. Il *silenzio* si impadroniva di lui, e a volte nascondeva *una lotta nel suo animo*. Continuava a *bere e fumare*, finché non si imbarcava in una di quelle conversazioni abituali, in cui riusciva ad *attirare l'attenzione degli interlocutori, raccontando le sue esperienze* in questo o in quel paese. Si chiedeva perché fosse rimasto qui. Tutto sembrava strano e affascinante, profondo e dolce. Gli sembrava di girare in un circolo vizioso. E le domande inquietanti che si poneva lo stancavano. Ogni giorno *aveva l'impressione che la logica non fosse in accordo con il suo obiettivo*. Non conosceva quale fosse il vero mezzo per passare dall'altra sponda. A volte fuggiva le domande che lo straziavano con alcune risate tristi. Oppure *scriveva poesie*.[12]

Whilst this passage offers only a brief allusion to memories, rather than articulating them, it offers evidence central to my analysis here in the form of a collection of motifs and elements which together stake out the territory for the experience and action in the present of memory in a number of migration narratives. The apprehension of Rome's antiquity transports the observer into the past, which becomes here – it seems – *his* past, and prompts a sequence of responses (the italicized words and phrases above): silence, interior struggle, smoking and drinking, the telling and exchange of stories, a fundamental sense of incomprehension and of loss, and creative

---

12   Melliti, *Pantanella*, 19 (italics added).

activity. All of these, in a sense, are both a response to and an expression of *ghurba*, and it is interesting that, like the experience of *ghurba* as defined by Melliti, they articulate at once a personal and interior experience and one which is not only shared with others but can be seen as constituting a shared experience and identity, thus positing a cultural as well as an individual condition. Importantly, this collection of responses also underscores that from a fundamental sense of estrangement from or loss of the past – the 'esilio' and 'nostalgia' discussed above – there develops a sense of dislocation which is cognitive as well as emotional. It suggests that logical strategies customarily used by the individual to make sense of experience are disabled by the experience of migration, the very synaptic connections linking the immediate sensory response to things with their rational explanation cut, so that logic cannot reach its 'obiettivo'. This has resonances, I think, with the point made in my introduction to this chapter about the disabling of habitual memory, in that what Ahmad expresses is a conviction that embedded and repeated practices, a form of knowledge so habitual as to go unnoticed as such, have been exposed through the experience of migration to be dysfunctional, and the process of establishing comparable 'habits' to fit the new environment seems unfathomable. In this sense, the operations of memory in the context of immigration are expressed in this novel as a fundamentally disruptive force, the very destruction they bring engendering, however, creative and constructive behaviours as well as confusion.

At the personal level, as indicated in the extract above, these positive behaviours include silent reflection and writing; they also move outwards into the socializing activities of smoking, drinking, and story-telling, and it is in these areas which *Pantanella*, as one of very few novels to narrate quite systematically, rather than incidentally, a collective experience of immigration, offers some specific images of the operations of memory. Conversation amongst migrants at night in or around the Pantanella building is a primary *locus* of memory in the novel, alongside Ahmad's private excursions into the past. Individual memories of home and stories of the past are told and are absorbed, digested, and responded to, often tacitly, by the listeners. In this way, they acquire the significance of something more than simple verbal exchanges (in fact, silence dominates in many): they establish friendship and solidarity, in that the individual entrusts his (the story-tellers are exclusively male) intimate and often painful story to the consciousnesses of those around him.[13] Night-time conditions, in a building with an only intermittent electricity supply, favour this process. Intimacy between individuals is enhanced by night-time: the darkness, silence and stillness associated with night help to suppress the interference which attenuates sensory perception in the active, daylight hours and instead to concentrate and accentuate perception of certain elements; vision may be impaired, but this in itself draws attention away from individual details to more harmonious impressions of texture and tone; hearing takes into account not only spoken words, but modulations of breathing and the interaction of lips, tongue, teeth. Night, in other words, allows for the barriers which separate individuals to be penetrated in emotional terms through the very process of physical boundaries becoming porous, affording a peculiarly powerful sense of shared experience, often fuelled by smoking and drinking alcohol.[14]

An example of the acutely physical sense of an intimacy rooted in emotional exchange is offered by an instance early in the novel in which a migrant named Mustafa tells Ahmad the story of his home, his wife, and his emigration. It is the silence which follows the telling which orchestrates an emotional symphony of sorts, expressed through bodily motifs:

> Gli animi ardevano e un dolore schiacciava i due cuori. Entrambi avvertirono quel dolore profondo e preferirono il silenzio. Il silenzio talvolta era una piacevole ebbrezza, più di un bicchiere di vino o di un fugace piacere sessuale. Forse attraversavano il deserto o i boschi. Forse andavano in giro sulle spiagge, nudi, senza vestiti, senza maschere. Ognuno di loro si sentì legato all'altro dai propri occhi scuri e dai capelli neri. In quegli istanti il silenzio assoluto dominava il loro universo. I battiti del cuore erano come il tocco di un orologio appeso al centro di un bosco silenzioso.[15]

---

13 On alternatives to the use of the Italian language for expression, see Jennifer Burns, 'Language and its Alternatives in Italophone Migrant Writing', in Jacqueline Andall and Derek Duncan, eds, *National Belongings: Hybridity in Italian Colonial and Postcolonial Cultures* (Oxford: Peter Lang, 2010), 127–47.

14 See Burns, 'Language and its Alternatives', 136, for comments on the role specifically of music in this process.

15 Melliti, *Pantanella*, 16.

Problematic though this fantasy may be in its vision of a cultural solidarity through primitivist images, in its privileging of the unity of dark eyes, black hair, and hearts beating as one, it articulates a transformation of personal memory into cultural memory, and also emphasizes the embodied quality of memory.[16] A gathering narrated later in the novel between Ahmad and three friends at night underscores this point: '[Ahmad] prese un bicchiere e rimase a guardare le bollicine della birra. L'amicizia dominava quel tavolo: quattro persone, quattro mondi diversi... Ognuno portava con sé la storia del suo paese. [...] Ahmad continuava a giocherellare con il bicchiere, se lo strofinava sulla fronte, sulle guance, mentre mille pensieri gli affioravano alla mente'.[17] The transfer of narrative focus between the bubbles in the glass, the glass rolled along Ahmad's forehead, and the thoughts inside his head of various pasts articulates a fluid co-penetration of exterior and interior experience which establishes in this novel a principle that the past is inscribed upon the body of the migrant and speaks through his embodied actions and movements in the present.

An embodiment of memory of a different kind is a powerful tactic used by Younis Tawfik in *Il profugo* to construct an image and an imaginary of the fate and future of a national culture. The symbolic body of the brother, Anis, of the novel's narrator is invested in as a figure of both the possibility and impossibility of freedom in Iraq under the regime of Saddam Hussein. Before examining this particular act of narrative figuration of the memory of a culture, there are broader aspects of the novel's construction of cultural memory which merit comment here. Firstly, the draw of the past described above, in relation to Melliti's *Pantanella*, in terms of the experience of the present being ever saturated with that of the past, is expressed still more emphatically in this novel by means of structure. The prologue and epilogue to the novel are situated in the present of the novel's publication (mid-2000s) and in the context of the first-person narrator living

---

16   The implicit reference to the paintings of Salvador Dalí here reinforces an imaginary in which historical periods co-exist; an explicit reference to the artist occurs later in the novel (Melliti, *Pantanella*, 153).

17   Melliti, *Pantanella*, 43.

and establishing a family in Holland, the destination which he has reached after migration from Iraq.[18] The body of the novel, however – all but the final pages of its seven chapters – is set in the past in Iraq, and then across the countries which map the migration journey of the narrator, Firas. In some ways, the novel offers a straightforward memoir of Firas's experience from age six to approximately thirty, in which the reader reconstructs a personal history by following, in real-time, the narrator's story; however, the albeit thin prologue, as well as a sense established very early in the novel of the inevitability of the narrator's departure from Iraq, have the effect of predicating the story of the past on a future in a different environment. In effect, then, the reader knows from the outset that what she is reading is a pre-history of the European citizen introduced in the prologue, which has the effect of heightening her consciousness of the double perspective of the narrative – then and now – and of the status of the story told as narrative memory. This novel very clearly meets the performative function associated with cultural memory, in the sense that what the narrator tells is manifestly intended to enact not only a representation but a realization, for the readership, of the recent cultural history of Iraq through the instrument of an individual narrative memory. Viewed within the wider context of Tawfik's textual production, which includes non-fictional works aimed at explaining Islam to an Italian readership, *Il profugo* takes its place in a portfolio of textual acts of intercultural performance and communication.[19]

18   The vision of a future in Europe through 'heterosexual entitlement', as noted by Derek Duncan, is replicated but also adjusted here, in that the narrator's wife is also a migrant from a Middle Eastern country. An imaginary future is predicated still on heterosexual reproduction, but in terms of the consolidation of a specific ethnic identity within Europe. See Duncan, 'Cultural Assimilation and Heterosexual Entitlement in Fortunato and Methnani's *Immigrato*', in Jennifer Burns and Loredana Polezzi, eds, *Borderlines: Migrant Writing and Italian Identities (1870–2000) / Borderlines: Migrazioni e identità nel Novecento* (Isernia: Iannone, 2003), 379–85.

19   Novels by Tawfik other than those discussed in the current volume, all examining Arab Islamic culture from different angles, include *La città d'Iram* (Milan: Bompiani, 2002), *La sposa ripudiata* (Milan: Bompiani, 2011), and *La ragazza di piazza Tahrir* (Siena: Barbera, 2012). In addition to fictional works, poetry and translations, Tawfik has written a work of history and explanation of Islam, *Islam*.

Less concerned than Melliti's novel with the psychological expression of the insistence of memory in present consciousness, the strategies Tawfik deploys in this novel for constructing a memory of a distant culture consist largely in the narration of events as they happened, or plausibly would have happened. Through the experience of Firas as a child, adolescent, and young adult, the story is told of Saddam Hussein's accession to power, of the Iran–Iraq war, of Iraq's invasion of Kuwait and the subsequent Gulf War, of insurrection and civil war within the country, and of the invasion again by Allied forces in 2003. Committed to freedom of speech and thought, secular in his convictions, and multicultural in his associations and friendships, Firas is constantly at odds with the dominant forces in his culture, and is from childhood subjected to prohibitions, censure and beatings, developing later into participation in armed resistance, and subsequently torture and imprisonment. The apparently straightforward construction of the narrator as a cypher for the experience of an entire nation and culture is somewhat complicated, however, by an imaginary of migration which, as indicated above, punctuates the narrative. For example, the early indication of the inevitability of Firas's emigration lies in the story of his (unnamed) eldest brother, who takes the decision to migrate to Italy in the late 1970s, shortly before Saddam Hussein's rise to power. The narrative establishes the shared values and affective affinity between the eldest and youngest of the siblings, and thus indicates that the only route to freedom for Firas will be departure. Interestingly, it is reunion with this elder brother in Italy, en route to Holland, narrated by the older man himself, that creates the narrative opportunity to stake the claim for Firas's story as testimony to the experience of an entire culture. He explains that Firas recounts his experiences in Iraq and his migration journey to him orally as they return home after Firas's arrival at the railway station: 'Ascolto, attento, la lunga storia del piccolo bambino che da un giorno all'altro è diventato uomo. Lui parla con la voce tremante e io scrivo'.[20] The elder brother is effectively

---

Dai califfi all'integralismo (Turin: Ananke, 2004) and a course in Arabic language, *As-Salamu alaikum. Corso di arabo moderno* (Turin: Ananke, 1999).

20 Tawfik, *Il profugo*, 224.

installed as the witness – and the scribe – of Firas's account, which he goes on to endow explicitly with the ethical value and moral imperative of testimony, addressing the readership directly:

> Il racconto che io vi lascio scritto, cari amici miei, sui muri delle vostre case, sugli alberi, sulla neve e sul vento è una storia vera. Sono le storie di milioni di persone, raccolti in una sola storia dipinta con le sofferenze e i dolori.
>
> Ve la racconto per fissare nella memoria del tempo il tormento di un popolo che continua a morire un giorno dopo l'altro, e dalle sue ceneri un giorno risusciterà per vivere libero. Non potevo tenerlo per me perché dovete saperlo, lo dovete raccontare ai vostri figli, agli amici e alla gente che cerca la verità. Affinché non ci sia mai più ingiustizia nel mondo, mai una lacrima di bimbi senza volto, un urlo disperato di una madre o un prigioniero che non torni più a casa.[21]

The assertion of the story's status as cultural memory could not be more explicit, and this statement illustrates, in its acutely lapidary quality, the process of memorialization which I indicated in my opening comments to this chapter. However, the statement is literally not the end of the story, and in that sense is somewhat parenthesized or mitigated by the ongoing and itinerant story of Firas himself, narrated by himself. The structure of the novel lends it a dialogical quality, despite the dominance of the first-person account, in the sense that each chapter narrated by the protagonist incorporates a shorter narrative voiced by one of its other protagonists: Firas's parents, siblings, and friends. In this way, the single and 'representative' voice of the survivor is inflected by other voices and perspectives, whose narratives are in turn interpreted critically in relation to Firas's own. In this sense, the elder brother's statement of ownership of the written narrative is somewhat undermined by Firas moving on from his brother's home in Turin to Holland, where his story continues not only to his apparent 'destination' in full citizenship in that country, but also back on a visit to Iraq some time later, where the narrative ends in his mother's death in a still war-torn and highly menacing environment. Whilst this ending in many ways underscores the message delivered in the elder brother's account, it also reintroduces into the narrative the very personal elements of restlessness,

---

21 Tawfik, *Il profugo*, 224.

uncertainty, dissatisfaction, vulnerability which have characterized Firas and his actions throughout the narrative and which serve incrementally to figure an impossibility of settlement.[22]

More powerful in establishing this sense of the necessity of departure or detachment is the figure – and figuration – of the older brother closest to Firas in age, Anis, as indicated above. The two share from late childhood a sense of not fitting into their changing political and cultural environment, having moderate and liberal values which are at odds with the militaristic nationalism of the regime, which seeks to recruit and control them in almost all areas of their lives, from school to friendships, and even in the home. Within the environment of the immediate (and ideologically liberal) family, the agent of this external extremism is the second eldest brother, Walid, who espouses the Ba'athist cause, enters the military, and becomes a fairly high-ranking officer in Saddam Hussein's regime. The clash between Walid and his younger brothers, especially as they increasingly resist conformity to the regime and so risk damaging Walid's reputation and career, is violent in both verbal and physical terms. It is during one of these arguments within the central courtyard of their home that Walid draws a gun to shoot Firas, and Anis, who steps between them to defend Firas, takes the bullet and is killed. This act of fratricide clearly carries symbolic value within the cultural memory which this novel constructs, embodying and enacting the inflamed sectarian hostility within the country which the author represents as having the capacity to destroy a rich and complex culture and deny it a viable future. That the fratricide is accidental or displaced, from the more rebellious to the more peaceful brother, underscores the destructive illogic of the regime's ideology of national supremacy.

What is of interest in the current discussion, however, is the way in which the memory of Anis is constructed in the novel from the outset,

---

22   Such an impossibility is also figured in the prologue of the novel, in which Firas, during the very wedding party in Holland which would seem to cement his future as an Arabic European citizen, feels violently ill and escapes to the bathroom where he almost collapses. That this crisis is prompted by his brother recalling moments from their past signals the insuperability of memory and the fragility of visions of the future. See Tawfik, *Il profugo*, 13.

making of him a figure or symbol even before his death, rather than a human character in the narrative. His death is tacitly understood to be predicated from the first chapter, in which he intervenes successfully between Walid and Firas during a punishment beating, in an event which foreshadows his murder. The sense is generated that he is vulnerable because he is immune to the anger which appears to inform relationships in the wider political and cultural environment, and this places him already in a realm apart from the everyday one. In fact, shortly after this incident, the two younger brothers withdraw from the celebrations for the end of the Iran-Iraq war, articulating amidst the victory a feeling of personal defeat: 'ci sentivamo soli e in un certo senso estranei a un mondo che non ci apparteneva'.[23] This principle of being not of this world is played out in alternative ways by the two brothers: by Firas, in his dogged ideological resistance to this world and his need to move elsewhere, and by Anis, in his more spiritual withdrawal from conflict.

Already, Anis is constituted, then, as a figure of a different realm of understanding, somewhat unearthly, and this is confirmed emphatically when the narrative turns to him in the second chapter:

> Nel mio paese il tempo si era fatto pietra e nemmeno le cose si muovevano, vi era soltanto la sensazione di essere presenti sulla terra per riempire lo spazio, in attesa che tutto si sciogliesse come cera sotto un sole che non sorgeva.
> Mio fratello Anis invece non amava molto stare con noi, ma saliva in tutte le ore libere sul terrazzo di casa per passare la giornata con le sue colombe.[24]

In contrast to a culture petrified by the absence of freedom of expression, Anis is identified with air and movement. The more detailed description which follows offers an almost angelic vision:

> A volte saliva sul muretto e stando in piedi apriva le braccia e si abbandonava il [*sic*] vento, come per decollare. La sua jellaba di cotone bianco si allargava e si gonfiava d'aria sventolando come due enormi ali. Teneva gli occhi chiusi e la testa puntata verso l'alto in attesa di sollevarsi in volo, facendo il giro di tutto il recinto.

23   Tawfik, *Il profugo*, 57.
24   Tawfik, *Il profugo*, 58.

> I suoi colombi gonfiavano il petto e stiravano le ali per aprirle bene, ruotavano l'uno attorno all'altro e qualcuno svolazzava sulla testa di Anis, come per proteggerlo. Un gruppo saliva, sbattendo le ali forte, verso il disco del sole e poi scendeva in volo geometrico radendo gli alberi e le antenne per risalire più in alto del minareto della moschea principale e disegnare un enorme cerchio di luci solari nello spazio aperto di un cielo terso, prima di scendere di nuovo in picchiata verso il nostro terrazzo.[25]

The way in which he is virtually disembodied here, his human physicality attenuated and transformed as he bodily projects himself from earth and stone towards air and light, establishes his figure in the novel as a liminal being inhabiting a space between life and death. With feet barely touching the upper surfaces of the building, and his gestures mimicking the flight of the birds whose movement seems eagerly to accommodate and enfold him, the image is constructed of Anis as a being already inhabiting a 'beyond' of some sort, and this is confirmed when, at the end of this same chapter, he is killed: 'Anis era a terra come un angelo affaticato, era sorridente'.[26]

Whilst the imaging of a prematurely killed adolescent and sibling as an angel may be in itself a somewhat crude and unoriginal literary figure, there are elements of the construction of Anis in this novel which offer more interesting insights in terms of migrant imaginaries. Given the powerful link established in the narrative between the two younger brothers in the family, the almost literal flight (or attempted flight) of Anis in his daily experiences on the rooftop acquires a more earthly counterpart in Firas's protracted attempt at 'flight' – i.e. migration – which the narrative recounts. As such, the figure of the fallen – or, rather, felled – angel is not simply an emotional or spiritual one, but also cements an association between the desire to escape an unlivable environment, chance or accident, human agency, and the proximity of death. Seen from this perspective, the rest of the five main chapters of the novel go on to recount the accidents, engagements with mortality, and human interventions which, in a much more empirical and physical way, punctuate and contribute to the sense of Firas's journey out of Iraq. In this sense, it is interesting, that – as quoted

---

25   Tawfik, *Il profugo*, 59.
26   Tawfik, *Il profugo*, 75.

above – Anis in death may bear a beatific or beatified smile, but he is 'a terra'. The political and cultural environment which he inhabits brings him literally back down to earth from the rooftop where he leans towards the ether, offering a neat refraction of the longer story (this novel) of Firas's heavily earth-bound struggle to move through and out of Iraq, Kurdistan, Turkey, Greece, Albania, Italy. Travelling largely on foot, sheltering in caves, Firas's is a 'flight' which keeps him attached firmly to or in the earth's surface, and that Anis too is finally 'brought down' in the central courtyard of the family home signals an emotional and figurative compromise between the imaginary of freedom and the struggle to achieve it. A reference to Anis and to flight during a delirium which afflicts Firas when he is seriously ill whilst stuck in Istanbul seals the association: 'Era il buio totale e mi trovai sopra la terrazza di casa nostra con Anis che mi sollevava in aria come un bambino e rideva divertito; io aprivo le mani per volare ma l'aria che mi sollevava per pochi secondi era fredda, mista a un gelo bianco che assomigliava alla nebbia e dava una sensazione di morte'.[27]

A different reading of the imaging of Anis in *Il profugo* might interpret him as a figure of trauma. The question of traumatic memory is one which I will address in the context of the further novels to be discussed in this chapter, and which is not immediately pertinent to Tawfik's novel, which tends rather to narrate the violence to the individual (and to the nation) as it occurs, rather than to investigate the more oblique and belated ways in which that violence might present itself to the individual consciousness. There is, however, an argument for identifying the figuration of Anis as precisely the symptom of the narrator's trauma, and this becomes apparent if one considers trauma in terms of possession of the violent event, following Cathy Caruth in her discussion of post-traumatic stress disorder. She identifies the disorder or pathology in the structure of the experience: 'the event is not assimilated or experienced fully at the time, but only belatedly, in its repeated *possession* of the one who experiences it. To be traumatized is precisely to be possessed by an image or event'.[28]

---

27   Tawfik, *Il profugo*, 203.
28   Cathy Caruth, 'Introduction', in Cathy Caruth, ed., *Trauma: Explorations in Memory* (Baltimore, MD: Johns Hopkins University Press, 1995), 3–12 (4–5); italics in original.

Whilst Firas seems otherwise to be entirely in possession of the events and images of the experiences he has, and organizes them into a coherent and largely transparent narrative memory, the image of Anis is one which could be said to possess him, in two ways. Firstly, that Anis is remembered and recounted in the narrative as, in part, a recognizable human character, but overwhelmingly as a symbolic figure who acquires larger-than-life resonance even before his death is narrated, suggests that the event of his death cannot be 'possessed' in straightforward, narrative terms by the narrator, but rather itself determines and balances the narrative and representational economy of Firas's personal memory. Secondly, and following the same logic, the image of Anis recurs throughout the narrative, possessively if not obsessively, from the prologue onwards, like no other image or event, including Firas's torture, the death of his father, and a later attempt by Walid, in armed combat, to shoot him. The figure of Anis, in the sense of the beyond-human image rather than the human body, dominates the narrative, and in so doing, arguably gives the lie to the control which the narrator appears to exert over his violent and painful memories. That Anis re-appears in the moment when the narrator himself is in a delirious state and perhaps close to death – as quoted above – and fails to 'save' Firas in that moment ('Non c'erano più le mani di mio fratello che mi reggevano e precipitavo nel vento'),[29] allowing him to fall, is perhaps the sign of the unresolved trauma, the lapse in the narrative memory. Transposing this traumatic event in Firas's personal memory to the level of the national and cultural memory which the narrative quite explicitly delivers by means of the story of Firas and his brothers, then one might read the novel as an illustration of a further point made by Caruth, that the centre of the pathology in traumatic experience is the truth of the event itself within history: 'The traumatized, we might say, carry an impossible history within them, or they become themselves the symptom of a history that they cannot entirely possess.'[30] Firas, in this sense, carries an impossible history, the very impossibility of which is signalled in the figure he, in memory, constructs of Anis.

29 Tawfik, *Il profugo*, 203.
30 Caruth, *Trauma*, 5.

Caruth's construction of the relationship between the traumatized teller and the history he bears might be applied still more compellingly to the narrative of escape from Algeria's civil war in the early 1990s which Amor Dekhis offers in *I lupi della notte*. In common with Tawfik's *Il profugo*, one effect of this novel is to memorialize a national and cultural experience and to do so in the imagination of a readership assumed perhaps to know *about* this national history but not to know what it was like to *experience* it. Dekhis lends a particular ethical accent to this operation in cultural memory by framing his narrative – relatively lightly – in the work of Primo Levi. The dedication on the title page of the novel refers to survivors, and specifically in the sense of those who have survived in the barest terms, with no hint of triumph: 'coloro che, pur vincenti, sono sopravvissuti senza volersi accaparrare alcunché'. A quotation from *Se questo è un uomo* opens the first page of the narrative, recording the imperative to survive in order to tell the story and bear witness.³¹ In this way, Dekhis establishes at the outset the import of his narrative and its function in communicating a history which only his narrator, as a survivor, is equipped to tell. In the implicit comparison his reference indicates between the Holocaust and the Algerian civil war, the author also makes a particular claim for a recognition of the events and strategy of that conflict as an instance of genocide, of systematic elimination of a particular population, rather than as a case of internal political and ideological conflict, as it has widely been understood in Europe. In terms both of narrating a history and of the truth of that history itself, the link Dekhis establishes with Primo Levi's Holocaust memoir frames the narrative he offers as the memory of a traumatic personal and cultural experience.

The structural features and techniques of *I lupi della notte* point to an interpretation of the experience it relates as a deeply traumatic one. The operations of memory in this novel are disruptive. In common with Tawfik's *Il profugo* and with numerous other narratives of migration, the novel has

---

31   The quotation reads: '... che in questo luogo si può sopravvivere, e perciò si deve voler sopravvivere, per raccontare, per portare testimonianza; e che per vivere è importante sforzarci di salvare almeno lo scheletro, l'impalcatura, la forma della civiltà' (quoted in Dekhis, *I lupi della notte*, 7; original text from Primo Levi, *Se questo è un uomo* (Turin: Einaudi, 1976), 35–6).

a double time-frame, set both in the past in the narrator's home country, Algeria, and in Italy in – interestingly – the proximate future (2015, so seven years ahead of the novel's publication).[32] Movement between these chronologies is not systematic in the narrative. A prologue and epilogue set in Florence in 2015 frame the past within the present in a relatively conventional way, but within the three parts which make up the body of the narrative, the structure of the double frame gives way: part one tells the past in Algeria entirely, and ends with the protagonist's departure towards Europe, but both parts two and three begin with the protagonist in the present-future in Italy, only to be hijacked, in effect, by the vision of the past offered by a photograph, which precipitates the narrative back to the past. The impression is thus created that the memory of the past is absolutely not in the control of the narrator; or, to put it in Caruth's terms, the traumatic events of the past 'possess' him.[33] A striking accentuation of the trauma thus indicated is the split of the narrating and remembering subject, who speaks in the first person as Salè in the present-future in Italy, and is remembered in the third person as Salah in the past in Algeria. What this draws attention to is not that the trauma of the civil war has generated a schizophrenic disorder, with the subject split into two distinct personalities; in fact, the continuity between the narrating and narrated subjects, as human subjects, is underscored. What is highlighted is rather the mechanisms of *telling* the story of traumatic events: the subject who speaks in the present-future in Italy cannot, it seems, speak directly the experiences he underwent in the past, but rather must displace the memory to a 'third person' in order to be able to articulate it. To claim possession through narrative of those memories remains beyond the emotional capacity of the remembering narrator: as the incursions of the past into the narrative of the present-future in Italy demonstrate in structural terms, it is the traumatic events which possess him.

---

32   The novel was in fact completed by 2003, twelve years earlier than the year in which it is set, and was short-listed for the Premio Calvino in that year. See Daniele Comberiati, *Scrivere nella lingua dell'altro: La letteratura degli immigrati in Italia (1989–2007)* (Brussels: Peter Lang, 2010), 266.

33   The reference to survival in the novel's prologue points to this interpretation: see Dekhis, *I lupi della notte*, 10.

Susan J. Brison identifies features of traumatic memory which appear very pertinent to Dekhis's construction of his remembering protagonist-narrator in *I lupi della notte*. 'The undoing of the self in trauma', she states, 'involves a radical disruption of memory, a severing of past from present and, typically, an inability to envision a future.'[34] This model is interesting in terms of my comments above, in that, again there is a 'severing' of sorts between Salè in Italy and Salah in Algeria, although, as noted above, there is also some narrative continuity between the two places and the two subjects: the 'severing' is not absolute. The 'inability to envision a future' is an aspect to which I will return, but again, the very setting of the novel in 2015 confirms an ability to envision a very near future, and more compellingly, the future of Salè is envisioned in the novel as in various ways compromised by his past, but nevertheless possible and in some ways desirable. Similarly, Brison goes on to address the question of possession of a traumatic history from a slightly different perspective from that of Caruth, and in ways which illuminate certain mechanisms of the construction of the past in Dekhis's novel:

> Working through, or remastering, traumatic memory (in the case of human-inflicted trauma) involves a shift from being the object or medium of someone else's (the perpetrator's) speech (or other expressive behavior) to being the subject of one's own. The act of bearing witness to the trauma facilitates this shift, not only by transforming traumatic memory into a coherent narrative that can then be integrated into the survivor's sense of self and view of the world. But also by reintegrating the survivor into a community, reestablishing connections essential to selfhood.[35]

This description fits the story of Salah-Salè, in that a striking condition of his existence in Algeria is that he finds his agency repeatedly annulled by the opposing forces which vie for dominance in the country: the Islamist rebels and the military. His attempts to assert control over his future and establish an identity to take pride in – for example, setting up a shop selling books and newspapers, as the organs of free expression and thought; buying a car

---

34   Susan J. Brison, 'Trauma Narratives and the Remaking of the Self', in Bal, Crewe and Spitzer, eds, *Acts of Memory*, 39–54 (39).
35   Brison, 'Trauma Narratives', 39–40.

in order to spend some time with his partner, Algyida, in Algiers as well as to care for his mother in his home village of Bou Z'nada – are quashed by the Islamists, who force him to close his shop and sequester his car as well as Salah himself, who is removed from society temporarily and abused by both the Islamists and the military. He is also forced to become a collector of 'taxes' in his community on behalf of the Islamists, and so to be the agent in his community of an ideology and a form of social organization which he absolutely rejects.

In this sense, his trauma is both physical and psychological, and he very manifestly becomes and is forced to be in his everyday life 'the object or medium of someone else's [...] speech (or other expressive behaviour)', as Brison phrases it. Indeed, the techniques of manipulation deployed by the Islamists include the elaboration of a powerful narrative in which the human subject takes on a particular function within their vision of society, and in this sense, Salah becomes their agent through, precisely, becoming the object of their speech.[36] When he eventually escapes from Algeria, he does so following the death of his mother, the absorption of his two brothers into the two opposing forces of the civil war, and the (presumed) murder and mutilation of Algyida. When Salah is given the evidence of the latter, in the form of Algyida's wedding ring found on the beheaded

---

36 A striking example is the rhetoric of the letter Salah receives requiring him to stop selling certain publications, which represents his chosen titles entirely differently from his view of them as the *loci* of open debate: 'Mentre si consiglia la lettura dei testi sacri ai nostri sudditi, sono categoricamente messi al bando quelli che professano idee sovversive e atteggiamenti spudorati. Sono state individuate come testate proibite i seguenti giornali comunisti, femministi e guidei: "Le Matin", "El Watan", "Liberté" e ogni pubblicazione che appartiene al potere empio e tiranno' (Dekhis, *I lupi della notte*, 35). A further example demonstrates that the capacity to construct the individual in speech according to the logic of the dominant ideology belongs to both sides in the conflict. An officer of the military, to whom Salah turns to report the crime after his car has been sequestered by the Islamists, offers his own narrative of the events: '"Hai trattato con loro. Vi siete messi d'accordo su come e quando ti renderanno la macchina. Poi ti hanno mandato da noi. Tutta una messa in scena". Salah ingerì come cianuro quelle parole, che oscillavano fra la semplice supposizione e la più assoluta convinzione' (Dekhis, *I lupi della notte*, 54).

and burned corpse of one of four women dumped outside the village, the narrative reports that, 'Pianse, Salah. Poi non ebbe più sentimenti'.[37] The naming here is a clue to the 'severance' which follows, in the sense that his loss of feeling – which amounts to, recalling Levi again, the loss or forced extraction of his humanity – is immediately demonstrated in him acting himself as the violent oppressor. He secures passage out of Algeria by threatening a lorry driver with his Kalashnikov in order to force him to take him on board, and again, his speech is uncharacteristically brutal and mimics that of his oppressors.[38] That he has become what his oppressors posited him as is, arguably, the motivation for the severance of Salah from Salè, and for the distancing and re-objectification of Salah as third person from the first person narrator in the present-future, in Italy.

Brison's description also draws attention to the telling of the story as 'a coherent narrative' as an act of overcoming the trauma, and – in common with other theorists of trauma – stresses the 'act of bearing witness' for a listening audience as therapeutic. The first-person account of the past in Dekhis's novel, from this perspective, perhaps signals his recovery from the past, and his recovery of a sense of individual selfhood. Brison highlights that this is a recovery within society: 'reintegrating the survivor into a community, reestablishing connections essential to selfhood'. It is this particular feature, I think, which points to the problem in Salè's recovery in Italy from the trauma of the past. The narrative constructs him, indeed, as integrated into a community, in the sense that he has a largely rewarding job in Italy, as part of a dedicated 'squadra multietnica' of the national police force in Florence, he speaks fluent Italian, he has a stable partner (Italian) and a solid network of multi-ethnic social contacts. However, this is a different community from the one in which he experienced the traumatic events of the past: he is absolutely not, in Brison's terms, '*re*integrated' and has not '*re*establish[ed] connections essential to selfhood'

---

37 Dekhis, *I lupi della notte*, 124.
38 For example: '"Chiacchieri troppo per i miei gusti" lo minacciò Salah puntandogli il mitra alla tempia. "Dammi i documenti! Così se fai il furbo, saprò dove trovarti"' (Dekhis, *I lupi della notte*, 126).

(italics added). In fact, what he has achieved is a new and quite markedly dislocated integration of himself into a community and a new construction of himself. Salah and Salè are, as noted above, continuous with one another but remain separate, the community he knew in Algeria insists in his life in Italy in that individuals from the Islamist groups he knew emerge within criminal networks in Italy, and, crucially, he discovers Algyida is alive and brings her to Italy, but the family he knew and imagined whilst in Algeria has been lost. It is perhaps the fact that Algyida is regained but their relationship cannot be reconstructed as it was before, at the same time as Ilaria, his Italian partner, remains in his life and forms a powerful bond with Algyida but again, their relationship cannot be reconstructed as it was before, that signals most powerfully the dislocation which persists at the centre of the protagonist's traumatic memory.

The story of Salah-Salè illustrates that the process of recovery through bearing witness within the community is disrupted by migration, which creates the conditions in which the listener is of a different community and experience, and the 'reintegration' is into a different community and a different construction of the self in that community. This suggests that the trauma cannot be completely overcome in a condition of such displacement from the environment in which it was experienced. Brison similarly asserts that:

> How (and even whether) traumatic events are remembered depends on not only how they are initially experienced but also how (whether) they are perceived by others, directly or indirectly, and the extent to which others are able to listen empathically to the survivor's testimony. The traumatic event is experienced as culturally embedded (or framed), is remembered as such (in both traumatic and narrative memory), and is shaped and reshaped in memory over time according, at least in part, to how others in the survivor's culture respond.[39]

Though there is continuity and reconstruction in the story of Salè in Italy, and it is not, as noted above, accurate to speak of a permanent 'severance' caused by the traumatic experience of the past, it seems that there remains

---

39 Brison, 'Trauma Narratives', 42.

a persistent breach between past and present, a point at which the narrating subject cannot tell with absolute coherence and without disruption the traumatic experience of the past. This, in turn, disturbs the '[ability] to envision a future', as Brison noted. At the end of the novel, Salè has lost not only the future he had imagined for himself in Algeria, centred on Algyida, but also the one he had constructed in Italy, centred on Ilaria, and what remains – and what he does look forward to as the narrative closes – is a professional future in the police force and within the community formed by his team. It is, however, a somewhat solitary and contingent future, based on a sense of exclusion from the partnership which the two prominent women in his life have formed. This element of contingency is perhaps reflected in the fact that the novel is set in the future, but in a future not distant in time, suggesting that a future beyond the framework set by current circumstances remains unsure and unimaginable.

An examination of two further textual examples offers insight into the working of specifically traumatic memory in migration literature in Italian. The first is a short story which speaks very interestingly to Brison's comments about the cultural or community response to the trauma story. 'La storia di Fatima', by Gertrude Sokeng (Cameroon), is markedly transnational or transcultural in its location of the therapeutic telling of and response to traumatic memory, disrupting conventional associations between communities and their geographic location.[40] In this story, it is the return to Italy from 'home', for the second time, which prompts the construction of a memory: Fatima returns after an absence of nine years, and remembers the morning of the death of her husband in Italy, Rachid. The narrative makes clear that these events, which she describes as 'la mia tragedia', are a story she has never fully told nor fully relived.[41] A gathering of her migrant friends in Italy provides the occasion, however, for her to break her silence. Between herself and her friends, a narrative of the morning is gradually constructed, piecemeal, from different perspectives. The friends contribute

---

40   Gertrude Sokeng, 'La storia di Fatima', in Alessandro Ramberti and Roberta Sangiorgi, eds, *Parole oltre i confini* (Santarcangelo di Romagna: Fara, 1999), 157–78.
41   Sokeng, 'La storia di Fatima', 157.

memories of their early days of struggle in Italy, and Fatima herself contributes information she first learned from the police after Rachid's death, about death threats he had received, for example. In this way, the mechanism of exchange of memories in the peculiarly transnational community of a multi-ethnic group of friends in their 'destination' country allows for a full memory to emerge both of Rachid and of the events leading to his death, and this has an intensely therapeutic effect on the 'primary' teller, Fatima. At the end of the evening, she feels liberated, anticipating a rebirth of sorts in the morning. The story suggests that only the combination of a community of migrants, who share a common experience, located in the place of migration in which their experience of migration is foregrounded, offers the cultural context in which the trauma can be fully remembered, and it is remembered and told as precisely a communal act.

The second example is *Scontro di civiltà per un ascensore a piazza Vittorio* by Amara Lakhous, which is amply discussed elsewhere in this volume, but largely in terms of its narrative of the present in Rome. What I wish to focus on briefly here is the relationship between the narratives given by others of the Roman citizen, Amedeo, and the reflections of Amedeo himself which alternate, as eleven 'ululati', with these witness statements. There are obvious comparisons to be drawn between the novels of Lakhous and Dekhis. In both, an Algerian migrant in Italy is troubled by the violence of his past: Amedeo alludes to the loss of a woman named Bàgia in the ninth, tenth and eleventh of his interventions, recalled first through a nightmare and subsequently within the stream of consciousness of his own troubled accounts. The statement of Abdallah Ben Kadour, placed between the ninth and tenth 'ululati', offers an historical account of Bàgia, Amedeo's partner, who, in a reflection of the true and presumed story of Algyida in Dekhis's novel, was killed following an ambush by Islamist rebels. The teller identifies this as a traumatic event for Amedeo: 'Ahmed non ha saputo accettare quella tragedia. È rimasto chiuso in casa per giorni, poi è scomparso'.[42] As the mismatch between names recalls, both novels articulate the 'breach', as I have termed it, or possibly the 'severance', in

---

42 Lakhous, *Scontro di civiltà per un ascensore a piazza Vittorio*, 162.

Brison's terms, between the subject who experienced the trauma and the one who attempts to tell it by means of names adapted to the environment in which remembering and telling takes place, Italy: Salah is replaced by Salè and Ahmed by Amedeo. A difference in this process draws attention to another, more profound convergence between the novels: Salè chooses to re-name himself whereas Amedeo becomes such by means of the narratives others construct of him. In other words, both novels identify significant effect in the ways in which subjects (objects) are narrated by others who possess political or cultural agency. Whilst I explored this issue in relation to Lakhous's novel and to questions of identity in my previous chapter, it acquires additional resonance in terms of memory, when examined in the light of trauma. As my discussion of Dekhis's novel has indicated, the subjection to the narrative construction of oneself as the object of another's discourse or modes of expression (following Brison) is an element of the traumatic experience, or arguably, a trauma in itself, and it is the belated playing out of this experience in Lakhous's novel, when the construction of Amedeo by external 'witnesses' comes to a head in the form of the police murder investigation, which perhaps prompts the collapse of his subjecthood which the later 'ululati' indicate, and the resurgence of the traumatic memory of the murder of his partner.

Numerous other convergences and divergences between these two narratives, in terms of memory, might be identified, but I wish to highlight here the questions of response and of form in the telling of the traumatic memory, in order to expand my field of enquiry in this chapter. Picking up first the question of who responds to the trauma victim's bearing witness to her memory, the rupture identified in relation to *I lupi della notte*, in that the audience is not one necessarily attuned to the experience, is evidenced still more acutely in Lakhous's novel, pointing to the ultimate isolation, again, of the individual who confronts his memory. Since Amedeo is regarded by the majority around him precisely as Amedeo, a Roman citizen with a Roman memory, there is almost no recognition of his trauma. When the traumatic memory erupts through the 'ululati', it does so as diary entries which record a painful interior articulation of his memory. The protagonist of Dekhis's novel seems able to bear witness in the present-future to his trauma, since he has come to terms with it, albeit in an awkward and disrupted fashion, through discovering the truth of Algyida's experience and taking (limited) action against the figure he identifies as perpetrator. Amedeo, by contrast, and returning to Caruth's terms, does not 'possess' his traumatic experience, which is denied almost throughout his narrative and instead, emerges unbidden to possess his consciousness. In this sense, the operations of Amedeo's memory seem to confirm the view of Bessel A. van der Kolk and Onno van der Hart, that 'in contrast to narrative memory, which is a social act, traumatic memory is inflexible and invariable. Traumatic memory has no social component; it is not addressed to anybody, the patient does not respond to anybody; it is a solitary activity'.[43] The sole addressee is, of course, the reader of the text, who alone acts as what Dori Laub describes as the protagonist's 'companion on the eerie journey of testimony'.[44]

The second question – of form – emerges also from the essay by van der Kolk and van der Hart, which explores Pierre Janet's theoretizations of trauma, based on work with patients at the Salpetrière in the 1890s, in relation to Freudian and other models. They argue that the model of repression of trauma, by which the traumatic experience is actively pushed away or 'down', is problematic, and that the term, dissociation, indicates a distinct process, more accurate to certain cases:

> Repression reflects a vertically layered model of mind: what is repressed is pushed downward, into the unconscious. The subject no longer has access to it. Only symbolic, indirect indications would point to its assumed existence. Dissociation reflects a horizontally layered model of mind: when a subject does not remember a trauma, its 'memory' is contained in an alternate stream of consciousness, which may be subconscious or dominate consciousness, e.g. during traumatic reenactments.[45]

Though I would hesitate to define Dekhis's and Lakhous's novels according to these alternative models, the description of a dissociative memory of trauma seems to me to articulate aptly the narrative process at work in

---

43 Bessel A. van der Kolk and Onno van der Hart, 'The Intrusive Past: The Flexibility of Memory and the Engraving of Trauma', in Caruth, ed., *Trauma*, 158–82 (163).
44 Dori Laub, 'Truth and Testimony: The Process and the Struggle', in Caruth, ed., *Trauma*, 61–75 (62).
45 Van der Kolk and van der Hart, 'The Intrusive Past', 168.

Amedeo's engagement with his traumatic past, and so to illuminate the difference between the modes of memory in the two novels. Certainly, Amedeo's memory of his trauma appears to be contained within the 'alternate stream of consciousness' which is expressed in the 'ululati', subconsciously at first, but latterly becoming dominant. Interestingly, though, the perhaps dominant – in terms simply of space – horizontal layer (or layers) of consciousness about Amedeo and his history is constructed by others, projected upon him rather than produced by him. The model which the novel thus offers is of a 'horizontally layered model of mind' in which the composite memory, traumatic and not, of an individual is constructed by multiple agents internal and external to the remembering subject, each offering different 'truths' of his past, from the trauma experienced in Algeria (Abdallah Ben Kadour) to his performance as a 'true Roman' in that city (Sandro Dandini), and each thus diverting attention away from the traumatic memory and allowing it to remain 'dissociated'.

Repression, on the other hand, seems more clearly to be the mechanism by which the memory of a trauma is controlled in *I lupi della notte*, and the triggers for the return of memory, the elements which 'hijack', as I described it, Salè's narrative of the present-future in Italy, merit some discussion. The traces of the past within the narrator's experience of the present in a different country and culture suggest a palimpsest, whereby the narrative of an earlier self can be discerned between and behind the narrative offered in the here and now, which seems intended to over-write the history of the past. Initials, allusions to earlier histories familiar to the narrator, and particularly photographs, serve as cyphers which allow him to decode the memory of his past from clues in the present. For instance, the trigger to the return to the narrative of life in Algeria in the second part of the novel is a photograph shown to him in which he recognizes the faces of members of the Islamist group who dominated him at home. The language used to described the recognition articulates very directly the Freudian return of the repressed: 'In una delle fotografie, molto vecchia, c'è un Ben Tabis più giovane, quasi irriconoscibile. Accanto a lui compare un altro uomo con un faccione enorme. Riconoscerei i suoi lineamenti perfino al buio. *Resuscitato dalle tenebre*, il suo volto mi scuote la memoria con orrore. *Un orrore che qualche istante fa credevo di aver seppellito.* […] La mia mente sprofonda nella mia stessa ombra. Nel passato di Salah, in una parentesi nera dominata dalla sigla BB'.[46] Photographs and initials offer the metonymic experience in the present of relationships, individuals, and experiences in the past, and afford the apparently lifeless images or letters in the present a history and a presence which allows the past to be re-lived.

The overarching metaphor for this process is, of course, the police investigation into Islamic extremism in Italy in which Salè is professionally engaged, and the novel fully exploits the trope of the detective's investigation into events leading to a crime as a figure for the individual's investigation of his own past experience in order to decipher, from clues and traces, the truth of a formative experience, if not of a trauma. Reading the story of Salah-Salè through this genre framework, it is possible to understand the trauma of the past in Algeria as being sited primarily in the unknowability of the subject's oppressors and of their actions. What troubles Salah even before the actions of the extremists impinge violently upon his existence is that he does not know when or where they will approach him, he does not know where they reside, he does not know what are the limits of the violence they are prepared to exert, and he does not know, ultimately, what they did to Algyida. The role he constructs for himself in Italy, as a police officer, endows him with the agency and with the technologies to know: by examining photographs, listening to intercepted phone calls, watching recorded images, reading medical records and other documented evidence, listening to the accounts of witnesses and amplifying them by exerting psychological and physical pressure, he makes his past knowable and assembles a narrative in the present from the traces he discovers of the past. He constructs a full human subject to attach to the face – the 'faccia d'ascia' – which he most prominently recalls from his past, which has haunted his memory, and to which has thus accrued all responsibility for the violences he has suffered.[47] He is empowered by his current posi-

---

46 Dekhis, *I lupi della notte*, 92 (italics added).
47 Salah notes the man with a 'muso a forma d'ascia' on the second time the Islamists visit his shop (Dekhis, *I lupi della notte*, 25), and thereafter, he is repeatedly referred to as 'faccia d'ascia', acquiring iconic value. Salè succeeds in putting a name, Antar Soukadji, to the face late in his investigation, revealing that not only has the man used

tion to control this individual physically, bringing him down by shooting him in the leg in a physical pursuit, and morally, ensuring that he will be tried within the Italian judicial system before also being extradited to face further charges elsewhere.

On the one hand, we might read this as the overcoming of trauma: in Caruth's terms, Salè takes dramatic possession of his traumatic memory. I think it is important also, however, to read the novel beyond the paradigm of the trauma narrative and to read further through the framework of the police investigation. Carlo Ginzburg offers the method to do this, in his essay, 'Spie', in which he examines the processes by which clues, traces, indications, signs are interpreted in order to arrive at knowledge of a certain kind.[48] Taking as his cue the paradigm shift in art history prompted by Giovanni Morelli's attributions of paintings, in the 1870s, based on the examination of minute and apparently inconsequential details of the artist's painting practice, Ginzburg marries this example to new critical and interpretative practices in the fields emerging at the time of detective fiction and psychoanalysis, in order to argue that the focus of interpretative activity shifts in modernity from the integrated, comprehensive whole to the isolated scrap of evidence. In constructing thus an epistemology by which the connecting and reading of apparently disparate traces and clues leads the observer to a form of knowledge of a complex reality which otherwise seems to defy apprehension, Ginzburg, as a historian, invites a reading of Dekhis's novel which includes its interpretation as a trauma narrative but also frames that individual history within a wider hermeneutical operation, by which the traces of a national and cultural history – that of the Algerian civil war in the 1990s – are visible and carry meaning in the context of Europe, and specifically Italy, in 2015. Following this deductive logic, sectarian strife in a distant country with a reputation for fostering

---

multiple names over time, but he has also had cosmetic surgery to become invisible even as the image of 'faccia d'ascia'. For further discussion of this figure, see Jennifer Burns, '*Lupus in fabula*: The Workings of Fear in Italian Migration Narratives', *Italian Studies*, 68.3 (2013, forthcoming).

48 Carlo Ginzburg, 'Spie. Radici di un paradigma indiziario', in *Miti emblemi spie. Morfologia e storia* (Turin: Einaudi, 2000), 158–209.

extremism in its remote mountains and deserts is not only graspable and comprehensible in Italy in the present, but, like the figures of Salè's past who appear in photographs and oral accounts in Florence in 2015, is in fact present and can be acted upon in that environment. Dekhis's novel underscores the notion alluded to in Ginzburg's essay (through reference to prehistoric cultures) that not only can another time be apprehended through the tracing of clues, but this is also in itself another place in culture and in geography.

A political and cultural history often regarded – or disregarded – in Europe as impenetrable is made knowable not only through Salè's re-discovery of it in Italy in the present-future, but also by the cultural memory which emerges through his personal memory of Salah in Algeria. By narrating daily life through the intimacy of one individual's public and personal experiences and positions, Dekhis constructs not just the cultural memory of Algeria's civil war, but a cultural memory broader in time and range of experience of what it is to be born and raised in Algeria, in North Africa, in a Muslim culture, etc. This more folkloric memory is encased in the novel in descriptions or vignettes of domestic interiors, domestic practices, everyday social life, business dealings, the conduct of sexual relationships, family relations and the fulfilment of roles, expressions of faith and practices of worship.[49] Albeit expressed through the filter of the young, male protagonist, Salah, significant insight is offered into how values, relationships, and presence in the community are organized and played out in the everyday, and, as tensions in civil life become more acute, how these elements adapt to or mutate in the face of various kinds of threat. For example, a notorious village gossip becomes a potential informer, and therefore a more dangerous figure than before;[50] family unity may be disrupted by contrary political

---

49 An early short story by Dekhis focuses on the role of the older generation, and particularly, the mother (central also to *I lupi della notte*) in calibrating and safeguarding religious identity through everyday practices and habits. See Dekhis, 'La preghiera degli altri', in Alessandro Ramberti and Roberta Sangiorgi, eds, *Le voci dell'arcobaleno* (Santarcangelo di Romagna: Fara, 1995), 185–97.

50 See, for example, the account of the character, Fumm il Mulino, who, in the context of Salah's heightened anxiety about his own and the community's vulnerability, is

affiliations within it, as illustrated by the relationships between Salah and his brothers. Tawfik's *Il profugo*, in a more orchestrated way, and Melliti's *Pantanella*, in a more fragmented way, as well as a number of other migration narratives, offer this insight into a culture remembered in a certain way. Dekhis's novel places a particular accent on this folk memory, however, by alluding to the force of myth and fable in organizing understanding of the world, since they together reinforce community values and anxieties. The wolves of Dekhis's title are the prime example, connoting a remote but vicious threat established as such through childhood fables, which acquires immediate and violent significance when extended to apply to the Islamists hidden in the mountainous regions, who are similarly invisible and unpredictable but ever present as a danger.[51] Evoked to perform the threat to individual safety by both factions in the civil war, the figure of the wolf allows the fear instilled in childhood of a distant menace to be very effectively inflamed in adults in the public arena by its application to a similarly unfathomable threat, and as such becomes in this novel perhaps the key figure of memory, dominating the recollection and telling of personal and national experience.[52]

It is precisely this level of everyday memory of cultural practices and beliefs which Connerton alludes to in the comment with which I opened this chapter, about the potential for the erasure of memory of local cultural practices which is a corollary of mass migration. As noted in my opening comments, the memory narratives I have discussed form one example of an attempt to counter such amnesia by recalling in the present the practices of the past. Not only is this, in the narratives examined here,

---

apprehended first as an annoying gossip, then as a familiar and so comforting figure, and subsequently understood to be a potentially dangerous pedlar of misinformation (Dekhis, *I lupi della notte*, 55–6).

51 On the operations of fear in this novel, see my article, '*Lupus in fabula*', forthcoming.

52 The military officer who interrogates Salah in part one of the novel alludes to the threat outside (of the Islamists who have just released Salah), saying "'Vedi com'è buio? E il paese è pieno di lupi pericolosi'" (Dekhis, *I lupi della notte*, 54). When the story of Algyida's detention by the Islamists is narrated, the scene of her arrival at their mountain encampment is marked by the summary murder of a young woman within the kidnapped group, and the leader of the rebels instructs his officers: "'Datela in pasto ai lupi'" (Dekhis, *I lupi della notte*, 174).

a consolidation of cultural memory, but also, recalled in texts written in Italian and published in Italy, these acts of memory have a performative function, bringing such practices into being in a different context and for a different audience, so producing a cultural condition and placing it into dialogue with others, rather than simply reproducing it in order not to lose it. It is tempting to argue that forgetting ought to be a privilege, or a need, or even a right: the anxiety about forgetting which is perhaps manifested by so many migration narratives, in the insistence of the past in the narrative of the present and future, has the potential to fetishize figures or fragments of past experience and to draw attention away from the injustices, atrocities, or simple frustrations which might have characterized the past and might indeed have generated the choice or necessity to migrate. As such, to forget 'roots' and past experience is perhaps to invest more positively in the process of migration, seeking opportunity and gain rather than dwelling upon loss. Why remember? However, the overwhelming weight of the past in migration literature in Italian suggests that the emotional, cultural, political and narrative value of engaging with the past is simply too great to let it go. Michel de Certeau perhaps offers the clue to this in his discussion of minority cultures having voice and influence. He speaks of second or subsequent generations of minority communities feeling that traditional points of reference have become 'extinct' (recalling Connerton), and observes that this brings 'a brutal return to local tradition, to a local language, but it is a return to something that has already become foreign. We return to something that still inhabits us (a means of identification), but it has already become other or altered'.[53] It is perhaps in anticipation of such an estrangement from past points of identification that narratives by the 'first generation' migrants I am concerned with here seek to keep memory alive through the telling of it, at the same time as they seek to bring it alive, for those (readers) for whom it is already 'foreign', through the telling of it in a second (or other) language. My next chapter turns from the processes to the dominant locus of memory – home – in order to probe further the resistance to amnesia.

53   Michel de Certeau, *Culture in the Plural*, introduction by Luce Giard, trans. and afterword by Tom Conley (Minneapolis, MN: University of Minnesota Press, 1997), 71.

CHAPTER 3

Home

Home is the focal point and location of many of the processes of memory which my last chapter explored. Home, in fact, offers the ground upon which to establish the kind of 'everyday' cultural memory outlined at the end of Chapter 2, recording the repeated and habitual actions and practices of a culture which is fixed through the processes of memory in a particular place and time. Just as in closing the previous chapter I questioned why an imaginary of migration might tend towards remembering and reconstructing the past, so it would be reasonable sense to ask why, in the terms of a condition – migration – predicated upon departure from an 'origin' towards other destinations, the notion of home might retain currency in the imaginary of that condition. A progressive interpretation of migration might seek figures of the creative production of new places and communities rather than of the reproduction of places left behind. However, home, along with the events of the past, insists in the imaginary which many narratives of migration to Italy express. This chapter will explore what exactly home is in these narratives, and in what terms it exerts such dominance in many narrative figurations of migrant life in Italy.[1]

Two principles related to home will inform my discussion in this chapter, each of them indicating methods by which the apparent permanence as a reference point of a home left behind might be understood and connected with wider migrant imaginaries. The first is the perhaps obvious principle that 'home' is a construction, imagined and put together from

---

1   For discussion of the relationship between the migrant subject and home in terms of exile, see Jennifer Burns, 'Exile within Italy: Interactions between Past and Present "homes" in Texts in Italian by Migrant Writers', *Annali d'Italianistica*, 20 (2002), 369–83.

affective, cultural and political principles and memories, and responding to an absence in the migrant's experience in Italy (or anywhere else that is not 'home'). Michel de Certeau articulates the specific risk the migrant takes in giving up home, and the relative repossession strategies:

> In particular, the immigrant has much more at stake: he or she loses more, but in order to gain a higher return. If we stick to the aspects of this defiance inherent in belonging, the loss first of all concerns the need to pursue a history outside of the territory, the language, and the system of exchanges that sustained it to that point. [...] Because of this distance, a representation of everything that happens to lack forms a representation: tradition is turned into the imaginary regions of memory; the implicit givens of life as it is lived appear with a strange lucidity that often rejoins – in many facets – the foreign perspicacity of the ethnologist. Lost places are transformed into fictional places offered to the mourning and reverence of a past.[2]

Representation, in this view, is the mode of reconstructing or retrieving home: in this sense, the invention of home in the direct or indirect narrative of migration serves to compensate a specific and painful lack; it is the antidote to nostalgia, construed literally as the 'pain of loss'. De Certeau's outline of the modalities of reconstruction highlights a further, notable element of the mechanism, in the 'strange lucidity' with which the lost home is imagined. The sense that the migrant estranged from a home tradition sees or imagines that tradition from the position of a foreigner, and of an observer with a trained eye for specificities of cultural practice, indicates that a relationship of continuity with home – albeit gradually distanced by migration – is in fact substituted by a relationship of detachment: the migrant's imagining of home deploys different methods and has different purposes from her experience of home. Lastly, I would note the language de Certeau uses here of 'mourning and reverence'. The processes of memorialization of the past that I noted in Chapter 2 are perhaps most powerfully in evidence in the memorialization of home, and this is enacted in the use in some narratives of figures and motifs of death and bereavement

---

2   Michel de Certeau, *The Capture of Speech and Other Political Writings*, ed. by Luce Giard, trans. and afterword by Tom Conley (Minneapolis, MN: University of Minnesota Press, 1997), 171.

in the expression of the relationship with home. In short, de Certeau's particular formulation here of how and why home might be constructed in the imaginary of migrants offers telling insights into the representational strategies of a number of texts I will discuss.

The second principle which will inform this chapter is that of the instability of home. Whilst my comments, following de Certeau, on the memorialization of home and on 'reverence' might suggest the opposite, in the lapidary fixity of something understood to be gone forever, the very mechanism of turning a 'lost place' into an imagined one exposes an ongoing exchange with home which maintains its presence and changeability. The act of representation, less an act than a process of the imaginary and of textual expression, repeatedly reinstantiates the currency of home whilst also acknowledging its extinction, and in this sense articulates one particular tension which disrupts the perceived fixity of a lost and desired home. There are other perspectives which spotlight such tension or instability, as argued by Sara Ahmed.[3] She takes issue with accounts which tend to extrapolate migration as a metaphor and thus to celebrate it as liberation and transgression:[4] 'The violence of this gesture is clear: the experiences of migration, which can involve trauma and violence, become exoticized and idealized as the basis of an ethics of transgression, an ethics which assumes that it is possible to be liberated from identity as such, at the same time as it "belongs" to an authentically migrant subject'.[5] This affects not simply our approach to the migrant subject but also to home itself, which comes to be described only in terms of what it is not:

> By being defined negatively in this way, home henceforth becomes associated with stasis, boundaries, identity and fixity. Home is implicitly constructed as a purified space of belonging in which the subject is too comfortable to question the limits or

---

[3] Sara Ahmed, 'Home and Away: Narratives of Migration and Estrangement', *International Journal of Cultural Studies*, 2.3 (1999), 329–47.
[4] The accounts she refers to are Rosi Braidotti, *Nomadic Subjects: Embodiment and Sexual Difference in Contemporary Feminist Theory* (New York: Columbia University Press, 1994) and Iain Chambers, *Migrancy, Culture, Identity* (London: Routledge, 1994).
[5] Ahmed, 'Home and Away', 334.

borders of her or his experience, indeed, where the subject is so at ease that she or he does not think. [...] [H]ome is associated with a being that rests, that is full and present to itself, and that does not overreach itself through the desire for something other. To be at home is the absence of desire, and the absence of an engagement with others through which desire engenders movement across boundaries.[6]

In taking issue with such an impossibly complacent and static perception of home and of being-at-home, Ahmed hints at the source of the almost forensic 'strange lucidity' of the backwards look of the migrant envisaged by de Certeau, when reconstructing home from elsewhere. What both theorists, differently, bring to light is the operation of desire, and of its corresponding lack or loss, in constructing a sense of home in relation to elsewhere. Referring to the vision which she describes and rejects above, Ahmed suggests that 'The problem with such a model of home as familiarity is that it projects strangerness beyond the walls of the home. Instead, we can ask: how does being-at-home already encounter strangerness? How does being at home already engender desire?'[7] This alternative model, which takes account of the historically determined experiences of a migrant, allows us to see the movement within the experience of home which is engendered by the desire to be elsewhere and to depart, and the sense of estrangement within the home which this produces. The secure space of home can thus be understood differently as a site of conflict, all the more pressing upon the individual because it exists within the home and therefore must often be suppressed or at least negotiated. Ahmed continues: 'The issue is that home is not simply about fantasies of belonging – where do I originate from – but that it is sentimentalized as a space of belonging ("home is where the heart is"). The question of home and being at home can only be addressed by considering the question of affect: being at home is here a matter of how one feels or how one might fail to feel'.[8]

Home as a construction in the imaginary which speaks to and speaks of the affects of being at home and of making homes, engaging with senses

---

6   Ahmed, 'Home and Away', 339.
7   Ahmed, 'Home and Away', 340.
8   Ahmed, 'Home and Away', 341.

of both belonging and non-belonging, is thus at the centre of the analysis which will form this chapter. What exactly I am defining as 'home' will in large part emerge from the discussions of specific texts themselves, since it is the imaginary of the individual migrant character or narrator which identifies what home includes and where its borders lie. Home envisaged as physical space, often understood metonymically to represent a home culture, is a central trope, encompassing details of architecture and domestic interior arrangements, light, climate, vegetation, food and culinary practices, etc. Within this space are the people who signify home: family, most prominently, but also friends and community figures. Amongst the people, but influenced also by the space, are the beliefs, practices, habits, and sentiments of home. As indicated above, I shall also consider 'home' away from the place of birth and upbringing, examining how home is imagined in various 'destinations' or crossing points along the routes of migration. In this regard, I shall pay particular attention to home and embodiment, looking at ways in which the migrant body – especially, perhaps, the female one – is figured (and contested) as an agent of reproducing home in new locations. These questions will be considered in terms of three novels primarily: *La straniera*, by Younis Tawfik, *Divorzio all'islamica a viale Marconi*, by Amara Lakhous, and *Lontano da Mogadiscio*, by Shirin Ramzanali Fazel.[9]

'Home', for the architect who is one of the two protagonists and narrators of Tawfik's first novel, is established as Turin at the beginning of the novel. He inhabits a domestic space which bespeaks middle-class Italian-ness, he inhabits the immediate locality as a 'native' (frequenting a particular bar, as noted in Chapter 1), and he inhabits the city as a citizen, confidently navigating its urban layout by car. No imaginary of a home elsewhere in time and geography appears to trouble him until his encounter with Amina, 'la straniera', which prompts both – the architect in particular – to revisit and relive the homes in which they were born and raised. It is interesting that the narrative establishes his refusal to imagine home in the

---

9   Younis Tawfik, *La straniera* (Milan: Bompiani, 1999); Amara Lakhous, *Divorzio all'islamica a viale Marconi* (Rome: e/o, 2010); Shirin Ramzanali Fazel, *Lontano da Mogadiscio* (Rome: Datanews, 1994).

first chapter by means of comparison with a male friend, also of Middle Eastern origin, whose use of Amina as a prostitute accidentally introduces her to the architect. The married friend seeks out casual sexual encounters with women, including women of his own nationality or ethnicity, and in this expression of the compensation for a lack or loss, he offers one model for the reconstruction of home by means of sexual fulfillment provided by someone who 'represents' that experience. The architect's sexuality, on the other hand, is represented through a failed marriage and a short-term relationship, both with middle-class Italian women: his investment in reproductive sexuality, such as it is, is directed rigidly towards the consolidation of Italian-ness, and away from any reproduction or extension of his home culture. The relatively few encounters between Amina and the architect in the book are dominated by story-telling, and it is the stories of their homes and of their migration that they exchange; indeed, this narrative communion is the substance of their relationship.

The architect's narratives of home in many ways illustrate the 'strange lucidity' highlighted by de Certeau, bearing in part the detail and the informative thrust of an ethnological enquiry. They form part of Tawfik's project, noted in Chapter 2, to inform an Italian readership about Arab Islamic cultures. At the same time, they perform within the narrative of the novel the representation of home of which de Certeau speaks, creating an imaginary of tradition – and also of political history – which articulates a lack hitherto denied by the protagonist. The rhythms and rituals of home life in an unspecified Middle Eastern nation are recounted with affection and a strong sense of stability, and at the core of this are the architect's mother and father: she seen, stereotypically, as a nurturing figure at the centre of the domestic space, associated particularly with the smell of freshly baked bread in the morning,[10] and he, stereotypically, as a source of under-

---

10 The same notion of the woman reproducing home by means of a body which regularly and systematically provides nutrition occurs in Tawfik's *Il profugo*, where, in the radically dislocated environment of the narrator's escape route via Kurdistan, the sight of a mother baking bread consolidates the sense that a new life outside Iraq is reachable, or that a new home is imaginable. Younis Tawfik, *Il profugo* (Milan: Bompiani, 2006), 173.

standing, not always 'accurate', in terms of full and up-to-date detail, but rather reliable, in being born of experience and long reflection. The figure of the father in this way comes to embody the tension in the architect's sense of being at home, functioning as the fulcrum at which a sense of identity and respect for tradition meet intense frustration at the very stability of such identities and traditions. The architect's straining away from home is encapsulated in an episode shortly preceding his departure to study in Italy. In response to rumours peddled by his uncle about petty criminality and lawlessness in Italy,[11] his father cites more accurate information about the dangers of contemporary Italy, mentioning the murder of Aldo Moro, the activities of the *Brigate rosse*, etc. This information comes through the network based in the café he frequents, whilst his son is aware of the same issues, but has heard about them on the radio. That the father's knowledge relies on community, and is bound within 'home', whilst the son's derives from technology operating largely in an extra-territorial space, demonstrates that the architect's imaginary at this point constructs a home where he will feel 'at home' as being elsewhere.

The figuration of the father, at home, as an embodiment of a cultural truth is, of course, a cliché, and one reproduced in a number of narratives of migration to Italy. Tawfik seals an association between the architect's father as a sort of *Ur*-text, furnishing human wisdom and understanding, and the desert as an *Ur*-location, constructing a highly romanticized cultural stereotype.[12] In response to his father's voicing of his veneration of the desert as his own cultural 'home', the architect comments, 'Col tempo, mi sono reso conto che aveva ragione, anche se non in tutto. Tutto quello che ho conservato dentro di me, nel mio cuore e nella mia anima, è il calore del deserto. Il sole che abbraccia tutto. Avvolge le creature e penetra nelle

---

11   The warnings about Italy delivered by the uncle accurately mirror both western prejudices against Arabic countries, and western prejudices against Italy – especially southern Italy – in a relatively recent past (persisting, arguably, into the present), e.g. 'Sono capaci di tagliarti un dito per rubarti la fede. Non portare niente di valore con te...' (Tawfik, *La straniera*, 21).

12   Tawfik's later novel exploits further this stereotype: Younis Tawfik, *La città di Iram* (Milan: Bompiani, 2002).

cose fino a renderle più irreali. La luce abbagliante che disegna la natura e la rende allegra. Più viva del solito'.[13] The imaginary of the desert, in particular, provides a striking example of the poetic representation of a symbolic feature of home, here represented from a distance by the migrant long absent from it.

Elements, however, of the architect's representation of his father – as place/culture as well as person – also bring to light tensions in the migrant's sense of what home is. During the second meeting between the architect and Amina, their encounter with African immigrants on the night-time streets of Turin (as discussed in Chapter 1, 'Identity') prompts the architect to recall hunting trips with his father, and his own unease at being involved in the killing of living creatures. The association between seeing migrants in the Italian city and hunting animals bespeaks a startling violence which, on the one hand, underscores the threat the architect feels that large-scale immigration poses to his identity, but on the other, in the terms of the current discussion, reveals a potentially violent ambivalence also in his apprehension of home. At one level, this concerns his response to the patriarchy. He recalls in detail not a hunt which he experienced, but rather a story of hunting told by his father and friends on one of their hunting trips, so constructing a cultural patrimony secured in the oral transmission of narratives amongst men and particularly in their collective balancing of an economy of violence and mercy in response to the vulnerable (and beautiful). The story tells of a gazelle wounded with a hunter's arrow, which enters a bedouin's tent and then is protected by the bedouin until his own death because the animal is his guest: 'Per quell'uomo, la gazzella era entrata nella tenda come un ospite che chiedeva la sua protezione. Era un dakhil, in cerca di rifugio. L'arabo era pronto a morire, secondo il codice d'onore del deserto, per garantire la vita e la sicurezza dell'ospite'.[14] The 'moral' of the story restores humanity and mercy where the threat of male (and patriarchal) violence had been evoked, but in reproducing this folk tale in the presence of migrants in Turin, and particularly of Amina,

---

13   Tawfik, *La straniera*, 131.
14   Tawfik, *La straniera*, 129.

clearly associated with the gazelle of the tale, the enchanting quality of the desert lore delivered is disrupted by the implicit stress on the vulnerability of the object of the hunters' gaze. Had the wounded animal not happened upon the bedouin's tent, the hunters (fathers) would have killed it.

The incipient possibility of violence in the home culture which this apparently idealized vision reveals is articulated more directly in a story the architect tells of home later in the novel, when he sees a boy, spotted by soldiers breaching a curfew, shot when he fails to respond to their calls: 'Il secco e determinato "Alt!", lo scoppio, la scintilla e lo spruzzo di sangue per me erano stati la fine del sorriso, dello sguardo, della parola. Avevo visto morire la libertà.'[15] The summary brutality of the scene marks the difference between the lucky escape of the gazelle within the traditional framework of desert lore and the historical reality of the Middle East after the Six-Day War of 1967. Home, at this point, becomes a site of physical danger and moral alienation, in which individuality is stifled. The sense of conflict with a male hegemony which surfaces in the hunting story is delivered as a socio-political critique (removed, in this instance, from association with the architect's father, who is represented as a moderate and liberal pan-Arabist): 'Con la politica era meglio non aver nulla a che fare. Da un momento all'altro si sarebbe potuti sparire dal mondo anche per un piccolo sospetto, per un'amicizia sbagliata o per una frase detta a caso. [...] Bisognava vivere a modo loro, e sotto la loro stretta sorveglianza'.[16] This surveillance, extends, in fact, to his early experiences as a student in Italy, where the architect meets, by chance, an individual whom he knew at home only by his reputation as a dissenter and rebel. He is impressed by the opportunity to meet and speak, as an equal, with this figure whom he acknowledges to have acquired something of the status of a folk hero and

---

15   Tawfik, *La straniera*, 108.
16   Tawfik, *La straniera*, 26. The sense of acute pressure to conform to the dictates of a political and/or military hegemony, for fear of one's life, in the home culture is figured also in Tawfik's *Il profugo* and in Amor Dekhis, *I lupi della notte* (Rome: L'ancora, 2008). On the effects on the individual of this external force, see Jennifer Burns, '*Lupus in fabula*: The Workings of Fear in Italian Migration Narratives', *Italian Studies*, 68.3 (2013, forthcoming).

who thus offers the opportunity to reconstruct a notion of home in Italy which accommodates and perpetuates the home he has left. The day after this casual encounter, however, the architect is approached in the university refectory by an older man from his own country, who warns him to choose his friends more carefully, for the sake of his own and his family's safety. That the oppressive force of the patriarchy has the capacity to hunt him even in his new life in Italy is sufficient for the architect at this point to sever contacts with home. Interestingly, in doing so, he articulates a comprehensive rejection of a certain imaginary of home, of community, of nation, in favour of a rationalist engagement with the here and now: 'Là continuavano a vivere nel sogno, e io quel sogno non lo vivevo come realtà, ma solo come fatica, sofferenza, lotta continua per la sopravvivenza.'[17]

Comparable critiques of the political realities of home and of the societies which acquiesce in these pernicious conditions are a feature of a number of other narratives by migrant writers. In Abdel Malek Smari's novel, *Fiamme in paradiso*, the political hegemony in Algeria is the object of specific and angry criticism, and is represented as the primary cause for emigration.[18] Smari's protagonist, Karim, engages the Algerian leader directly: 'E sarebbe poi questa la democrazia? Imbavagliati da sempre nella parola e nelle azioni; assassinati nello spirito da coloro che eran stati i padri della nostra indipendenza. Caro signor Boudiaf, in questo paese, noi, non l'abbiamo mai visto la democrazia.'[19] Again, the perpetuation of attitudes and prejudices related to this hegemony in Italy, amongst the community of Algerian migrants, is an element of acute frustration for Karim. Reflecting on this community and particularly on its centre in the mosque they all attend – stronghold in Italy of the values and practices of home – he reflects: 'Ripetevano sempre le stesse cose, le stesse che aveva lasciato in Algeria, per cui aveva lasciato l'Algeria. E ora le ritrovava anche qui. Chiusura e ostilità verso gli altri, tutti gli altri. Ripetizione, infinità di gesti ritualizzati e parole che davano loro la garanzia assoluta di essere nel

---

17   Tawfik, *La straniera*, 35.
18   Abdel Malek Smari, *Fiamme in paradiso* (Milan: Il Saggiatore, 2000).
19   Smari, *Fiamme in paradiso*, 10.

bene, di essere *il* bene. Gli faceva un po' paura cominciare a sentirsi estraneo a loro'.[20] The conflict insistent within the home before departure is, again, seen clearly from the perspective of a different home (in Italy), and the sense of alienation this produces is tacitly accepted. Interestingly, Smari's narrator draws attention to a logic of ritual, repetition, and mimicry as the vehicle for the reproduction at a community level of a home in a new geographical and cultural location.[21]

A comparable logic is observed by the character, Sofia, in Amara Lakhous's *Divorzio all'islamica a viale Marconi*. She uses a call centre in her neighbourhood in Rome to telephone home (as will be explored below), but whilst she uses it for personal reasons, she also notes the function that the call centre fulfils for the community, by reproducing home in Italy. Fittingly, the name of the call centre is 'Little Cairo'. It functions as a hub for the migrant community in part simply as a social space: paths cross there, repeatedly. The effect which Sofia particularly notes, however, is in terms of the cultural and ideological imaginary of the community, in that the call centre screens Al Jazeera programming on a rolling basis. It thus endlessly reconstructs a particular view of the world and its current events – a view indeed dominated by a particular visual imaginary – which dominates the consciousness, and sense of self and community, of those who pass through the call centre and are drawn to its images and commentary. Sofia's comment on it is highly critical:

> Il Little Cairo è affollato, molti clienti non si limitano come me a telefonare, ma si fermano a guardare Madame al-Jazeera. Il televisore serve ad attirare i clienti e a farli sentire a casa. Purtroppo sono in tanti a cascarci. Non so come fanno a stare ore e ore a seguire le notizie di attentati, bombe, kamikaze, guerre, morte. È un bombardamento mediatico quotidiano. Un autentico doping della mente e della memoria.[22]

---

20 Smari, *Fiamme in paradiso*, 107.
21 On the 'stylized repetition of acts' used to perform a particular cultural identity, see Judith Butler, *Gender Trouble: Feminism and the Subversion of Identity* (London: Routledge, 1990), 140.
22 Lakhous, *Divorzio all'islamica a viale Marconi*, 145.

In this sense, the call centre, which in some ways expresses a mobility of place in its interchange of voices and communications across the globe, in fact becomes the organ for a unilateral vision of the world. This vision constructs a simulacrum of a culture – a little Cairo – which is introspective, self-affirming, hostile or indifferent to other voices from other communities, and therefore socially and culturally dysfunctional. Though displaced from its original 'home' – or indeed because of this – it articulates an imaginary of home which rejects any sense of mobility and interprets the intercultural possibilities afforded by the presence of an Arabic Muslim community in Rome as the grounds for a dogged production of monoculturality. Echoing Smari's character, Karim, Sofia identifies this as a dangerous form of delusion. As such, both characters articulate that 'strangerness', following Ahmed, might insist for individuals as much within the new 'homes' posited by migrant communities in destination countries as within the culture of departure: the introspective reproduction of home, at a community level, serves simply to transplant its tensions and dangers.

Returning to the question of 'strangerness' within the family unit, similar figures of homeliness as reproduction exercise a different but determining effect. As suggested in relation to the architect in *La straniera*, if an unequivocal sentiment of being at home is figured at all, it is figured and embodied in the mother. In both *La straniera* and *Il profugo*, by Tawfik, and in *I lupi della notte*, by Amor Dekhis, the mother is figured almost exclusively within the domestic space, and within one place within the home (the central courtyard of the home in Tawfik's novels and the central living area in Dekhis's). As such, she is presented as rooted, her body, which endlessly and unconditionally supplies emotional and alimentary sustenance to those around her (figured predominantly as men), permeating the physical fabric of the domestic interior, so that she embodies the nucleus of the domestic sphere. Recalling my discussion in Chapter 1 (see pages 54–5) around the notion of fixity and stasis in relation to women's occupation of domestic space, in which I followed Irene Gedalof and others in identifying movement within this apparent stasis, I would note that in the case of these elderly mothers, there is little evidence that they are other than 'grounded'.[23] Their very affective value in the emotional economy of the various male protagonists is predicated upon the fact that, physically and emotionally, they do not shift or develop: their existence is as figures of being rather than becoming, and it is in the constancy of their unequivocal being that they permit the men in the household to 'become', which is also to move or migrate.[24] The references – themselves repeated in the narratives – to baking bread, as cited above (from *La straniera*), to a particular way of making tea for her husband (in *Il profugo*), to specific rituals of faith (in *I lupi della notte*) all create an imaginary of motherhood which is defined absolutely by the endless and reassuring reproduction of the domestic household through repeated acts and gestures. This centrality and fixity is perhaps most emphatically figured in the epilogue of Tawfik's *Il profugo*, where the narrator's return, mid-2000s, to an Iraq more than ever riven by conflict generated internally and externally, finds his mother still seated in the enclosed courtyard at the centre of the home, where she then dies.

How, then, is home figured in the narratives of female protagonists in Italian immigration literature? Tawfik's *La straniera*, in its bifocal structure whereby male and female protagonists narrate in the first person in alternating chapters, and in the insistent presence of home within both narratives, offers one kind of case study through which to explore my question. Imbalances exist within this structure, however: the novel comprises a prologue and six chapters, the first, third and fifth of which are narrated in the first person by the architect, and the second and fourth by Amina. The sixth is narrated in the second person singular, addressed to the architect. In terms of textual space, the architect's consciousness thus

---

23   Irene Gedalof, 'Taking (a) Place: Female Embodiment and the Re-grounding of Community', in Sara Ahmed, Claudia Castañeda, Anne-Marie Fortier and Mimi Sheller, eds, *Uprootings/Regroundings: Questions of Home and Migration* (Oxford: Berg, 2003), 91–112.
24   I would note that the mother figure in *I lupi della notte* is figured with slightly more complexity, in that her failing health and increasing dependency disrupt the emotional and physical geometry of the household: she can no longer function entirely as 'centre' of the home, and accordingly, Salah himself begins to move, travelling back and forth from Algiers to be with both her and Algyida.

dominates, and more specifically, a binary logic underpins the structure of the text, in that the very title of the novel invites the reader to adopt the perspective and the gaze of the architect, the 'straniero integrato' upon the less definable and integral character marked as 'other', or 'la straniera'.[25] Viewed within the context of Tawfik's broader enterprise to raise awareness of Islamic cultures within a wide Italian readership, his initiative to create a migrant Islamic woman who tells her own story and thus his construction, through Amina, of what aims to be an account of Arab Islamic culture (in Morocco) from a woman's perspective, offers particular insight into the representative strategies used in relation to home.

Amina's imaginary of home shares some of the idealizing thrust of the architect's, in terms of creating images of local space, climate, tastes and aromas. Much of her representation of home performs, however, a critique of the status accorded to women in her home society. Amina depicts herself as struggling to assert her independence and to make her own choices against the familial and cultural forces which aim to exercise what they believe to be a right to determine how she lives and behaves. Full consciousness of the pervasiveness of this instance of oppression comes after she has moved from her rural home to Casablanca, to work in a factory, and realizes that the independence this affords her is both limited and impermanent. The appearance, and what she knows of the personal histories, of her female co-workers tell her that hers is not an isolated case of struggle but a universal condition in that culture. She comments: 'Nella nostra società, la donna passa dalla schiavitù dei genitori a quella del marito. Non ha il diritto di vivere nel mezzo una vita tutta sua, un momento privato per capire se stessa, esplorare la sua natura, senza dover per forza fare chissà che cosa o quale strana esperienza'.[26] Her marriage shortly afterwards only serves to confirm this: under her husband's impetus, they migrate to Italy, using all the money

---

25   I use here the notion of binary opposition associated particularly with feminist post-structuralist thinking, whereby the 1 of the binary denotes male integral subjecthood and the 0 denotes female lack. See Hélène Cixous and Catherine Clément, *The Newly Born Woman*, trans. by Betsy Wing, introduction by Sandra M. Gilbert (Manchester: Manchester University Press, 1986).

26   Tawfik, *La straniera*, 74.

they have – mostly deriving from her dowry and possessions – to pay the trafficker who organizes their boat passage to Spain. Not long after arriving in Turin, her husband goes, unannounced, to a job in southern Italy, only to return eventually in the narrative present of the novel, when he physically and sexually assaults his wife. Mirroring the architect's accounts (in such a way as again to underline the pre-eminence of his perspective in the novel), her account of home stresses, within the sphere now of personal relationships and the domestic economy of power, that the structures of patriarchy extend from the physical location of a home as origin through the routes of migration to insist in new homes posited elsewhere.

This recent story of Amina's exploitation confirms a lifelong history of being expected to bow to the will of others – either of men or of women acting according to men's expectations – and of constantly seeking opportunities to gain and to demonstrate some degree of agency in her own affairs. The stories of home which Amina first tells are of her birthplace, childhood and family, and though shot through with some nostalgia, the dominant tone is of shame and anger. The shame, her stories establish, is a cultural condition created for any woman whose conduct is not perceived to be impeccable; the anger is generated herself in response to this condition. She reveals that she was deemed responsible for her six-year-old younger brother's death, because she was supposed to be supervising him when he fell in a ditch, after which he developed a fever from which he did not recover. This, she recalls, was the first time that her mother called her a whore, and this establishes a principle of intense personal shame which governs her attitudes to herself from then on, whether she rebels against it or concedes. It is significant that it is specifically a shame rooted in sexual behaviour which is attributed to her, despite the fact that her perceived neglect of her little brother on this occasion had nothing to do with sexual activity. It is also fitting that, in a culture in which the text suggests that a woman's individual worth is entirely equated with her sexual purity, any apparent transgression is associated with – indeed, defined as – a sexual transgression, and the perpetrator permanently marked as a result.[27] Recalling Ahmed,

---

27 This recalls the conviction of Sofia, in Lakhous's *Divorzio all'islamica a viale Marconi*, that any cancellation of her marriage will be attributed by the community to her

it is clear that 'being-at-home already encounter[s] strangerness' for a prepubescent girl in this environment, in which inclusion in the household is so finely calibrated according to perceived sexual purity, or indeed, to a perceived disposition towards such purity even in childhood, that the possibility of being forcibly estranged or rejected is ever present. The condition of 'being at home' is thus suspended uncomfortably between the desire for inclusion and the desire to reject such arbitrary conditions of acceptance.

The sexual resonance of Amina's shame is complicated and accentuated by a manifestly sexual element, in that she is sent by her mother during the period of her brother's illness to a local 'healer', a man in his fifties named Sidi Ahmed, to collect medicine for her brother. Sidi Ahmed tells her she is the cause of the affliction which has taken hold of her brother, because of her incipient and dangerous sexuality, and that the only remedy is for her to return to him in a week's time so that he can rid her of this 'lupa nera', obviously by having sex with her.[28] She does not return on this occasion, but a year later, when her father is seriously ill, she takes the decision herself to return to Sidi Ahmed to complete the sexual transaction. This episode is problematic, in terms of the representation of a woman, and specifically of a woman in Islamic culture, at two levels, and these merit some analysis here in order to expose what is at stake in the reconstruction of a 'home' in a distant culture for a 'foreign' readership. Firstly, at the level of the textual construction of Amina, the reader is invited to read her transaction with Sidi Ahmed as a seizing of sexual consciousness and an action of empowerment; an interpretation which appears to confirm that a woman's value – her negotiating power in any transaction – resides uniquely in her sexuality (and maximally, in her virginity). That it is through Amina's consciousness that the encounter is constructed as such is particularly uncomfortable, especially since Amina represents the sexual encounter with Sidi Ahmed as a personal triumph, eliding the subjugation she has experienced – and, at a cultural level, thus confirmed – with a somewhat mystical notion of empowerment through sexual self-discovery: 'Da allora,

---

future husband's presumed discovery that she is not a virgin, rather than to a choice made by herself on moral grounds. See Chapter 1, page 49.

28   Tawfik, *La straniera*, 56.

sono una donna. Una donna violentata. Una donna ricattata e violata, una donna prigioniera, ma che, con l'alba del risveglio, è riuscita a trovare se stessa, a capire bene il suo vero essere. Dietro le sbarre del corpo, trovai la mia femminilità'.[29] That this reconstruction of her first sexual experience is intercut in the narrative with the account of sex in the present (with the architect's friend), for money, confirms that her 'femininity' is defined by the commercial value of her female sexuality.

At a different level, the wider imaginary of Amina's sexual initiation is populated by images which exoticize the encounter. Sidi Ahmed himself, as 'healer', is an exotic figure in the very threat he represents, whose home is filled with a darkness 'trafitto dai raggi della luce proveniente dalle fessure nei muri', with 'nuvole d'incenso, come spiriti di follia', in which there is 'un'anfora di vetro mezzo piena di una bevanda color rosso bruno', and where he mixes unidentified powders and speaks of jinns.[30] When she returns to have sex with him, Amina describes her 'vestitino [...] quasi trasparente', 'seni ancora piccoli ma sodi e ben visibili',[31] and other elements of her orchestrated seduction of the older man in detail, before recounting the pleasure she enjoys in this sexual initiation. The detailed narrative of intercourse between an older man and a fourteen-year-old girl, who initiates the encounter and participates enthusiastically and somewhat expertly, offers a fantasy of young female sexuality from which the reader is invited to derive untroubled pleasure.[32] Any moral, emotional, even physical, negative responses can be anaesthetized precisely because the event is so emphatically justified by distance, or 'othered', through the exoticizing detail of location, circumstance, and participants, that any discomfort which the event might otherwise – elsewhere – provoke can readily be attributed to, and thus dissociated from the reader as, 'cultural difference'.

---

29 Tawfik, *La straniera*, 59.
30 Tawfik, *La straniera*, 54.
31 Tawfik, *La straniera*, 57.
32 The cover image of the 2001 edition of the novel tends to confirm this view, showing, in extreme close-up, the upper half of the face of a girl who looks to be between childhood and adolescence, wearing heavy make-up presented as part of a traditional costume.

Recalling my comments above about the binary logic underlying the narrative in *La straniera*, it is possible now to extend that discussion, and thereby to uncover further elements of the construction of home in this and other narratives. Through Amina's accounts of the establishment of her sexual identity, and the architect's anxiety about her performance of her cultural identity in Italy, it is possible to view the architect, again, as an integral whole, and Amina as an empty signifier, the nil value upon which he is able to inscribe a rationale of his own experience of and identification with his home culture. In narrative terms, Amina prompts him to revisit home in his imaginary and memory, after long absence, and in the terms of his interiority, her stories of home enable him to engage in a discussion about his own relative Italian-ness and Middle-Eastern-ness. Her body, the currency of transactions within and between cultures, both at home and in Italy, is made the carrier, under his gaze, of the value of his home culture, hence his desire for it/her and his acute anxiety about its devaluation through free commerce between cultures. In contrast to the grounded and reproductive figure of the traditional mother, Amina certainly moves, in terms both of emotional development and physical migration, but in response to the desires of men: Sidi Ahmed, her husband, her customers. Despite the insistence in both her own and the architect's narratives on her relentless efforts to claim and assert agency, she functions as the object of the architect's gaze and, increasingly, the object of his quest for home which becomes, in the latter part of the novel, a quest for Amina, a missing woman. As such, she peculiarly illustrates the point made by Sara Ahmed, Claudia Castañeda, Anne-Marie Fortier and Mimi Sheller, that '*Being grounded is not necessarily about being fixed; being mobile is not necessarily about being detached*'.[33] Her very mobility, viewed through the eyes of the architect as her primary respondent, charges her all the more oppressively with the values and principles of the culture and the traditions associated with home, so that she is fixed within the culture which she describes, despite her explicit critique of it. Her body cannot be detached from that

---

33   Ahmed, Castañeda, Fortier and Sheller (eds), *Uprootings/Regroundings*, 1 (italics in original). See my discussion of this principle in Chapter 1, pages 48–55.

economy of female sexuality, despite her repeated efforts to force a detachment through radical sexual choices. Tawfik's novel thus offers one, somewhat difficult, model of the embodiment of home in the female figure.

The characterization of Sofia, in Lakhous's *Divorzio all'islamica a viale Marconi*, offers a productive counterpoint to Amina in terms of the imaginary of home. In relation to the expectation that a woman will embody and perpetuate the home environment, it is interesting to recall Sofia's positions with regard to the wearing of a veil, as discussed in Chapter 1. In Egypt, she did not wear nor was expected to wear one; in Italy, both those in her own culture (her husband) and Italians expect her to wear it in order to mark her as of a different culture and to make her, and that culture insofar as she embodies it, impenetrable and 'other'. The covering of her body which it affords serves to give her an integrity as a representative of another culture in Italy to which a certain value accrues in everyday life on the streets of Rome, and as such, she comes to accept and even to play that identity. What is most interesting, in the present context, about the character of Sofia is, however, the way in which she envisions and negotiates home. Her emotional and imaginary investment in a notion of home is channelled in quite complex and mobile ways between locations in space and time. Her vision of a home of the future is constructed around an image of herself as a successful businesswoman in Italy, and, later, around the possibility of a future in Italy with Issa. Her home, in the sense of her country and culture of origin, is more or less absent from this construction – she seems not to be compensating a loss, as de Certeau articulates a migrant's imaginings of home, but rather envisaging a gain. Her mode of constructing a home in Italy is not by reproducing the culture, the environment, and the practices of home, but rather by producing in her imaginary an entirely new social and physical location for herself, as a hair stylist to the stars in Rome. Indeed, as will be noted in the next chapter, she rejects absolutely the models of migrant culture in Italy which insist on reproducing home via television (Al Jazeera rolling news and commentary for men in public spaces; Egyptian *telenovelas* for women in the private sphere). Accordingly, the sociality she constructs for herself in her immediate locality in and around viale Marconi mimics no one cultural construct of community, but mixes eastern European migrants, Arab Islamic migrants, and Italians.

The way in which Sofia inhabits and constructs her new home finds distinct resonances in Ahmed's analysis of being at home, less in the notion of 'strangerness' discussed above, and more in Ahmed's insistence on the passage between plural homes, and on the experience of self in relation to locality. She argues:

> Home is [...] not a particular place that one simply inhabits, but more than one place: there are too many homes to allow place to secure the roots or routes of one's destination. It is not simply that the subject does not belong anywhere. The journey between homes provides the subject with the contours of a space of belonging, but a space which expresses the very logic of an interval, the passing through of the subject between apparently fixed moments of departure and arrival.[34]

As the novel recounts Sofia's arrival and establishment of a life in Rome, with a degree of uncertainty and possibility about her future there which dissolves any sense of this being a definitive destination, the notion she constructs of being at home in Rome is provisional and mobile in the way which Ahmed describes. Sofia's sense of self, place, and attachments seems absolutely to be in movement, responsive to her local surroundings and to possibilities that it offers as well as to principles and affects established in the country and culture from which she departed. Her adaptation of her name (Safia to Sofia) to suit her new environment marks this passage. Moreover, her articulation of criticisms of social organization in contemporary Italy, of the hierarchies and outdated practices of her culture of origin (such as infibulation),[35] and of the tics and fetishes of the migrant culture in Italy which she inhabits (such as dedication to Al Jazeera)[36] demonstrate the process she is engaged in of making critical connections between 'homes' and testing their boundaries. As such, her imaginary of belonging seems itself to be predicated upon the 'logic of an interval', and she offers a model of home which not only can move, but derives from movement.

Sofia also illustrates Ahmed's point, however, about the difficulty or impossibility of being freely transgressive ('nomadic') and entirely liberated from a primary identity established within a specific cultural environment.

---

34 Ahmed, 'Home and Away', 330.
35 Lakhous, *Divorzio all'islamica a viale Marconi*, 123–7.
36 Lakhous, *Divorzio all'islamica a viale Marconi*, 145–6.

Home – in the sense of Egypt, Arab Islamic culture, and family – draws Sofia back as powerfully as it does, for example, Tawfik's architect, even though the mode and means of this return are contained as everyday events within the here-and-now of Rome, rather than as prolonged narrative recollections of experiences at home. Sofia's regular visits to the 'Little Cairo' call centre to telephone her family allow her, within the acutely confined and sealed space of a telephone cabin, to re-enter emotionally and imaginatively the home she no longer physically inhabits, and the effects – indeed, the affects – of this are striking: she tends to vacate the cabin in tears, and acutely aware of the contradiction this demonstrates in terms of her self-possessed performance of being at home in Rome, she anxiously dries her tears each time. Interestingly, it is not that the substance of the conversations carries a high emotional charge, but rather the opposite, in that the detailed updates about everyday life in her family and home locality recreate an experience of the ordinariness of home which at once articulates her sense of belonging and serves as a reminder that she no longer belongs there. This is accentuated by her mother's question, repeated each time, whether she will be able to return home for a visit that year. This carefully regulated and contained engagement with home, every Friday in a small cabin in the same call centre, suggests that the positive habitation of an interval or passage between homes which Sofia's experience of Rome seems largely to construct depends upon an underlying rhythm of re-inhabitation of the home from which she departed. Notably, Issa regularly visits the same cabins in the same call centre to engage in conversations with family members who are entirely invented, as part of the construction of his 'cover' identity as a Tunisian migrant. The same minutiae of everyday life, albeit reported to him by a fake mother in relation to fake sisters etc., have a comparable (and comic) effect in stimulating his curiosity and sense of emotional belonging to a community. At the same time, he notes that he communicates less and less with his own family and partner in Italy. This suggests that the power of an imagination of a home felt to have been lost has a determining influence on the individual's sense of being 'at home', or not, in other homes established in other moments and places, and that this power is felt especially acutely where there is a geographic, and particularly, cultural boundary which has been crossed.

Foregrounding distance from a reference point, the title of Shirin Ramzanali Fazel's book, *Lontano da Mogadiscio*, also indicates the fundamental or primary importance of the place and culture of origin. Unusual amongst particularly the earlier texts by migrant writers, it certainly tells of migration, but tells of it through an imaginary of the place of departure rather than of that of destination: this is not a narrative of migrating to and through Italy, but a set of reflections from Italy on leaving Mogadishu behind. The imperative propelling the account is to recreate, in the imaginary of the author and in that of the reader, the lived experience of Mogadishu, but, where de Certeau suggests that this representation is brought to life in 'the imaginary regions of memory', Fazel rather seeks to make the city *present*, in terms of time and space, in Italy. As distinct, then, from Tawfik's representation of Iraq for Italians in *Il profugo*, which uses the vehicle of a personal memoir, Fazel's imaginary of Somalia plays explicitly nostalgic recollections against direct interpellations of the reader in the present tense. In this very play, the text thus articulates a different, but associated, kind of mobility of home from that indicated by the construction of Sofia in Lakhous's novel. Home – Mogadishu – is all-pervasive in the text, but it is a home which is both lost in the past and dynamically visible in the present, and at the same time, a home which is radically, sometimes exotically, different and distant from Italy and insistently connected to everyday life in Italy. Fazel, writing with the direct authority of the author – rather than through a character, as in the examples discussed here so far – suggests that, as she migrates through different countries and cultures, including Italy, she carries home with her. Home travels with her not only as a personal and emotional totem, but rather as an entire, mobile *habitus*; the cultural, political, moral, geographical, and affective reality of her home country.

The precise modes of Fazel's reconstruction of Somalia merit some attention, since the 'play' referred to above involves, stylistically, a range of techniques which deploy alternative and almost contradictory figures and images of the country. The text opens with an explicit recall of the form and the language of the fable – 'Il mio paese un tempo era il paese delle favole' – suggesting that the distance noted in the title is, apart from considerations of geography and chronology, one of perception and epistemology.[37] If Somalia is to be recreated and understood in the consciousness of the reader, it is through recourse to a childhood imaginary of 'cantastorie nelle piazze', 'frutti dai colori vivaci', 'immensi campi di granturco', 'tartarughe giganti'.[38] The direct invitation to share a nostalgic imagination of place draws at once upon the author's reconstruction of a specific location which she has experienced and the reader's parallel recollection of childhood, along with his imaginary of Africa or otherwise distant cultures and climates, creating the conditions for a representation of a home in which both author and reader, cross-culturally, can imaginatively invest. The sensual and affective charge of this form of imaginary of place is stretched and massaged in the first parts of the book, which work to endow the reader, by means of participation in the author's imagination of home, with a powerful sense of belonging to a place which is, in fact, 'lontano'. Rich and detailed description, and the confidential use of the second person (singular and plural), create a degree of intimacy intended to make the reader feel at home in this representation of place: 'Tutto era scandito da uno scambio di voci, risate, canti e pettegolezzi che incominciava a far parte della tua vita sin da piccolo e di cui era inconcepibile dover fare a meno'.[39]

Within this fable of a long-lost land, Fazel inserts references to the present of Somalia which disrupt the illusion of belonging to another world precisely by activating an imaginary of a current and violent crisis, perhaps equally familiar to readers from television images, but likely to generate a sense of detachment and distance, or of non-belonging. For example, a detailed explanation of rituals related to death is offered, in relation to the memory of the death of the author's grandmother, but this somewhat homely recreation of a family bereavement is closed with a much more disturbing image: 'Ora, nella tragedia che ha colpito la Somalia manca perfino l'acqua per lavare i morti che vengono sepolti in fosse comuni'.[40]

37 Fazel, *Lontano da Mogadiscio*, 13.
38 Fazel, *Lontano da Mogadiscio*, 13.
39 Fazel, *Lontano da Mogadiscio*, 15.
40 Fazel, *Lontano da Mogadiscio*, 16.

These jolts to the reader's sense of comfortable inclusion in a reconstructed and appealingly different home are signposts towards an alternative rhetorical mode of inclusion which takes precedence in the fourth part of the book. The opening section of this part interpellates Somalia itself, in five short paragraphs beginning each with that name, in order to stress the passage from a rich commercial nation connected globally via a series of opulent trade routes, to a 'terra di conquista'. The breach is identified with the name of Vasco da Gama, but the focus is much more recent: 'Vennero i colonizzatori europei e stuprarono la terra, seminando il germe degli orrori futuri'.[41] In this way, the Italian reader for whom a strong sense of belonging in Somalia and participation in its culture has been established is confronted with a radically alternative vision of her engagement with that country, and invited to recognize her 'participation' in the form of historical complicity in oppression. That Fazel does not swap one mode of dialogue with the reader for another, but rather combines images of violent civil warfare with dedications to a personified Somalia and 'le tue città dai cieli azzurri e odorose di gelsomini, le tue belle donne', maintaining the sensualized and exoticized imaginary of place alongside one which is politically and morally charged, demonstrates the play of modes of representing and imagining home in this text.[42] Such play intends to hold the reader's attention tightly to the discourse of what Somalia was, is, and might become.

A further element of play operates between history and story. On the one hand, Fazel claims the authority of one who knows and can tell of her country in part through recourse to a formal history of the nation, as indicated by the reference to Vasco da Gama. This invitation to the reader to participate through knowledge is counter-balanced by the telling of specific stories of recent atrocities. These are told in the mode of accounts of everyday life within a community; part of an oral exchange within kinship and friendship circles rather than a recorded history of events. The author herself refers to them as 'racconti' and 'testimonianze', and, strikingly, records the

---

41   Fazel, *Lontano da Mogadiscio*, 42.
42   Fazel, *Lontano da Mogadiscio*, 43.

names of the individual sources of these stories – Mumina, Dahir, Abdi.[43] In this way, the reader is again drawn into a local and 'homely' circle of news and information, and invited to participate through empathy for those who harbour various traumatic visions of atrocities they have witnessed. Viewed from a postcolonial perspective, this puncturing of the dominant narrative of history by means of sharp insights into the lives of individuals countering oppression at the periphery serves to undermine the notion of Somalia as the object of other national or regional narratives and to present it rather as the subject of its own narrative, still in the making.

Other homes than Somalia are, however, imagined and told in *Lontano da Mogadiscio*. The author speaks of Italy from a position of – compromised – inclusion, again indicated by the title which denotes a particular perspective from which Somalia is viewed. This position is articulated with some equivocation by the author, in ways which recall the somewhat critical, somewhat curious, somewhat desiring engagement of Lakhous's Sofia with Italy. Mediating in this relationship is the media itself, which provides, from the perspective of Italy/Europe, visual images and verbal commentary of a home that she knows and imagines differently, and yet which offers the only source she has of information on what her home has become. She is thus a critical viewer of television news, recognizing her own participation as both subject and object of the discourse of Somalia constructed and of an imaginary of Africa which it both feeds from and feeds. Watching television images of children and adults suffering famine in Africa, she acknowledges her proximity to them: 'Sento allora una fitta al cuore nel vedere la mia gente ridotta così'. Almost immediately afterwards, she also articulates the position in which the very act of watching those images has placed her, voicing a very different inclusion: 'Noi siamo belli, bianchi e la nostra pelle è liscia. [...] Quelli invece non hanno un nome, una storia. Sono solo immagini, immagini di fantasmi che non ci appartengono'.[44] In this way, she demonstrates Ahmed's point, discussed in my opening comments, about home and affect: 'being at home is [...] a matter of how one feels or how one might fail to feel'. However, she also

---

43 Fazel, *Lontano da Mogadiscio*, 46–7.
44 Fazel, *Lontano da Mogadiscio*, 48.

complicates this equation by expressing first how she feels ('sento'), and then how, once positioned in a particular cultural context ('noi'), she can recognize how it is possible, there, to fail to feel ('non ci appartengono'). She acknowledges, with a critical self-awareness, a sense of the possibility, at least, of belonging to her Italian or European 'home'.

In this way, Fazel posits a mode of home-building which follows the model neither of reproducing home in a new environment, nor of recreating home in the imagination in order to compensate for its lack, but which accepts the impossibility of being at home fully either in the place of departure or in the destination/s. On this basis, strategies are assembled for inhabiting in the imagination both the place which has been left and the place which is present (and, perhaps, others to come) in order to create a sense of being at home, albeit consciously contingent, in different places at once. Fazel thus offers a further illustration of how, in Ahmed's words, home may be less concerned with a defined geographic and cultural location than with creating, in movement, 'the contours of a space of belonging'. Her references in *Lontano da Mogadiscio* to living in Rome, Milan, Los Angeles, New York, London and Paris underscore this notion that home is a practice of negotiating and (re)constructing affective attachments in and between places. Since all those locations are collectively defined by being 'lontano da Mogadiscio', however, the text also cements the notion that there is an origin, an *Ur*-home, to which all others refer in a shifting economy of affects.

It is this compelling, or indeed, compulsive, presence of Somalia in both Fazel's first book and in her novel, *Nuvole sull'equatore*, published more than fifteen years later, which suggests a form of the centrality of home in migrant imaginaries which is relatively unfamiliar, expressing a violent nostalgia rooted in memory and distance, but at the same time insisting on the urgent proximity of home in Italy.[45] This proximity is, of course, furnished by the colonial relationship between Somalia and Italy, which makes the presence of Somalia in Italy traceable, even if these traces have tended to be hidden or denied. The first subtitle of *Nuvole sull'equatore*,

---

45 Shirin Ramzanali Fazel, *Nuvole sull'equatore. Gli italiani dimenticati. Una storia* (Cuneo: Nerosubianco, 2010).

Gli italiani dimenticati, draws attention to the principle which the novel expresses – and which it embodies in its mixed-race protagonist, Giulia – that the relationship between Italy and Somalia is in fact an inclusive one: the history of Somalia incorporates that of Italy and vice versa. That such a notion that two national histories and two cultures are so tightly imbricated with one another that one is present in the other is a factor of the imaginary only of postcolonial narratives is not the case, I would argue: *I lupi della notte* by Amor Dekhis is inflected with a similar sense that the recent history of Algeria can be traced and read in the present/future of Italy. However, as Igiaba Scego's novel, *La mia casa è dove sono*, demonstrates, it is perhaps in the specifically postcolonial narrative of Italy that the function of the text as a palimpsest through which other stories may be read is most vividly demonstrated.[46] As both of Fazel's works suggest, the relationship between present and temporary homes or destinations and previous ones, including the home of origin, is perhaps less accurately grasped according to a vertical model, where the place of origin is buried deep in a past which is also geographically distant, than by a notion of horizontality, whereby different homes are layered and superimposed over one another as sites of historical memory and experience, both for the individual and the nation or culture, at the same time as they offer sites of belonging for the present and future.

In conclusion to this discussion of home(s), and by way of introduction to my discussion of place and space in Italy in the next chapter, I will turn finally to two examples of places or spaces which raise questions about how to locate home and crystallize the sense, explored in various ways in this chapter, that it is both in the culture of origin and in the destination culture at once, or indeed, between them. The first emerges from both of

---

46   See Igiaba Scego, *La mia casa è dove sono* (Milan: Rizzoli, 2010), in which she recounts both her personal history and the history of Somalia through a structure constituted by sites in Rome. For histories of Italy's colonies (Somalia and Eritrea respectively) told through presence in Italian cities (Pavia and Rome), see also the combined books/documentaries: Simone Brioni, ed., *Somalitalia: Quattro vie per Mogadiscio* (Rome: Kimerafilm, 2012) and Ribka Sibhatu, *Aulò! Aulò! Aulò! Poesie di nostalgia, d'esilio e d'amore*, ed. by Simone Brioni (Rome: Kimerafilm, 2012).

Fazel's works, but features in countless other narratives of migration, and this is Stazione Termini in Rome. Sandra Ponzanesi has identified this location as an example of a 'non-place', following Marc Augé's argument, primarily because of the association it cements between migrants and social marginalization.[47] However, as a place of passage and movement, the station also comes to be invested, in the imaginative economy of many novels, as the location which accommodates and makes visible migration, and thus as a place of belonging. It is the place to go to to make new contacts or revive old ones, to gain intelligence and information, and, crucially, to participate in a sense of community. The notion which Ponzanesi highlights that this is a community 'out of place', in some ways, serves in fact to consolidate the sense of belonging and familiarity which the contact with a mix of others from the same and different countries and cultures generates in the individual. A striking example is that of Giulia, in Fazel's *Nuvole sull'equatore*, who slowly establishes a sense of being at home in Rome through recognition of the city itself, but also through the access that Stazione Termini offers her to Somalia. She actively chooses to visit the station in order to realize a connection between Rome and Mogadishu which allows her to feel genuinely at home: 'Molte volte bastava andare alla stazione Termini, e anche se non ci si conosceva risultava facile individuare i propri compaesani, dalla fisionomia e dalla parlata somala. Ti potevi avvicinare e iniziare a raccogliere notizie sulla Somalia, c'era continuamente qualcuno che era appena arrivato'.[48] In the terms used in this chapter, the station is an endlessly productive space, offering networks which shift and change shape according to the logic of a physical space created to organize travel. It thus produces a 'home' which in some ways resolves through performance a tension inherent in migration, by being identifiable neither as place of origin nor of destination, but rather by offering a spatial and social realization of passage.

---

47 Ponzanesi, Sandra, 'Imaginary Cities: Space and Identity in Italian Literature of Immigration', in Robert Lumley and John Foot, eds, *Italian Cityscapes: Culture and Urban Change in Contemporary Italy* (Exeter: University of Exeter Press, 2004), 156–65 (158–9). She refers to Marc Augé, *Non-places: Introduction to an Anthropology of Supermodernity*, trans. by John Howe (London: Verso, 1995).

48 Shirin Ramzanali Fazel, *Nuvole sull'equatore*, 201.

My second example again is played out in a 'non-place', and a place of transit, which on this occasion is an Algerian airport. Tahar Lamri's short story, 'Solo allora, sono certo, potrò capire', brings together a second-generation French Algerian, Jean-Marie, and Akli, an Algerian migrant to Sweden, as they await a flight to Paris after respectively their first and last visits to Algeria.[49] In this location, they exchange the views generated by their different experiences of being at home, or not, in Algeria on core issues related to migrant identity, such as names, linguistic competency, cultural and historical knowledge of the 'home' country. The cancellation of the flight they are awaiting prompts a more prolonged engagement between the two and allows Akli to invite Jean-Marie to stay overnight at his brother's house. This experience serves to fuel the desire for Algeria which Jean-Marie harbours in response to his father's strict prohibition of any return to Algeria or engagement with its culture. Mirroring his own fetishization of French-ness, Jean-Marie's father has created the conditions in which his son has constructed a partial notion of Algerian-ness which dominates his emotional engagement with this absent 'home' to the exclusion of all wider information on or understanding of the place. On the contrary, Akli, who chose to leave Algeria behind, has such a strong sense of non-belonging that he greets the death of his mother, whom he has been visiting on this trip, as the release from any further forced association with the country. Each man expresses a radically different perception of home. Akli states: 'Io non ho paese. Il mio paese è il mio corpo. Il mio paese è dove sto bene.'[50] As such, he articulates a radical interpretation of Ahmed's notion that a sense of belonging is formed around the mobile body of the migrant.[51] He goes on to justify his rejection of place as an anchor of belonging by violent rejection of his specific space and culture of origin. His 'paese' is 'sicuramente non questo merdaio. A te lo posso dire, sei quasi straniero: io odio gli arabi. Quando c'erano i francesi qui, non c'era mica tutta questa

---

49 Tahar Lamri, 'Solo allora, sono certo, potrò capire', in Alessandro Ramberti and Roberta Sangiorgi, eds, *Le voci dell'arcobaleno* (Santarcangelo di Romagna: Fara, 1995), 35–53.
50 Lamri, 'Solo allora, sono certo, potrò capire', 39.
51 Ahmed's discussion in the article to which I refer in fact opens with the airport as a prime example of 'the in-between space, the interval'. Ahmed, 'Home and Away', 330.

sporcizia, poi abbiamo avuto l'indipendenza e questi sono i risultati'.[52] Jean-Marie, by contrast, recalls de Certeau's description of the process of reconstruction of a home lost, signalling himself the 'strange lucidity' of the images of places which he has never in fact seen before: 'Ognuno di noi è legato a qualche cosa: un'immagine, un ricordo, un sapore dell'infanzia o dell'infanzia dei suoi genitori. I paesaggi di questo paese mi sembrano familiari, certi paesaggi che vedo per la prima volta sono così nitidi nella mia memoria, che non mi spiego il fatto. Forse è il presente che diventa per me passato all'istante, perché ho bisogno di inventarmi una storia, delle radici'.[53] He concludes with the intention to migrate to Algeria.

To close my discussion with these two apparently opposing views of the value and significance of 'home', and of how it might be located, is not simply to state that ultimately, home is anywhere we might imagine it. Rather, I would like to underscore the location of this story, which is, primarily, an airport, in which two characters travelling immediately in the same direction, but in terms of life trajectories, travelling in opposite directions, meet.[54] In such a place of transit, and particularly the no-man's land of an airport from which passengers departing immediately leave the ground, the sense that the story of the two men underscores is that 'home' is only fully constituted through mobility and detachment: it is the experience of leaving or returning, and the tensions towards and against, which animate that experience and which construct an imaginary of home. The territorialized physical reality of home is a real and potent source of images and affects, but it does not in itself constitute a home until it is animated by the imagination, negative or positive, of the subject envisioning it from a distance and contemplating the possibility, or impossibility, of return.

---

52 Lamri, 'Solo allora, sono certo, potrò capire', 39–40.
53 Lamri, 'Solo allora, sono certo, potrò capire', 53.
54 Ahmed notes the particular fertility of the airport in an imagination of home-in-migration: 'the familiar place, the place that is comfortable and comforting, is the in-between space, the interval, of the airport. Such a space is comforting, not because one has arrived, but because one has the security of a destination, a destination which quite literally becomes the somewhere of home' ('Home and Away', 330).

CHAPTER 4

Place and Space

To identify a body of writings as 'migration literature' posits movement across geographical space as somehow inherent to the stories that those writings tell and the ways in which they tell them. Indeed, in all the texts to be discussed in this chapter, including the majority which do not explicitly narrate a journey from one country to another, the imaginary which colours and animates the narrative is built upon notions of mobility. 'Immigration' might suggest a simple passage from one nation state to another, from origin to destination, but in all cases I shall discuss, arrival and even prolonged residence in the destination country is articulated through a sense of continued displacement or restlessness, a sense of being also elsewhere. This sense is, as the previous chapter demonstrated, a product in large part of the feeling of absence from and loss of home, with all the emotional and cultural load which accrues to that term once it is left behind, but also of the investment in possibility, the faith in a different experience in the future, which motivated departure. In other words, the completion or resolution which a single journey from origin to destination might imply is disrupted by a tension back towards the point of departure – the possibility/dream of return – and a simultaneous tension forwards towards other possible movements. As a range of novels will illustrate in this chapter, the territory of the destination country, Italy, and the territory of the migrant's imaginary in that location, remain territories to be explored, measured, invited into or excluded from. As such, the presumed stability of arrival is revealed to be simply the transfer into a different experience of flux or instability, but one in which, alongside risks and restrictions, opportunities and freedoms may emerge.

This chapter will look, then, at how Italy is apprehended, engaged with, and expressed by characters in Italian migration literature, and at how migrant writers collectively, but unprogrammatically, construct an image of the country, and especially of its major cities, which both draws upon a long-established and widespread imaginary of the physical and architectural landscape of Italy, and also answers to it, offering different perspectives on what it is to travel or to reside in that country. Enjoying the perspective both of an outsider (migrant) and an insider (resident), the migrant gaze is specially equipped to see what a tourist sees or seeks, and at the same time to see or know what else happens at or near to tourist sites, who inhabits or uses them at other times of the day or night, and which other parts of the city hold comparable centrality in its everyday life but are barely touched by the presence of visitors. The question of the migrant's position in relation to the Italian city will be key to the discussion in this chapter, since it functions as the fulcrum at which everyday experience of the city meets with affective and speculative response to that experience and to the objects and effects which make up the city itself. In other words, I will look at empirical experience of being a migrant in an Italian city and examine the emotional, psychological, and aesthetic figures and processes which take their cue from that experience.

The same fulcrum might be identified with the two terms of the chapter's title – place and space – but with significant caution. Indeed, place in my discussion tends to be associated with an identified or named location, with a demarcated and real urban area, whilst I use space to refer to the experience of spatiality, of proximity and distance, and of movement within or across an area which appears boundless or at least indeterminate. As such, there is a correlation between, on the one hand, place and immediate, empirical experience, and on the other, space and the realm of the speculative or the imaginary. However, the distinction is not so neat, and what the use of both terms in my title aims to promote is the perception not of a clear dichotomy but rather of, precisely, the slippage and overlapping between the terms themselves and also between the experiences to which I have approximately attached them. Both terms have, of course, been interrogated fully in theoretical writing on space, along with alternative terms, such as location, but I do not intend to use here a specific model, but rather to exploit the play between a range of descriptive terms whilst also privileging 'place' and 'space' for the connotations they carry which seem to be particularly pertinent to the texts I will address.[1]

In thinking about place in Italian migration literature, what I shall be looking at in detail is the ways in which migrants are figured as moving in and inhabiting particular urban settings in Italy, namely, Rome, Milan, and Turin.[2] A particular kind of intimacy is established between the migrant individual and the physical fabric of the city, especially (but not exclusively) in texts which narrate the early experience of migration and of subsistence, often clandestine, in the city. I will consider the privileging of places of passage and of anonymity – stations, parks, central city thoroughfares – in which individuals may make contact briefly with others, but not consolidating any kind of concrete association between individual, surrounding individuals or community, and location, as one might in a private house, school, or place of worship. As noted in Chapter 3, these are what Sandra Ponzanesi, after Marc Augé, terms 'non-places', since they defy notions of placement and tend to erase rather than establish individual presence within them.[3] A further important characteristic of such (non-)places is their public nature, which brings to light a key feature of place in Italian immigration literature: the habitation and use for private experiences and functions of public places. In fact, even in texts in which migrant characters have 'a place' in Italy and are securely housed, the enclosed domestic space figures faintly in the texts, which tend quite systematically to foreground

---

[1] A sample of key theorists on space, in this context, would include: Marc Augé, *Non-places: Introduction to an Anthropology of Supermodernity*, trans. by John Howe (London: Verso, 1995); Homi K. Bhabha, *The Location of Culture* (London: Routledge, 1994); Henri Lefebvre, *The Production of Space*, trans. by Donald Nicholson-Smith (Oxford: Blackwell, 1991). Further examples will be cited below.

[2] Engagements with rural or provincial space are present in Italian migration literature, but far less common, and it is engagements with urban space which tend to generate the more intense activity of the imaginary. For these reasons, I deal only in this chapter with cities.

[3] Sandra Ponzanesi, 'Imaginary Cities: Space and Identity in Italian Literature of Immigration', in Robert Lumley and John Foot, eds, *Italian Cityscapes: Culture and Urban Change in Contemporary Italy* (Exeter: University of Exeter Press, 2004), 156–65 (158–9).

exterior, public space as the theatre for various kinds of encounter, between strangers or intimates. What this emphasis collectively generates is a sense of exclusion, which is often underscored by the immediate hardness and impenetrability of buildings and streets as they are presented in these narratives. Life is lived on the outside, under the public gaze, even in more intimate or determining moments, and even when the sense of operating constantly within a wider community which this creates is figured as a positive and vital one, the fundamental impression created is often that migrants cannot be 'at home', in the strongest emotional sense of that expression, in Italy.

This sense of continual, restless movement is expressed very prominently in the texts through the activity of walking. These tend not to be fixed journeys from a defined location to another, for a specific purpose, but rather walking in search of opportunities or encounters, or away from risks, wandering without a fixed itinerary, or simply filling time and space. Michel de Certeau analyses the activity of walking in the city and comments: 'To walk is to lack a site. It is the indeterminate process of being both absent and in search of the proper, of one's own'. This makes of the city, he argues, 'a universe of places haunted by a non-site or by dreamed sites'.[4] This suggests that the activity of walking through the city is in fact constructive, opening up and developing spaces which have the potential to satisfy the walker's aspirations and thus serving as a spatial realization of individual projections, even if these remain ultimately just projections or visions, rather than concrete buildings or marked-out places. As this indicates, walking tends to articulate a particular, and perhaps limited, mode of possession of places in which the migrant is often figured as feeling to be an unwelcome outsider. A specific kind of knowledge of places is derived from walking through and around them: an intimate and immediate knowledge which is able to take account of minute and momentary changes in the fabric of the place, which may be repetitive in whole or in part, so constantly reaffirming or readjusting knowledge of the place, and which

---

4   Michel de Certeau, *The Practice of Everyday Life*, trans. by Steven Rendall (Berkeley, CA: University of California Press, 1984), 103.

includes interstitial and apparently featureless zones in equal measure to sites regarded as noteworthy and marked on the map of the city. Walking also offers an epistemology of the urban which conjoins temporal and spatial experience: there is no acceleration of the passage between significant sites, but rather all sites – central, peripheral, interstitial – take their place in a continuum which also encompasses, at similar pace, the stretches of pavement, intersections, tunnels, etc. between them. Perhaps most striking is the sensory experience opened up by walking, which heightens intensely the intimacy of contact between individual and urban fabric: the rhythmic, direct contact between foot and pavement, and the sounds, smells, and flavours which parts of the city produce at different moments, compound the slow, searching vision of the city to allow the walker almost to live the city as an organism and thus to have a privileged knowledge of its physical contours, consistency, and movement. This particular 'privilege' is one which I think many migrant writers in Italian assert, and the impact of which I will foreground through my discussion of various texts in this chapter.

In discussing walking and citing de Certeau, I have already called upon one significant tranche of theoretical work on the modern-postmodern city, and further areas of my inquiry in this chapter will call upon others. Walking is, of course, associated with the figure of the *flâneur* and his particular mode of engagement with urban space and the urban community, as theorized by Benjamin in response to Baudelaire.[5] In my opening paragraphs above, I identified the observational position of the migrant in the city as crucial to the apprehension and expression of the Italian city in the texts which I will analyse, which further indicates the model of the *flâneur* as a productive one for investigating the migrant's view of Italy. Although a somewhat modernist conceptualization and expression of the city is indeed sketched in some of the texts I will discuss (chiefly, Abdel Malek Smari's *Fiamme in paradiso*), and I will explore the implications of this in

---

[5] Walter Benjamin, *The Writer of Modern Life: Essays on Charles Baudelaire*, ed. by Michael W. Jennings, trans. by Howard Eiland, Edmund Jephcott, Rodney Livingston and Harry Zohn (Cambridge, MA: Belknap Press, 2006).

those instances, the figure of the *flâneur* is ultimately some distance from that of the migrant observer of contemporary Rome, Milan, or Turin.[6] The distinction lies predominantly in the *flâneur*'s active choice to detach himself from all but observational contact with the city and its crowds, which is to some degree a choice made by some migrant observers, but is also disrupted as such by the sense that it is a forced detachment from the city and its crowds that the migrant experiences: generally speaking, he has little option but to look on or in from the outside.[7]

The practice of walking, and reference to de Certeau, point this discussion to the questions of the everyday which have animated discussion of contemporary experience, especially urban experience, since the 1980s, and continue to produce insightful analysis into how individual subjects and communities form and perform themselves in a multiplicity of social and cultural contexts.[8] Amin and Thrift in particular place emphasis upon the unexpected opportunities which might arise within the complex mix of everyday experience, and on the capacity of individuals to uncover accidentally, in the apparent monotony of the everyday, the routes to challenging ideas and experiences which might radically undermine the hegemony of

6   Abdel Malek Smari, *Fiamme in paradiso* (Milan: Il Saggiatore, 2000).
7   The authors I shall discuss in this chapter, and the majority of their characters, are male, and because I think there are differences, outlined earlier in this volume and briefly here, between the position of migrant women in the Italian city and that of migrant men, I think it is more accurate here to use the male pronouns and possessive adjectives to note that it is a masculine experience to which I generally refer.
8   The analysis of everyday life has vast scope and crosses disciplines, but a selection of key theorists informing this discussion includes: for early formulations, Walter Benjamin, *One-Way Street, and Other Writings*, trans. by Edmund Jephcott and Kingsley Shorter (London: Verso, 1997), and *The Arcades Project*, trans. by Howard Eiland and Kevin McLaughlin (Cambridge, MA: Belknap Press, 2002); in terms of theories of space, Henri Lefebvre, *Critique of Everyday Life*, trans. by John Moore (London: Verso, 2008), and *Writings on Cities*, trans. and ed. by Eleonore Kofman and Elizabeth Lebas (Oxford: Blackwell, 1996); for recent discussions, Ash Amin and Nigel Thrift, *Cities: Reimagining the Urban* (Cambridge: Polity, 2002), Michael Sheringham, *Everyday Life: Theories and Practices from Surrealism to the Present* (Oxford: Oxford University Press, 2006), Nigel Thrift, *Non-Representational Theory: Space, Politics, Affect* (London: Routledge, 2007).

that monotony.⁹ This seems to me to offer a highly productive framework within which to approach what is presented as the sometimes relentless disillusionment of life for migrants in Italian cities, as well as the capacity to think and to source satisfaction and pleasure beyond that immediate experience which narratives of migrants' experience express vividly. Within the aims of my project in this volume to explore the construction and the effects of 'migrant imaginaries', the engagement between the individual consciousness of the migrant city-dweller, as expressed by the writer, and the sometimes abrasive, sometimes utterly banal, but always compelling and somehow penetrable surfaces of the Italian city, is a particularly fertile moment to interrogate. It is this moment, in a range of manifestations, that this chapter will dwell upon.

Before moving to the textual examples or manifestations, however, it is helpful to dwell a little longer on the processes and on the images of the mechanism noted above of transfer from the immediate and often negative experience of the city in Italy to the stimulation and pleasure of spaces beyond it. The spaces I intend here may be those with which this chapter closely concerns itself, that is, experiences of extensive and undetermined spatiality; they may almost be places, having some measure of geographical determinacy; but they are also spaces of the senses or of experience beyond individual consciousness. Dreams, daydreams, hallucinations and vividly visualized memories or projections are all features of narratives of migrant experience which seem to have structural and expressional significance in negotiating the difficulty for the individual of engaging with a reality which tends to confound expectations.¹⁰ There is peculiarly productive ground for literary and cultural inquiry, I think, in the relationship – and the ways in which this relationship is figured – between places in Italy and spaces elsewhere, as apprehended in particular instances by migrant subjects in narratives.

---

9   Amin and Thrift, *Cities*, 128–9.
10 Amin and Thrift, referring to Baudelaire and Benjamin, comment on the centrality of dreams to constructions and understanding of the city in social and cultural theory (*Cities*, 122).

These 'elsewheres' overlay geographical locations or positions with multiple other dimensions of human experience, as indicated above. They operate by a relational pattern which is not a fixed matrix of correspondences, but rather any one 'elsewhere' – a place, time, emotion, thought, or identity – functions and holds meaning, albeit fleeting and contingent, by means of the distance and position it bears with reference to other instances. Similarly, the location in the Italian city which stimulates the passage to elsewhere is not stable: whilst specific, often minute, features of an urban landscape or architecture might acquire a certain quiddity simply by virtue of attracting the attention of the onlooker, it is precisely this attention which invests the site with meaning and activates its relations with 'elsewheres'. In other words, its location is ultimately unstable, open to dislocation or relocation in terms of the particular network of relations in which it figures at a given moment. To sum up theoretically the workings of this process or mechanism, before proceeding to textual examples, it is as if the topographical map of Italian cities were lifted from the ground which it accurately represents and somewhat dislodged and shaken, with the effect that one-to-one correspondences are loosened and the possibility of other, more plural and casual correspondences opened up. As such, the map becomes applicable or at least connectable to other spaces, at first geographical but potentially emotional or cognitive. The experience and the understanding of the Italian city is thus radically re-arranged by the migrant's observational attention, making it possible to inhabit in the imaginary other spaces not conventionally visible nor even conceivable in the centre of Rome, Milan or Turin.

In order to illustrate the ways in which an Italian city is placed in relation to a number of different kinds of 'elsewheres', I shall consider in this chapter six novels in total, offering a range of modes of narrating migration and a range of imaginings of Italian cities and other spaces. In considering closely how these forms of expression of place and space might be read and responded to, my aim is to communicate a clear sense of the significance which engagements with physical environment bear in Italian migration literature.

I first return to Mohsen Melliti's *Pantanella*.[11] As noted in Chapter 2, the Pantanella of the title is the name of a disused factory and warehouse complex near the centre of Rome, occupied by a multinational community of migrants, almost exclusively non-European, from around 1989 to 1991. Melliti tells the story of this community in a polyphonic narrative dominated by the consciousness of a young migrant named Ahmad. The positing of this separate and somewhat self-contained community as an alternative or parody to the city of Rome in the novel is an important element to which I shall return below, but my first concern is with the persistent interactions between Ahmad and the physical fabric of Rome itself.

The first strategy I would highlight, and which is not exclusive to narratives specifically of Rome as viewed by migrants, but is something of a theme of approaches to Italian cities, is the systematic disruption of the established historical account of the city. Instead of referring to well-known monuments and buildings in terms of their period, the political or economic moment which they embody, or their prominence as examples of cultural or artistic achievement, migration narratives tend to advance a notion of the instability of place and chronology. Sites are not named or definitively placed as historical monuments or topographical features; rather, buildings or locations exist in relation to one another within a particular, possibly improvised context, which may well be no more universal than the aesthetic and emotional reality of an individual observer.

A number of examples from *Pantanella* illustrate this strategy, all of them occurring more or less by chance in the narrative, and notably, often at night. As foregrounded in Chapter 2, night is the privileged moment in the novel for the indulgence of interior anxieties and ambitions, and for the exchange of these amongst friends. The softening of visual distinctions and of the boundaries between conscious and unconscious activity of the mind which night-time brings facilitates a particular mode of engagement which eschews historical determinacy and instead privileges a less

---

11   Mohsen Melliti, *Pantanella*, trans. by Monica Ruocco (Rome: Edizioni Lavoro, 1993). On engagements with Rome in this novel, see also Jennifer Burns, 'Provisional Constructions of the Eternal City: Figurations of Rome in Recent Italophone Writing', in Christian Emden, Catherine Keen and David Midgley, eds, *Imagining the City*, 2 vols (Oxford: Peter Lang, 2006), II, 357–73.

circumscribed experience of pleasure: 'Dormivano tutti profondamente, regnava il silenzio. La notte estiva era piacevole. Ahmad uscì a passeggiare per le strade della città, scrutando i palazzi e le mura antiche. Si fermò davanti a un grande teatro. Le porte e le finestre erano chiuse. Si sedette ad ammirarlo'.[12] Conditions of night-time, silence, and the fact that this means the building is closed to him together create the favourable environment in which Ahmad can observe the building simply as an object, and an object of pleasure ('ammirarlo'). Were he to visit in daytime, he would be likely to see, enter, and engage with the building within history; to read about it, hear about it, place it somehow in a specific context. Under night-time conditions, he can apprehend it as pure and palpable form, and so endow it with substance which he determines, rather than that dictated by history. Indeed, in common with other historical references in this novel, no indication is offered of the period to which the theatre belongs: significant are its connotations of past-ness, rather than any chronological denotation.

The instance that I have cited describes a shift, prompted by observation of the cityscape of Rome, from the tangible to the indeterminate, from the solidity of an empirical object to the flux of individual, interior experience. Arguably, this could happen in any act of observation by more or less anyone. Where one might argue, I believe, that Melliti, through the eyes of Ahmad, enjoys and communicates a privileged perspective on Rome's architectural and urban fabric is the frequency with which such moments of minute observation instantiate a passage towards home. The pasts evoked by Rome's unburied remnants correlate with the migrant's past experiences in what are felt to be an irrevocably distant time and place, and a time and place which, like features of ancient Rome, are encountered in the present but often as deracinated objects, floating free from any coordinates in a precise historical and cultural context. A chronology of precise dates, monuments, and events is erased and as such serves the migrant observer as a pretext to revisit in his consciousness dates, monuments, and events of his own experience which are rendered similarly indeterminate, in order to enable the experience of the pleasure associated with the past to prevail over the trauma of loss.

12   Melliti, *Pantanella*, 53.

A particular perspective on Rome allows Ahmad to exploit the potential the city offers for sensory and imaginative stimulation. He repeatedly looks out at night from a window of the derelict tower of the Pantanella building and engages with a panorama of Rome which has resonances of de Certeau. In the opening of his 'Walking in the City' essay, de Certeau notes the experience of looking from the 110th floor of the World Trade Center across what he describes as the 'texturology' of Manhattan, drawing attention by that term to the sensual, almost haptic, logic of what he sees before him.[13] Similarly, Ahmad identifies the 'texturology' of Rome: he appears to feel the city rather than to map or plot it, referring not to named monuments or streets as he views the skyline, but to the velvet texture of the darkness, the jewel-like quality of lights. The experience of surveying the urban environment is presented as a sensual interaction and as aesthetic practice, in the sense that his interrogative observation of the cityscape seems to mobilize that environment so that it begins to speak to his creativity and to his desires. I cite one specific example, taking place, typically, as night falls:

> Si sporse su un davanzale, al sesto piano, e cominciò a guardare la strada, il ponte, le macchine. Erano circa le sei del pomeriggio, il sole stava per tramontare. Durante la giornata si era sentito come un fuggiasco, perso fra le strade e i marciapiedi. Si fece notte. C'era la luna, il vento. Allora Ahmad fuggì lontano con i suoi ricordi lacerati dalla nostalgia, dal rimpianto e dal timore di un futuro ignoto. Le rovine delle antiche mura di fronte alla 'città', gli facevano rivivere la potenza e la grandezza che Roma aveva conosciuto in passato, un passato molto lontano. Dalla Pantanella viaggiò verso quel mondo lontano, quell'era antica dove le cose erano diverse, il mondo era diverso.[14]

The passage from present to past here may seem at first to set up a rather rigid opposition between contemporary and ancient Rome, mourning the loss of its 'potenza' and 'grandezza'. However, reading more closely, what is striking is the indeterminacy of the place which is being imagined, where 'le cose erano diverse', 'il mondo era diverso'. What emerges, particularly through the references to his own sense of loss and regret, is that the traces

---

13 De Certeau, *The Practice of Everyday Life*, 91.
14 Melliti, *Pantanella*, 19.

of ancient Rome are a thin tissue which overlays the more substantive object of Ahmad's desire, which is his own 'lost civilization', distant in space as well as in time; that is, his own country and culture of origin. Neither distant location is excluded in this somewhat painful reverie; rather the two are both equated and differentiated at once in a dense relation which draws attention to the contingency or instability of any coherent identity of Rome, which here seems almost literally to be undermined by other worlds and other histories.

A slightly different, and differently telling, example is offered by a vision which another migrant inhabitant of the Pantanella complex, Khaled, recounts in the novel:

– Immagina che quando cammino per Trastevere mi ritorna alla mente la mia città...

Sotto l'effetto di questi pensieri e di queste sensazioni, le immagini cominciarono a confondersi, ad andare a zig zag e poi di nuovo dritte, danzando sulle acque del Mediterraneo. Il rumore assordante delle onde altissime e il flusso della marea lo riportavano sull'altra sponda. Lì, vicino e lontano, sotto e sopra. Stendeva le mani e abbracciava gli archi della città, i suoi mercati coperti, il movimento, la folla, la lunga strada con gli alberi allineati, le mura bianche, i piccioni sulle case, le case sulla terra e sulla terra una ragazza bruna.[15]

The complexity of the set or system of relations between 'here' in Italy and 'there' at home is vividly imaged in the erratic movement of images and sensations which transport Khaled south. A moment of sensory confusion close to a loss of consciousness is experienced in the passage from one experience to another, until calm is restored through a process of refamiliarization and restabilization which notably happens through visual but also haptic means, as Khaled's outstretched hands rediscover the contours of his home town and its features, which are notably animate as well as architectural ('la folla', 'i piccioni', 'una ragazza'). The gradual downward movement from the high arches of the city to the ground, together with the repeated stress of the final three clauses which seems to drive both Khaled's and the reader's image of this experience relentlessly down into

15 Melliti, *Pantanella*, 20–1.

the earth itself, articulates a sense of being rooted in such a way as again, to uproot Rome in the present and render its materiality and its history relative to the elsewhere here imagined. The empirical experience of Rome's Trastevere is again a mere pretext.

A final note on the extract above is that the contact, albeit somewhat cross-wired by the zig-zagging passage of images across the Mediterranean, between Rome and the unnamed home city is relatively simple and coherent. More frequently in the novel, as illustrated in earlier quotations above, the transfer is to a much less determined time and space, and interestingly, this space is often figured precisely as the desert. As such, it offers a radical alternative and challenge to the heavily determined European city; a space which bears no walls, monuments, street-plan, nor visibly inscribed history and instead offers simply a limitless space which in form and appearance is not even constant from day to day, still less so from century to century. This association with the desert places the Italian city in relation to a spatial model with which it seems to have no match, and its identity and singularity are thus disrupted. In figuring urban spaces in Italy – layered in history and each monument, street, or zone labelled with significance – in relation to a space which lacks particular places and a time which lacks periodization, the substance of our understanding of what cities mean and how they function is thrown into question. The alternative model proposed is one which appears deaf and blind to periods or eras and to the ideologies which underpin them, and which encourages instead an attention to rhythms and to spaces which are significantly less determined. Such a contrast might appear, of course, to appeal to essentializing and even orientalizing strategies for comparing east with west or south with north (as noted in my discussion of the figuration of the desert in Chapter 3), especially in view of the emphasis placed on the sensual in the imaginary of the distant spaces accessed from Rome. However, I think the key to understanding the relations set up between here and there is in the mode of observing Rome, which deliberately applies the principle of prioritizing sensory perception in search of aesthetic stimulation. What is thus suggested is that there are ways other and more revealing than a conventional historical, civic, or even social, perspective in which to experience and engage with place and space, and that these are not just appropriate to particular kinds of space, but have the potential to stimulate more widely and freely if deployed in any context, including, perhaps, one of the most heavily over-determined spaces in the globe, i.e. Rome. In other words, it is not the spaces themselves nor the culture of the observer which is being interrogated, but particularly and precisely the mode of apprehending space. A city – or indeed a desert – can be differently imagined, this novel suggests.

Turning attention now to a slightly different aspect of the mode of apprehending space in *Pantanella*, it is helpful to refer back to de Certeau's comments on the 'texturology' of Manhattan.[16] He contrasts the vertical aspect upon the city, revealing the continuous and undulating texture of forms, with the horizontal, street-level experience, which reveals the immediate kinesis of human movement and activity around buildings, signs, lights, crossings, traffic, and around each other. Melliti's novel embraces this view as well, figuring the movement of Ahmad and other migrants through the streets of the city and around the Pantanella building itself, and so drawing a different kind of map of Rome, and one which makes contact more consistently with the known topography of the city, naming key thoroughfares or hubs such as Via Nazionale and Piazza Venezia, and Stazione Termini.[17] The novel thus communicates very powerfully, as its underlying pulse, the everyday experience of migrants as they follow routes through the city, largely on foot, and so become part of the system which constitutes it, part themselves of the everyday of Rome. Interestingly, of course, the experience often expressed by migrants is of not being part of the city at all: in the second quotation from the novel above, Ahmad narrates his experience of the opportunities which viewing night-time in the city brings by means of a direct and negative comparison with his experience of being in the city streets during the day, where 'si era sentito come un fuggiasco, perso fra le strade e i marciapiedi'.[18] Whilst the movement of population in the streets of a city is, from the point of view of human

16   De Certeau, *The Practice of Everyday Life*, 91.
17   Mario Fortunato and Salah Methnani, in *Immigrato* (Rome: Theoria, 1990) refer to a 'mappa alternativa' of Rome, produced through migrants' different use of and passage through the urban space (57).
18   Melliti, *Pantanella*, 19.

geographers and cultural theorists, part of the city itself, it is interesting that from the point of view of the migrant subject in narratives of the migration experience, that experience is an index of anxiety and estrangement, of being on edge and on the edge.

Where these perspectives meet interestingly in *Pantanella* is in the ready co-existence of the two conditions, of going about one's business in the city and of being radically dislocated from it. Many of the examples discussed above of escape through the imaginary from the city to 'elsewheres' insert themselves into the business and the conversations of everyday life, with the effect that the narrative leaps quite abruptly at some points from the mundane to the particular kind of sublime which this novel constructs: for example, a pragmatic conversation about the detail of setting up a restaurant in the Pantanella complex prefaces one of Ahmad's flights of consciousness, prompted by apprehending ancient buildings in the centre of Rome.[19] To some degree in this novel, the proximity of – perhaps, interdependence between – the difficult experience of the everyday and the imaginary of worlds beyond it articulates the notion of the everyday as the environment in which unexpected possibilities are born of expected and familiar routines, as Amin and Thrift suggest.[20] However, the particular inflection which Melliti adds to this conjunction lies, I think, in the migrants' sense of not in fact being part of the everyday, but being uncomfortably out of the ordinary, both in terms of their own experience and familiarity with the Italian city and of the ways in which they feel they are viewed or surveyed by other occupants of the streets. In this way, the trigger for the mechanism of being in a place – Rome – and elsewhere is acutely sensitive and exposed for migrants, as Melliti presents them.

The Pantanella complex itself articulates this condition of being at once within and outside the ordinary, in a place and in indeterminate space. The complex originally comprised a mill, pasta factory, and warehouse space in which the first building was erected in 1915, with significant additions in the 1920s and 1930s and refurbishment after World War II, and was

19 Melliti, *Pantanella*, 33.
20 Amin and Thrift, *Cities*, 128–9.

abandoned once the business it housed began to decline in the 1960s.[21] It sits on the via Casilina, towards the edge of the centre of Rome, and for its size (particularly height), location, and industrial history, is a monument of modern Rome in many respects. Melliti plays on this monumental status in the narrative, positing the complex, as noted in my opening comments on this novel, as a parody to the city of Rome by naming it the 'città' (in quotation marks) and all of its improvised infrastructure similarly as parodic labels in quotation marks ('caffè', etc.). The choice of 'città', rather than, perhaps, 'casa' – since the building is the mock-home of migrants – not only sets it in comparison or opposition with the city of Rome, but also signals its status as a (would-be) fully functioning community, rather than simply domestic space. In fact, Melliti makes significant efforts to underscore that this 'città' provides the environment in which its inhabitants can not only sleep, but also work, worship, eat, devise projects, do business, socialize, organize themselves culturally, socially, and politically, and so on. It is at once public and private space. It houses a range of ethnicities and religions and it provides the theatre for their conflicts as well as for their constructive interaction and collaboration.[22] In many ways, the Pantanella and its community offers a model for how a multicultural city – a multicultural Rome, maybe – might operate.[23] Melliti's sharp parody arises at the interface between this not idealized but generally functional social model and its physical reality: it exists within a derelict and unsafe set of buildings, with absent or unreliable services (electricity, water, sewerage), and subsists outside the law. Openly penetrable as a structure to wind and rain, it is

21 See http://www.acquamarcia.it/website/projects.aspx?pid=45&sid=2&cid=1&lid=1 (accessed 6 December 2012). A series of photographs of the complex, dating from 1929 to 1979, can be viewed at http://www.romasparita.eu/foto-roma-sparita/tag/via-casilina/page/1/ (accessed 6 December 2012).
22 For a further perspective on the life of the Pantanella community, see Carmelo Albanese, 'Via Casilina n.0 – storia del Pantanella, nel 1990', http://www.youtube.com/watch?v=aR62UXhhyRU (accessed 6 December 2012).
23 A comparable notion is expressed by a much more recent anthology, which tells of migrants' experiences in the 'Hotel House', a complex at Porto Recanati. See Ramona Parenzan, ed., *Babel Hotel: Vite migranti nel condominio più controverso d'Italia* (Castel Gandolfo (Rome): Infinito edizioni, 2011).

penetrable to human traffic from the community outside its walls only for circumscribed groups with specific interests in visiting it: police officers, social workers and volunteer intercultural organizations, journalists, illegal traders. The Pantanella inhabitants, on the other hand, move readily out of the complex to seek opportunities but live a precarious existence as much outside as within the buildings, since their status on the streets of Rome is in many cases illegal and generally they are made to feel unwelcome, or a 'fuggiasco', as noted by Ahmad in the quotation above.

Melliti makes of the Pantanella complex, however, more than simply a metaphor for a kind of improvised multiculturalism in Italy which is structurally unsound, and, as with the fabric of the other 'città', Rome, it is through the migrant's particular mode of affective and imaginative investment in the Pantanella 'città' that the significance of the buildings and the community they temporarily shelter is amplified. The Pantanella name, standing as the title of the novel, suggests it is personified as the protagonist of the novel, and in many ways, it is. As mentioned above, it is a polyphonic novel whose narrative voices slip between individuals or sometimes choruses which are both identified by name on occasion and not; as such, the complex is seen to speak for itself at moments in the novel. The end of the novel plays upon real events and the imaginary constructed around the building, figuring the raid by police and civic authorities which emptied the building of its illegal inhabitants as an apocalyptic inferno in which Ahmad himself, standing metonymically for the notion of multicultural community, is consumed in a suicidal leap into the flames. In this way, the parody I have described is more complex than a direct and ironic comparison between the established community of Rome and the community of migrants which subsists in or alongside it as a damaged para-community.

Analysis of an early, and apparently somewhat inconsequential, exchange which takes place within the Pantanella offers a sense of how the building signifies both for its inhabitants and for outsiders. The excerpt below stages a particular kind of scene which offers at once a vignette of the everyday within the community and an indication of how the identity of that community is constructed for and/or by outsiders:

Uno rispose:
 – Siamo diventati un museo archeologico, da visitare in occasioni speciali.
 Tutti risero alle sue parole.
 Il barbiere si trovava dall'altro lato. Tagliava i capelli a un cliente. Aveva messo un grande specchio su una sedia davanti al cliente per vedere il suo volto pallido o per sorvegliare meglio il movimento delle sue forbici fra i capelli. Vicino al barbiere c'era una ragazza che lo fotografava, forse una giornalista e quello, trascurando il cliente che gli stava davanti, sorrise allo scatto del flash e solo dopo riprese a lavorare. Il cliente gli disse:
 – I giornalisti e i fotografi ci vendono come se fossimo oggetti.
 – No, amico mio, sono i primi a difenderci.
 – Sei un illuso!
 Tacquero dopo questo breve dialogo, nonstante la proverbiale loquacità dei barbieri.[24]

Couched within a discussion of what the Pantanella is in the terms of the community which surrounds but remains firmly outside it, the scene of the barber at work offers two clear representations of the migrant community. First is the mirror image which is somewhat sober and even eerie: the pale face of the customer and the metal of the scissors working through his hair. Second is the photographic image captured by the journalist (if that is who she is), for which the barber performs, turning away from his work to the camera and smiling. Both images draw attention to an anxiety of representation around migrant activity and community: how migrants individually or collectively construct an image of themselves may be different from and even at odds with how others imagine them, and much is at stake, in terms of community, in the ambiguity which operates between those images and their dissemination. The gender divide here underlines the tension between representations by and for different constituencies whose responses are unpredictable: the homosocial domain of the barbershop, conventionally constructed as a locus of male grooming and of a particular and confidential kind of male intimacy, is infiltrated by a woman who will construct its image for another audience outside. What the import and impact of that

---

24 Melliti, *Pantanella*, 17. Albanese's 'Via Casilina n.0 – storia del Pantanella, nel 1990' features a comparable scene of an improvised barbershop.

image will be, taken entirely out of the hands and of the imaginary of its subjects, is left as an open question from which the interlocutors within the scene withdraw, leaving the reader to consider it.

The question of control over the construction of images is threaded through the subsequent section of the narrative, firstly through a very brief interjection which notes that the barber is untypically taciturn because he is in fact a law graduate expelled from his home university and now trying to find a living in Rome, and then into a discussion between two other migrants about the architecture of the Pantanella complex itself. Mustafa comments that it is 'l'unica città al mondo senza stile architettonico e senso estetico. Sembra impossibile che siano stati degli architetti a progettare un edificio simile'.[25] He implicitly marks a connection between the everyday experience of living and working in the 'città', glimpsed in the description of the barber at work, and the broader aesthetic which informs the way in which the complex appears in its architectural and social context, or how it performs as an element of the urban cityscape. He also implicitly responds to the comment which opens the excerpt quoted above, that the site has become a museum. As the brief exchange about the design of the Pantanella develops between Mustafa and Aziz, their emphasis is consistently on how the complex can be or could have been imagined: Aziz identifies an architectural coherence in its structures, Mustafa poses the question of how to realize the image of the building in film. It is Aziz who arrives at the conclusion that 'la nostra nuova città ha resistito a un bombardamento aereo!'; adding that this was 'Forse negli anni Quaranta', to which Mustafa responds, 'Dunque questa immagine ti ha fatto pensare alla guerra'.[26] Aziz identifies the bombing correctly (as will be mentioned below), though his stress on the possibilities or probabilities offered by the creative imagination, rather than on the certainties recorded by history, tellingly underscores the deliberately parenthesised form of realism which the novel employs. This somewhat whimsical, apparently non-penetrating commentary thus uncovers the centrality of damage and violence to any

---

25 Melliti, *Pantanella*, 17.
26 Melliti, *Pantanella*, 18.

image of community, and of the future, which might be constructed around the inhabitants of the Pantanella. Having entertained various images of the complex for inhabitants and outsiders, the one which prevails is that it has survived an attempt to obliterate it, and that it cannot but display its scars.

Melliti thus promotes the notion that a city, or any place of community, exists above all in the individual and collective imaginary: the dreams and will to succeed of the Pantanella community realize that community, even if only in compromised terms, and equally the failure of collective imagination of the community which surrounds the inchoate multicultural society posited by the Pantanella results in the irresolution of a social crisis, in empirical terms: the migrants are simply unhoused and moved on. Remaining within the empirical, it is perhaps revealing to note that the Pantanella complex has in the twenty-first century been fully refurbished and re-developed to offer a huge residential, commercial, and leisure complex. The development company who realized the project, a well-established and powerful organization, are careful to present the Pantanella as a historic monument of Rome, and in their description, refer to its early twentieth-century industrial architecture, the air raid (identified by Aziz) on 19 July 1943, which targeted thirteen bombs at the complex, and its abandonment during the widespread economic decline of the 1960s and 1970s, all as evidence that the complex has consistently been a landmark of the capital throughout its modern history, and a barometer of economic and social change.[27] Strikingly, the Pantanella's status as a landmark of economic, social, and cultural change in Italy at the end of the 1980s and into the early 1990s – as a site occupied by migrants – goes unmentioned in their publicity, again demonstrating both the force and the limits of the imaginary in particular contexts and for particular constituencies.

The element of imagining the city from an individual or collective point of view, but also of constructing images of the city – and particularly

27 The company is the Società dell'Acqua Pia Antica Marcia, founded in the nineteenth century with a project to restore the Marcian aqueduct: see http://www.acquamarcia. it/ (accessed 6 December 2012). Their description of the 'Mulino Pantanella' project is at http://www.acquamarcia.it/website/projects.aspx?pid=45&sid=2&cid=1&lid=1 (accessed 6 December 2012).

Rome – is also alluded to in a brief episode of Younis Tawfik's *La straniera*.[28] Recounting his first arrival in Italy, the male narrator of this dually narrated novel describes arriving in Rome as his first destination in Italy and defines it as 'la città dei sogni e della libertà'.[29] Rome is envisioned according to its mythologized status in western culture, and the narrator tacitly acknowledges this by pointing out that Rome is familiar to him, he knows it before he encounters it, because of his readings of history and his viewings, as a boy in Iraq, of Italian peplum films of the 1950s. Accordingly, in his very brief stay in Rome, he visits two of its iconic sites – the Colosseum and the Sistine Chapel – and here his somewhat circumscribed 'knowledge' of the city can be realized: 'Entrando al Colosseo, avvertii un brivido lungo la schiena. Le urla della folla, il rumore delle armi e il galoppo dei cavalli si materializzavano tra gli archi e i sottopassaggi. Mi sentivo come un antico guerriero mediorientale nel santuario della civiltà mediterranea'.[30] He recalls Shakespeare's *Julius Caesar* as well, neatly underscoring both the sense of an ongoing dominance of western or European cultural models in global education, and the notion of the fictional and/or spectacular re-telling of history. His image of Rome is soon punctured by the sharp experience of contemporary Rome's human and vehicular traffic, however, and his response is to reject the city which challenges his imaginary of Rome: 'Non era più la Roma dei miei sogni né quella della mia storia. Mi si presentava ora come una metropoli corrotta dalla modernizzazione'.[31] His abrupt refusal to recognize here is interesting: he relinquishes ownership of the city ('mia', 'miei') and the city itself becomes indistinct, non-individuated ('una metropoli'), and deprived of all historical and cultural texture. Since the city no longer matches the description constructed in his imaginary, it in effect ceases to exist for him.

Once inhabiting another Italian city – Turin – the migrant's perspective on the city becomes a more complex interplay of empirical experience

---

28 Younis Tawfik, *La straniera* (Milan: Bompiani, 1999).
29 Tawfik, *La straniera*, 28.
30 Tawfik, *La straniera*, 28.
31 Tawfik, *La straniera*, 29.

and imaginary, which is comparable in some ways to the interactions with place and space outlined in *Pantanella*. The position of the male narrator in this novel, unnamed and identified only (and tellingly) as 'the architect', is, unlike Ahmad in Pantanella, that of the 'straniero integrato', as he defines himself, and, as I demonstrated in Chapter 1 (see pages 35–40), the novel examines the extent to which the architect experiences life in Turin from an insider's or an outsider's point of view. He initially, superficially, responds to the city in which he lives – Turin – as might a young-to-middle-aged professional man of Italian origin, i.e. with a degree of indifference. It is interesting that Tawfik again – as in the vignette of encounter with Rome – deploys quite pointedly a somewhat clichéd image, this time of the contemporary white male in the city, to reveal his narrator's construction of a sense of self on the basis of place. The first two chapters narrated by the architect open with a view of the city at night, in the rain or fog, from behind the windscreen of a car: the city is an indistinct and monotonous blur, punctuated but thus made all the more repetitive by the orderly geometry of nineteenth-century urban architecture. This is an image which connotes disaffection and boredom, and is immediately familiar to the reader from modern-postmodern urban fiction and film, from *noir* to postmodern American fiction.[32] Seen from the driver's seat of a car, on a journey between a place of work and a place of permanent residence, it is explicitly not the familiar migrant's perception of the city.

It is interesting to compare the architect's view of Turin with the panorama which Amina recounts assembling on her first journey through the city, having arrived after a tortuous and dangerous journey by boat, foot and train, from Morocco through Spain and France into Italy. She and her husband are collected from the station by Moroccan friends already resident in Turin, and she too sees the city through a car window (as passenger not driver), but with the eagerness and apprehension of a new arrival:

> Era la prima volta che vedevo una grande città europea. Osservare dal finestrino dell'auto le strade, le piazze, i palazzi e i monumenti suscitò in me una sorta di

---

32   Examples are Bret Easton Ellis, *Less Than Zero* (London: Picador, 1986) and Jay McInerney, *Bright Lights, Big City* (New York: Vintage Contemporaries, 1984).

inquietudine. L'ordine con il quale strade e case erano esposte. Lo stile, di gusto raffinato e tipico, che caratterizzava le facciate, i negozi e i portici. Tutto in me suscitava una certa perplessità inspiegabile.[33]

It is the marked and cohesive architectural style of the city and its general sense of order which alienates Amina: there is nothing recognizable, nothing she readily understands, and so she is able only to observe at a distance, not to engage with the city. Both she and the architect articulate a powerful detachment from their urban surroundings in Italy, but in Amina's case, this detachment is engendered by unfamiliarity and awe, and in the architect's, by over-familiarity and disillusionment. Interestingly, however, when the architect at one point recalls his early days in Turin, as a student newly arrived from the Middle East, he too notes its architectural austerity and comments that it fills him with 'inquietudine'.[34]

The difference referred to above also indicates, however, that for neither migrant is the city centre, and the architecture which articulates the city, penetrable. Returning to Amina's account of her arrival in the city, it becomes evident that, as a clandestine immigrant, she has – of necessity – access to areas of the city which in effect appear to be penetrable. She notes a break in the monochrome order of the city which indicates a space for her: 'in una zona attorno a un mercato, iniziai a notare i colori della pelle e dei vestiti delle persone radunate nella piazza. Avevo visto alla stazione molti stranieri, ma non tanti così, da sembrare di essere capitati in una casba. Il nostro ospite c'informò che eravamo arrivati'.[35] The simile of the casbah underlines the familiarity and habitability of this part of the city, and it is interesting to note that here it is the inhabitants, not the buildings, which characterize the area, whereas in the city centre, there was no reference to the human, implicitly dwarfed and rendered insignificant by the majesty of the architecture. There is a sense that migrants here have taken possession of an area of the city, by means of a colourful performance, and in turn, this hints at a possibility for Amina to make it

---

33   Tawfik, *La straniera*, 89.
34   Tawfik, *La straniera*, 36.
35   Tawfik, *La straniera*, 89.

her own ('eravamo arrivati'). These are possibilities closed to the architect, who, moving in different circles and almost exclusively amongst Italians, appears to have adopted the mask of middle-class Italian-ness in order to find a habitation in the city.

It is, however, after an evening spent at dinner with Italian friends that he drives home and sees the city in its live, human detail, rather than as a grey, architectural backdrop: 'Lungo la strada osservo attentamente i marciapiedi appena illuminati. Per la prima volta, noto delle figure sbandate. Persone, spesso sole o in piccoli gruppi, che popolano le strade della notte. Stranieri caratterizzati dai loro modi di camminare e di vestire'.[36] He identifies these migrants specifically with the street (pavement), and in depicting the 'marciapiedi appena illuminati', locates them explicitly in both an instantly recognizable urban space and in a social position which is liminal and barely visible. This community which populates 'le strade della notte' can be directly associated with the migrants in *Pantanella* who stake their limited claim to the spaces of central Rome at night-time, and represents a distinct alternative to the day-time occupants of the city, who are implicitly not 'stranieri'. The migrants' mode of being in the city, of being present but largely invisible, might be described as a mode of 'non-dwelling', articulating a presence which is impermanent and almost untraceable, as opposed to the fixed visibility of 'dwelling'. Again, there is a theatrical element to this very vivid scene, in which the city streets at night serve as a theatre in which the 'stranieri' can display their identities and activities. The architect's references to their costume and gait accentuate the theatricality of this moment, as do the descriptions of the lighting ('appena illuminati') and *mise-en-scène* ('figure sbandate', 'persone [...] sole o in piccoli gruppi'). The 'audience', however, is the architect, enclosed in the sealed cabin of his car and unable to interact directly with the actors in the scene. Although this live city theatre also provides a space in which his own identifications can be played out, his position remains detached and almost prurient: he is more a voyeur than a participant. Nevertheless, this

---

36   Tawfik, *La straniera*, 121. See also the analysis of this passage, in terms of its significance regarding the protagonist's identity, in Chapter 1, pages 37–9.

dramatic scene illustrates that the architect's first encounter with Amina has made visible to him – though, as indicated above, not yet accessible – parts of the city and a mode of being in the city of which he was hitherto ignorant or which he denied.

Amina's influence on the architect's modes of engagement with the city he has adopted is, however, complex. She both alerts him to an alternative level of habitation of the city, and, by her very difference and the difference she thus exposes to him, consolidates his sense of belonging in the environment conventionally delineated by the city. For example, when they meet for the second time, the actual presence of Amina with him in the city, again at night-time, sketches a complex process of shifting between engagement with and estrangement from the city. On this occasion, he is walking through the city, rather than driving, and walking aimlessly, route-lessly, in the manner of a migrant. He can thus feel, smell and hear the streets directly, rather than observing them from within the sealed compartment of his car. This engenders an immediate intimacy something like that expressed by Ahmad in Melliti's *Pantanella*, but rather than digging under the skin of the city as does Ahmad's intimacy with Rome, the architect's intimacy with Turin here is a romantic one which articulates a respectfully preserved distance between the individual and the city, and which represents the city as a named and integral whole, rather than the rather formless collection of secret parts which Rome appears as in *Pantanella*:

> Passeggiando di notte, per la prima volta con una straniera, la mia città ha proprio un altro aspetto. Torino è 'la mia città' perché non potrei definirla diversamente. [...] L'amo come la mia città natale e, a volte, mi sembra di vivere in due posti. Una parte di me è rimasta nella mia città d'origine, l'altra è rinata qui.[37]

Amina's presence here, rather than estranging him from the city he has adopted, prompts a declaration of ownership of it. Indeed, this is the first time Turin is named in the novel (hitherto it has been identified simply as a major northern Italian city). A poetic description of the choreography of their walk through the centre of the city, in which the physical features of

---

37   Tawfik, *La straniera*, 127–8.

the city play a part in their growing intimacy, belies, however, an underlying threat of exclusion: 'Le nostre ombre camminano insieme. Alcune volte vengono interrotte dalle colonne dei portici, altre s'intrecciano tra di loro, per poi staccarsi'.[38] The presence of the city in their relationship seems to be romantically underscored here, but again, a close reading reveals that this presence is in fact an obstructive one: the shadows of the porticos which characterize so powerfully Turin and its architecture of political and cultural supremacy fall like barriers between the two individuals, forcing a separation between the accepted foreigner and the unacceptable one, the 'architect' (with all the social standing the term implies, and its close association with the language of buildings and of place) and the outcast, the prostitute.

The city of Turin, then, is used in this novel as a physical and visual medium to express the crisis of integration which the narrative recounts, and also, in a more active role, as antagonist, forcing confrontations and creating situations which prompt self-questioning. As the crisis develops, the city becomes less the grey cushion to the architect's monotonous self-satisfaction and becomes an increasingly abrasive environment which stimulates new kinds of behaviours and desires in him. Having lost touch for some time with Amina, and pursued a relationship with an Italian woman, he decides to trace Amina again and the space in which he seeks these traces is described as:

> Un immenso piazzale, che una volta era uno spazio abbandonato di ghiaia e fango, pieno di piante selvatiche, e che adesso funge da parcheggio. E pavimentato di cemento, recintato con transenne di metallo e adiacente a un edificio: la palestra di una scuola abbandonata. E una costruzione a scatola rettangolare, fatta di blocchi di cemento, ferro e lamiere.[39]

Whilst it is clear that he has left the ordered world of the city centre and moved into a space more 'chaotic', as I described Amina's home area, it is striking that there is none of the colour, human vivacity, and implicit

---

38 Tawfik, *La straniera*, 128.
39 Tawfik, *La straniera*, 175.

hospitality here that that environment seemed to connote. The space described above is a hostile environment, articulated through hard, impenetrable surfaces and massive forms which seem threatening rather than accommodating. These forms are also remnants of other buildings or installations now abandoned or re-used: they present no coherent narrative. In confronting an urban location of this kind – dislocated and broken – the 'architect' confronts the collapse of his own design for a 'straniero integrato' and replaces his imaginary of successful insertion into Italian society – orderly, coherent, and dominant – with an imaginary of sharp fragments.

It is the latter environment that the architect increasingly inhabits, and in doing so, he re-locates Amina, who is terminally ill and in that sense already in a world beyond the confines of the city. His own final engagement with the city of Turin pursues the same logic of passing beyond it. He sits in a square near the station (he is on the street, and in the migrants' part of the city) and looks longingly at a tall tree there (a natural, rather than architectural, feature), tracing its form up into the blue sky. The tree seems to act as a huge conductor, transmitting to him the sounds of home: 'La piazza si colma di suoni provenienti da molto lontano. Suoni e voci che solo tu riesci a comprendere. Rumori di mercati, di piazze e di cortili corrosi dal tempo e dall'umidità'.[40] Tawfik is here using an imaginary of the city very similar to that used by Melliti in *Pantanella*, in the sense that a fragment within the Italian city, closely observed by the migrant, creates the conditions for an affective flight elsewhere, to the past in the home culture. Khaled's vision in that novel, quoted above, stresses the visual and haptic, whilst the architect's apprehension here relies on the auditory and olfactory, but the impact of being led by the senses elsewhere, to an environment heavily marked as culturally different, is similarly emphatic. At the end of the novel, the architect climbs the tree, opens his arms like wings, and flies into the void.[41] It is a vision of madness, and the second-person narration of this closing chapter suggests a schizophrenic splitting

40 Tawfik, *La straniera*, 199.
41 There are resonances here of the figure of Anis in Tawfik's *Il profugo* (Milan: Bompiani, 2006), as discussed in Chapter 2.

of his migrant and 'integrated' performances of self. It is significant that his newly dismantled perception of the city, privileging its remnants and anomalies rather than its grand design, allows him to turn the place which has – in some senses – confined him into the location which contains the means or medium for him to escape into infinite and satisfying space.

A different inflection on 'elsewheres' is offered by *Fiamme in paradiso*, by Algerian writer Abdel Malek Smari, which was published in a similar moment to *La straniera* but recalls, in its emphasis on the primary experience of immigration, earlier novels, such as *Pantanella*. The novel is set in Milan, and narrates the difficulties of life as an illegal migrant, employing a narrative structure which is more conventional than that of *Pantanella*, centred on the individual story of a clear protagonist, named Karim. Two specific features of the novel are of interest here: firstly, its structural foregrounding of the oneiric, in the sense that the story is told in diary form, a chapter per day, with night-time and sleep occupying a privileged space in the structure of the novel. The parenthesis between day and night, between waking consciousness and other forms of mental activity, affords the opportunity for the passage of consciousness from the present in the Italian city to 'elsewheres', recalling somewhat the mechanisms of engagement with place and space discussed with reference to *Pantanella*. However, in Smari's novel, the passages to elsewhere remain untold: the narrative signals them, demarcates their space, but offers no details. As such, they tend to invite the reader's most intense creative engagement in filling the 'gaps' opened up, and so gain an interpretative weight in the novel which disrupts the apparently primary position of the more transparent narrative of the daytime life of the migrant in Italy.[42]

---

42   I refer to reader response theory and the notion that the unsaid or unspecified in a text offers the opportunity for the reader to engage creatively in the production of meaning. See Wolfgang Iser, *The Act of Reading: A Theory of Aesthetic Response* (London: Routledge & Kegan Paul, 1978) and Umberto Eco, *Opera aperta* (Milan: Bompiani, 1962). This mechanism also recalls Wayne Booth's comments, discussed in my Introduction, on the creative work required of the reader in interpreting figurative expression: see Wayne Booth, *The Company We Keep: An Ethics of Fiction* (Berkeley, CA: University of California Press, 1988), 298–9.

The second feature of the novel which is productive to examine in my current discussion is the engagement of Karim with the urban structures and architectural features of Milan. He takes the now familiar position of an observer and enquirer, intent upon the apparently impossible task of gaining the measure of the city:

> Preferiva camminare, dove il caso lo portava. Osservare tutto. Guardare; ci credeva a malapena che la gente qua fosse italiana. Guardava con occhi non ancora abituati a tutto quel nuovo che gli stava attorno, occhi non abituati a quel salto così brusco da inferno a paradiso. Un paradiso d'un grigio sbiadito, velato di nebbia inquinata. Karim desiderava vedere i limiti estremi della città. Ma le strade gli parevano lunghe, senza fine. Si perdeva di continuo. Sbagliava strada.[43]

The greyness and fog recall the vision of the city articulated by Tawfik's architect, but here, the protagonist is in the midst of this grey continuum and eager to explore and to understand it. The description above indicates that the city, and Karim's condition within it, are boundless, and as such the text seems to articulate almost a postmodern view of the city as endless horizontal spread, lacking in monuments or structures which might orientate the visitor's gaze and thus determine the topographical panorama. The greyness and fog blur still further any distinctions between centre and periphery, between identifiable architectural periods or styles and the histories they indicate.

The emphasis in the description above on observing and on unprogrammatic wandering, attentive to the truths which the city might reveal, offers, however, a more modernist sense of Karim as *flâneur*, albeit the absence of the crowd removes a key element of the experience of the *flâneur* as identified by Benjamin. The partly late nineteenth-century tone of Karim's engagement with the city is underpinned by the presence of death which seems to inform the narrative, intimated by the references in the quotation above and in the novel's title to the world/s of the afterlife, and articulated more directly, via spatial means, in Karim's accidental visit to Milan's Cimitero Monumentale. The necropolis within the city

---

43 Smari, *Fiamme in paradiso*, 43.

becomes the desired destination of Karim's walking in Milan, visited both in physical, spatial terms, and as a spiritual and intellectual 'end'. This place of death but also of the display, even celebration, of the passage of time and of human life, monument not just to a series of individual lives but to a defining period in the development of the identity of the city, is figured as a place where Karim feels at home, in a way which, unlike Benjamin's *flâneur*, the Algerian migrant generally cannot in Milan. He meets the crowds there, in the sense that he comes face-to-face with the photographs of the deceased in a silent environment which allows him a moment of intimacy and sympathy with the citizens of Milan which his experience in the 'living' city generally denies him.[44] It offers the capacity to reflect upon existence beyond the immediate demands of everyday life and this fuels his imagination and brings him emotional and spiritual relief: 'Malgrado la tristezza del luogo Karim provava piacere, godeva di quest'insolito panorama. Si sentiva trasportato per incanto in un museo di scultura, un museo della morte. Quel luogo si spalancava sul gran precipizio senza fine'.[45] To an extent, this monumental locus is a coordinate of stability, but its physical location at the end of the seemingly endless and directionless streets shrouded in grey, coupled with its location in Karim's consciousness at the 'extreme limits', occupying a space associated with the dreams which take him elsewhere at the end of each day, mean that the identifiable location on the map of modern Milan serves a different purpose. It figures as a portal to other, undetermined spaces, and – like Rome in Melliti's novel, *Pantanella* – the identity and integrity of the Italian city is destabilized by its relation to other places differently located in space and time.

The proximity of death in the novel, maintained within the reader's imagination by Karim's activities as a somewhat macabre *flâneur* in the city, is realized in its ending, in which, in an allusion to a recorded incident in Milan in 1993, Karim, having seen a vehicle parked in a city street begin to

---

44 Smari, *Fiamme in paradiso*, 70. Examples of human encounters here are that he buys a flower to offer at the plaque of a deceased young woman, and makes an affective contact with an older, living woman whom he watches visiting the tomb of a relative.
45 Smari, *Fiamme in paradiso*, 70.

smoke, runs to help and is killed as a car bomb explodes.⁴⁶ This somewhat voluntary propulsion of himself towards physical eradication fits with the narrative pull in the novel towards the 'extreme limits' of the city and of consciousness, and offers a closure of sorts to Karim's disruptive desire always to be elsewhere, beyond the confines of the city which he struggles to locate, and beyond the confines of conscious experience in the present. The closure of the novel fits also with the broadly suicidal endings of the novels previously discussed in this chapter, and so helps to consolidate the figure of a kind of death by misadventure as the only possible ending to the narrative of migration.⁴⁷ Misadventure here is intended as an adventure into the future, an imagined possible narrative of a different life for the subject, which has been compromised by the real experience of living as a migrant in an Italian city. The tragic, and therefore also spectacular and somewhat triumphant, passage beyond the confines of the condition of being a migrant is figured in each case as a passage, albeit fantastical or preposterous, beyond the confines of the city. Smari's example adds a rather different note to those of Melliti and Tawfik, and one which calls upon the imaginary of the modern Italian city in a different way. Karim's death in a terrorist attack in the heart of the city (perhaps particularly since the city is Milan) offers a vignette of a particular kind of modern urban Italian history, and calls to mind a series of well-known images in the popular imagination of Italian terrorism, from Piazza Fontana to the kidnapping of Moro to the explosions which killed Giovanni Falcone and

---

46 The 'strage di via Palestro' was accompanied by bomb attacks also in Rome and attributed to the forces of organized crime as an attempt to stall or halt the *Mani Pulite* investigations into political corruption. The Milan bomb exploded in via Palestro at 11.14pm on 27 July 1993, killing three firefighters, a police officer and a Moroccan migrant reported to have been sleeping in the nearby park. See http://archiviostorico.corriere.it/1993/luglio/29 (accessed 6 December 2012).

47 On endings – particularly suicidal – in Italian migration literature, see Maria Cristina Mauceri, 'Andare e non tornare: I finali in alcuni romanzi della letteratura della migrazione in Italia', in Franca Sinopoli and Silvia Tatti, eds, *I confini della scrittura. Il dispatrio nei testi letterari* (Isernia: Iannone, 2005), 89–99.

Paolo Borsellino.⁴⁸ By placing a non-Italian as the central victim (in the reader's view) of this incident, Smari suggests through this resolution of the novel a way of rewriting the modern Italian city and of perceiving its rather rigid and introspective national political history from a more pluralistic and diversified point of view. The author both points toward and problematizes this conclusion, however, immediately confirming Karim's demise by means of the newspaper headlines reporting the incident: 'Quattro persone e un marocchino morti in un attentato terroristico in via Palestro'.⁴⁹ The highlighting of the death of four 'persons', followed by the term, 'marocchino', implicitly denying the victim human status as well as an accurate nationality, suggests that the presence of a migrant as a victim in the attack is nothing more than an accident or a trivial footnote to this Italian urban event: a 'misadventure' of a more casual kind.⁵⁰

In the last part of this chapter, I shall consider novels which offer, in different ways, a more radical and perhaps postmodern, or postnational, imaginary of place in Italy. The novels of Melliti, Tawfik, and Smari envision named Italian cities in a way which is largely realistic and appears to be predicated on an assumption of the migrant's fundamental and ineluctable marginalization in urban society in Italy, figured through his (potentially also her) desire to experience the Italian cityscape as a palimpsest through which it becomes possible to occupy with the imagination spaces which are distant from the immediate topography of the city. The challenging charge of these novels lies, as I argued it, in the disruption of the integrity

---

48   A contemporary, spectacular imaginary of Italian urban terrorism and organized crime, from the 1970s to the 1990s, has been cemented by recent films such as *Romanzo criminale*, dir. Michele Placido (2005) and *Il divo*, dir. Paolo Sorrentino (2008).
49   Smari, *Fiamme in paradiso*, 158.
50   Interestingly, the comments on the event of the then recently elected Lega Nord mayor of Milan, Marco Formentini, underscored the rigid boundaries of the national. Referring to the victims, he eliminated the migrant entirely in commenting: 'Uno era nato a Milano, un altro a Terni, uno a Napoli, uno a Bergamo. C'è proprio tutta l'Italia in questa tragedia che abbiamo vissuto', http://archiviostorico.corriere.it/1993/luglio/29/svolta_Formentini_appello_all_unita_co_0_9307296791.shtml (accessed 6 December 2012).

and historical substance of each city which results from the process of displacing their recognized features by positing them in fluid relation to other spaces and times. The final novels I will consider progress further along the track of uprooting Italian urban space by imagining it as a place without 'place'; that is, as a vibrant and functional urban space which may or may not possess certain recognizable coordinates of an Italian city but is articulated without significant recourse to Italian political, cultural, or architectural history and as such can be imagined as – almost – anywhere.

My first object of analysis – Ron Kubati's *M* – situates an unnamed *io narrante* in an unnamed city, and tells the story of his relationships with a network of individuals within which he casually establishes himself.[51] These relationships are heavily regulated and commentated by the city itself, and the author sensitizes the reader to the incessant, insistent presence of the city in the narrator's social life; a presence which can be both oppressive and vitally liberating. The overground city is the source of some anxiety to the narrator, however, and it is the underground network, signalled by the 'M' of the title, which speaks to the narrator. The city under the ground seems vibrant, active, promising, and crucially, it is mobile. There are two points about Kubati's narrator's interaction with this underground metropolis which I think are pertinent to my investigation of space. Firstly, this novel takes further the notion posited above, in discussing Ahmad in *Pantanella*, that the environment is active in the experience of subjecthood. Kubati's narrator apprehends the underground city as a place of infinite possibility where individual agency is pleasurably annulled and substituted by an immense opportunity to be taken somewhere significant or fulfilling. In fact, on his first visit below ground, he describes that world twice in the space of two pages as a roulette.[52] The issues which trouble this individual in the overground world – issues broadly of identity and of placing himself in an environment in which he is not at home – dissipate underground and become meaningless. Subjecthood itself appears to become absurd, and the individual melts into a sort of continuum which exists beyond time

---

51 Ron Kubati, *M* (Nardò (LE): Besa, 2002).
52 Kubati, *M*, 8–9.

and beyond the human individual. It is not beyond space, though: it exists absolutely in a circumscribed space, but this is a relational one. This brings me to the second important point about being in the city in this novel, and that is that the model of mapping or of knowing the city that it posits is, in a much more direct way than in other novels discussed above, a topological rather than topographical one, as is the custom of representing the city in maps of its underground rail network. Locations are apprehended not in terms of physical distance from one another but in terms of how they connect to other places; as such, space is privileged over time in knowing or growing to understand the city. Kubati's narrator moves through the underground city by means of connections and numbers of stops, following a chain of relationality which insistently displaces him, thus liberating him from the anxiety experienced above ground in the search for a place and for an identity predicated upon fixed, visible collocation.

Kubati's underground in this novel is perhaps a more radical example of the expression, alluded to at the beginning of this chapter, of the restlessness of migration, better understood in this context as mobility. As witnessed in some of the novels discussed above, migrants, mostly dwelling or operating in the streets, trace networks of lines of passage through the city (and through wider spaces, such as across the Mediterranean or across European countries and their borders), but what is interesting is that those lines tend to be evanescent, and to disappear immediately. They establish presences and networks which exist and do not exist; which erase themselves through continued movement. De Certeau comments on this (without reference specifically to migrants):

> It is true that the operations of walking on can be traced on city maps in such a way as to transcribe their paths (here well-trodden, there very faint) and their trajectories (going this way and not that). But these thick or thin curves only refer, like words, to the absence of what has passed by. Surveys of routes miss what was: the act itself of passing by.[53]

---

53 De Certeau, *The Practice of Everyday Life*, 97.

This dynamic of presence and erasure, bodies and ghosts, is interesting. De Certeau mourns somewhat the visibility of human presence as it is replaced by lines on a map, and certainly, thinking of this discussion specifically in terms of migration, there is an anxiety about invisibility which regulates much of the discussion of identity and of inter-cultural encounter in migration literature. However, as I have noted, there is also an anxiety about visibility in these texts; about being too readily identifiable as 'other' and not ever being able to pass, unnoticed, as any other passer-by. Kubati's novel draws attention, somewhat provocatively, to the pleasure to be derived from being no more than an anonymous trace and to the opportunities offered not by 'the act itself of passing by' but rather by being gone, no longer visible and identifiable, accountable not to one's actions and presence in a place at a time but rather to one's movement through space.

M is important to my argument in this chapter because it quite radically dispenses with the interruptive presence of pasts – the pasts of the city itself or of the migrant inhabitant – in the migrant's expression of the city and figures the city as the space of the possible. As noted above, the city above the ground, in daylight and in the everyday, curbs somewhat the play of the imaginary, but below ground, as the references to roulette indicate, an immense sense of freedom is derived from the notion that any connection is possible, and that no destination need be that but will always offer a possibility to move on. Kubati's vision is perhaps a hyperbolic expression of the concept insisted upon by Amin and Thrift, to which I referred in the introduction to this chapter, that the everyday experience of the urban harbours unexpected opportunities. Positing cities as 'virtualities', they state:

> We understand the trajectory of cities not as being instanciated [*sic*] through replications of the present, but as a set of potentials which contain unpredictable elements as a result of the co-evolution of problems and solutions. Each urban moment can spark performative improvisations which are unforeseen and unforeseeable. This is not a naïve vitalism, but it is a politics of hope.[54]

Arguably, Kubati's novel imagines the city as just such a virtuality.

54   Amin and Thrift, *Cities*, 4.

From the 'virtuality' of Kubati's *M*, significantly displaced from Italy and from any inscription in specific national or local space, Amara Lakhous's second and third novels lead this discussion firmly back within the recognizable map of Rome, as their titles announce: *Scontro di civiltà per un ascensore a piazza Vittorio* and *Divorzio all'islamica a viale Marconi*.[55] The spaces demarcated and described in the texts are, unlike those of Kubati's novel, immediately real and almost palpable in their groundedness: there is a powerful sense of locality in each novel. Indeed, the action of each takes place within the area identified by the novel's title, and that the protagonists – all migrants, to some degree – inhabit their area is never questioned. Whilst the migrant protagonists' knowledge of each zone and facility in moving around declares a certain dominion over each area, this dominion does not necessarily in the novels equate with possession. The novels' titles may indicate ownership, but the very action of the first in particular in many ways works to interrogate the degree in which migrants are active agents in the transformation of urban space in contemporary Italy, or remain ultimately outsiders, tolerated but monitored, resident in terms which are precarious rather than permanent.

In *Scontro di civiltà per un ascensore a piazza Vittorio*, the lift in an apartment block is used as the fulcrum around which to examine the attitudes and prejudices of a multicultural community in Rome. This microcommunity is multicultural in the sense not only of harbouring different ethnicities, but more strikingly, inhabitants of different classes, ages, and genders, the identity of all of whom is defined in terms less of personal history than of their experience in the here and now of the small urban area which they inhabit. As discussed in earlier chapters, the novel is composed of eleven statements by neighbours about Amedeo (Algerian migrant, Ahmed), interspersed with eleven diaristic reflections by Amedeo himself. The structural privilege accorded to the migrant, Amedeo, and the sense that he is the point of constancy and even of truth amidst the variety of somewhat partial, prejudiced perspectives on the murder case, is underscored

55 Amara Lakhous, *Scontro di civiltà per un ascensore a piazza Vittorio* (Rome: e/o, 2006) and *Divorzio all'islamica a viale Marconi* (Rome: e/o, 2010).

by the fact that it is Amedeo's very knowledge of the city in which he lives which is one of the reasons for his neighbours being blind to his colour, ethnicity, and civil status.

In almost a parody of assimilation, Amedeo is pictured in the novel as a citizen of Rome because he inhabits his culture and his locality and knows them so well and so widely that his difference has become invisible to others. As discussed in Chapter 1, he passes for Roman. Indeed, if any difference is remarked, it is because he knows Rome more intimately than do the Romans in his community: bar owner, Sandro, comments, 'Per quanto riguarda la conoscenza della storia di Roma, Amedeo non ha rivali, conosce l'origine dei nomi delle strade e i loro significati'.[56] In turn, Amedeo himself reflects that:

> Non mi rendevo conto di avere tutte queste informazioni su Roma. Tutto il merito va ai miei piedi. Io adoro camminare, detesto il metro, l'autobus, le macchine e gli ascensori, non sopporto la folla. Amo camminare per godermi la bellezza di Roma in tutta calma, la fretta è nemica dell'innamorato. Sono paziente e sogno di bere da tutte le fontane di Roma e scoprire i suoi angoli più nascosti.[57]

Furthermore, it is Amedeo, a migrant (albeit an 'invisible' one), who acts as agent for others in negotiating Rome as a civic and bureaucratic entity and as physical space. For instance, he arranges with the police inspector for his friend, Parviz, an Iranian refugee, banned from feeding pigeons in piazza Vittorio because of a new policy of reducing the number of pigeons bothering residents and tourists in Rome, to be permitted to continue to feed the pigeons if the feed he uses is the approved one, containing a contraceptive chemical. The identification between Parviz and the pigeons, a connection through the imaginary of inhabiting the streets, being identified and controlled as a pest, but retaining the freedom to fly, is thus protected and perpetuated by Amedeo, who acts as the facilitator of urban living for his friends of all provenances.[58] Apparently, the relationship in this novel

---

56 Lakhous, *Scontro di civiltà per un ascensore a piazza Vittorio*, 134.
57 Lakhous, *Scontro di civiltà per un ascensore a piazza Vittorio*, 140–1.
58 The imaginary of the possibility of flight, and of 'homing', attached to the pigeons recalls (again) the figure of Anis in Tawfik's *Il profugo*, as discussed in Chapter 2.

between migrant observer and Italian urban space is one of pragmatic and straightforward habitation, perhaps facilitated by the fact that the action takes place almost exclusively in a multicultural zone of the city, generating almost none of the troubling confrontations between migrant consciousness and remnants of Rome's pasts which appear to disrupt narrative, psychological and emotional continuity in other, largely earlier, novels.

Ancient Rome is, however, very much present in this novel, and in the consciousness of its migrant protagonist. The title of the original version of the novel in Arabic translates as *Come farti allattare dalla lupa senza che ti morda*, and, as outlined in earlier chapters, the sections containing Amedeo's reflections in the novel are named 'ululati'. References to the wolf, to being accommodated or attacked by it, punctuate these reflections. In other words, the protagonist adopts the foundational myth of Rome within his own narrative rationalization of his experience of the city and of being at once an outsider and an insider in Italy, recalling the trope in earlier narratives of the migrant's conscious and unconscious investment in the history and myth of the empire. In fact, Amedeo refers in the text to Rome's imperial enterprises in North Africa, and comments on the complicity of the colonized in the colonizing process, drawing a parabola between the ancient colonial and the contemporary postcolonial which draws attention, by its absence, to Italy's modern colonial experience, in a way which articulates quite subtly the displaced position of an Algerian migrant in relation to the history of modern Italian colonialism. What Lakhous seems to compose in this novel, then, is a layered figure of Rome and its history in which traces of multiple experiences and lives, individual and collective, in the past and in the present, are sketched over one another to create an intricate web extending across times, cultures, and the relatively small but striated space of a specific zone of the capital. In many ways, the novel responds directly to the figure posited in much earlier novels of the migrant in the city, seeking footholds of the imaginary in a space both familiar and unfamiliar, by presenting an apparently unproblematic habitation of Roman space which is in fact revealed to be intersected with the problems embedded in the physical fabric of that space.

Lakhous's later novel, *Divorzio all'islamica a viale Marconi*, as I noted in Chapter 1, plays the notion of 'passing' as an Italian or as a migrant in the opposite way to the Ahmed/Amedeo characterization, in that the male protagonist and narrator here is in fact of Italian birth and citizenship (and named Christian), but, as a police detective, is required to 'go underground', posing as a Tunisian migrant named Issa amongst the largely Islamic community of viale Marconi and thereabouts. Given the space already dedicated to this novel in my earlier chapters, I shall note just three important aspects of its engagement with Rome as place and space. Firstly, the frame story of Issa's operation in the viale Marconi area immediately sets up an opposition between this multicultural Rome and the more central areas of the capital. The former is the theatre of engagement in which he is professionally committed to operate, and from which he is implicitly expected to retreat once his mission has been completed. In order to receive instructions and report back his findings, Issa periodically meets his superiors in a flat on via Nazionale. Here, rather than living in shared accommodation with inadequate sanitary provision, he can shower, change his clothes, make telephone contact with his family and partner, drink alcohol, and talk business. Whilst his passage between the two zones creates and repeatedly reinstates a correspondence between them, and on an intellectual, ethical, and affective level he becomes increasingly estranged from the world of central Rome and engaged with the multicultural periphery, at the same time, the narrative finds its form in large part in the fact that what faces Issa – and, in a different way, his female counterpart, Sofia – is a distinct choice between two worlds. In similar ways to those which operate in Lakhous's earlier novel, the vital and generally productive multicultural interaction which is developed in the zones in which his novels are situated is figured as in some ways delimited to those fairly well demarcated areas, and other parts of the city, especially its central and historical zones, are distant and separate. Arguably, the viale Marconi community is a more embedded and better housed, but still precarious, development of the Pantanella one as Melliti's novel envisions it.

My second point relates specifically to the construction of an imaginary of Rome, and shifts focus to the Egyptian second narrator of the novel, Sofia (Safia). Disdaining *telenovelas* and Al Jazeera, as discussed in my previous chapter, Sofia stakes her claim to a different kind of imaginary of a possible world, liberated in some ways from the constraints of both her culture and her gender which animate much of her reflection in the narrative. Whilst Tawfik's architect, arriving at the Colosseum for the first time, inserted himself into a re-visioning of a peplum movie (in a straightforward manner), Sofia narrates in detail a dream which places her at the centre of the Trevi fountain scene of Fellini's *La dolce vita* (1960). In her vision, she, as well as Sylvia (Anita Ekberg), enters the fountain and it is she to whom Marcello (Marcello Mastroianni) turns. Marcello's face is then revealed as that of Issa, whom Sofia has encountered but does not yet know, and who hereafter in the narrative is identified as 'il Marcello arabo'. By choosing one of the most iconic (and clichéd) images of modern Rome and inserting herself as an alternative to Anita Ekberg's character in the scene (and, moreover, the alternative which Marcello chooses), Sofia somewhat hyperbolically and ironically draws attention to the use of powerful, globally known images to construct intimate, personal realms of the possible.

Actually, Rome is – as in Fellini's film – simply the set for the creation of this image and in this instance I think to read any comment specifically on Rome as urban space or as community would be misguided. What is enormously significant in Sofia's re-imaging of this scene is the insistent visualization of and imaginative investment in transgression. Not only does she re-model one of Italy's most prominent and familiar screen stars as Arabic ('il Marcello arabo'), staking a direct claim to a valuable piece of territory in Italy's modern cinematic and cultural tradition, but she places herself into the vision as well, directly ousting the Hollywood star whose image has dominated understanding of the scene, the film, the period, the city, and, arguably, Italy, for half a century. With wit, Sofia's dream vision seems to claim that this is 'our' scene and 'our' image, where 'we' are new inhabitants of Italy and its cultural traditions. Perhaps the most powerful transgression lies, however, in Sofia's re-staging of the transgression which Anita Ekberg enacts in entering bodily into the monumental fountain, and doing so fully dressed in an evening gown. As Sofia narrates her dream, she describes, as an observer, the scene as it appears in Fellini's film, and the moment of her own entry into the scene comes as she notes, 'Non resisto a lungo, mi tolgo il foulard ed entro anch'io nella fontana'.[59] This 'foulard' is, as I demonstrated in Chapter 1 (see pages 48–54), at the

---

59   Lakhous, *Divorzio all'islamica a viale Marconi*, 100.

centre of her negotiations in the novel of her identity in Italy. To discard the veil is therefore a transgression which reflects not so much Sylvia's entry into the water in this scene of Fellini's film, as her mock-priestly costume which she wears to visit St Peter's Church in an earlier scene, and which articulates a much bolder assault (in 1960) on religious and cultural values considered unassailable. The motif of Sofia's love of classical Italian cinema offers, then, a complex tool by which, firstly, to illustrate an imaginary of place which also generates an imaginary of a set of cultural values; secondly, to articulate an acutely personal appropriation and reconstruction of that imaginary; and thirdly, to indicate by means of an apparently whimsical vision a cultural and personal radicalism which harbours transformative potential. Her dream offers an imaginative example of the sort of 'performative improvisation'[60] discussed with reference to Kubati's *M* above.

My third point about *Divorzio all'islamica a viale Marconi* relates to the particular mode of kinship and community which is highlighted in the novel. As discussed in my previous chapter, the hub of the multicultural community which Lakhous enquires into by means of his narrators is the 'Little Cairo' call centre. The name itself, within an urban zone accommodating a significant Egyptian minority, suggests a capacity to be at once in one place and, quite immediately and meaningfully, in another, which offers a new inflection on the passage to 'elsewheres' that I outlined above with reference to Melliti's *Pantanella*. To many intents and purposes, this part of Rome *is* Cairo: its community inhabits it on that basis, transposing practices of the everyday established in other cultures to this zone,[61] and indeed outsiders view it as such, hence – following the logic of the forces of the law – Issa's deployment there to investigate an Islamic terrorist plot.[62] As well as overlaying one urban reality with another, the call centre, and

---

60   Amin and Thrift, *Cities*, 4.
61   Sofia comments on the presence of Cairo in Rome: 'Nei primi giorni mi sembrava di vivere ancora al Cairo. Vedevo tanti egiziani in giro e mi chiedevo un po' stupita e perplessa: "Ma questa Roma, dov'è?"' (Lakhous, *Divorzio all'islamica a viale Marconi*, 41).
62   Issa's mission is revealed at the end of the novel to be a test fabricated by his superiors: no terrorist plot existed.

its name, establish a line of connection across the Mediterranean which is virtual; constituted, as noted previously, by the phone calls which are carried in and out of its booths. At the same time, this connection has a vital solidity in maintaining kinship and community across the globe and passing sustenance – be it financial, moral, or emotional – between distant locations. 'Little Cairo', in effect, eliminates the distance between 'here' and 'there', and vivifies in the rhythms of its constant transmission and reception of telecommunications a mobility which disrupts the rigid opposition associated with immigration and articulates instead a constant and multi-directional flow of human contact and experience.

It is useful to set the above observations within the framework of one of Amin and Thrift's key visions of the city. They discuss issues of propinquity and its alternatives throughout their exploration of cities, and draw attention to the model of 'distanciated cities' as one which emerges in twenty-first century culture, in which models of co-habitation, community, and encounter based on face-to-face contact are displaced or complemented by networks of contact and kinship which reach across the globe. Following a direction indicated by Deyan Sudjic, they suggest that the contemporary city must be approached with:

> a strong emphasis on understanding cities as spatially open and cross-cut by many different kinds of mobilities, from flows of people to commodities and information [...]. This is not just a simple statement of multiplicity, but a recognition that urban life is the irreducible product of mixture. Further, this mixture increasingly takes place at a distance, so challenging conventional notions of place. Even face-to-face contact increasingly involves a vast penumbra of distanciated interactions (for instance, via the internet, global travel, or wire-less communication).[63]

Probing further this form of community, which is not dependent on consistent physical proximity and interaction, they identify as a key example:

> diasporic communities, where the belonging and identification is anything but local. The close-knit family, clan, kin, and ethnic connections within a diaspora enable it to set up circuits of migration and subsequent mobility (in contrast to old-style

---

63 Amin and Thrift, *Cities*, 3.

migration) which are clearly dependent on a few very particular cities. Thus as bell hooks writes, 'home is no longer one place, it is locations' (1991: 148). Some of these locations are sites around the world, but others are relationships and imaginaries of a different kind, which also contribute to community. With the intensive growth of global migration and travel, many cities have seen a remarkable flowering of these new forms of mobile sociality whose chief characteristic is that they can and do thrive over long distances.[64]

With the obvious proviso that to distinguish so clearly between diasporic and migrant communities in Italy is less appropriate than in, for example, the United Kingdom or the United States, the description above of 'new forms of mobile sociality' is strikingly fitting to a range of migrant narratives in Italian, but particularly to Lakhous's *Divorzio all'islamica a viale Marconi*. This novel (as, in different ways, Lakhous's earlier one) endows with some human substance and empirical functionality the model constructed in earlier novels of Italian cities as to some extent a metonym and to some extent a proxy for wider affective and aesthetic experience. Envisioning Rome as globally connected in a constantly mutating communication network, Lakhous offers a more rooted imaginary of an Italian city as still offering access to elsewhere – and by this means, to affective stimulation – but also creating and fostering a mixed and mobile community within its own space.

It would be helpful, in conclusion, to offer some kind of theory (albeit tentative) of which anxieties and affective mechanisms, and which figures, are widely, if not constantly, operative in the expression of space by migrant writers. Whilst resisting, as I have consistently tried to, any characterization of earlier examples of immigration literature as somehow undeveloped, the texts themselves draw attention to different historical experiences of social and cultural acceptance which are envisioned in the literary text by means of different senses of physical space. The first texts considered in this chapter construct a sense of extreme exclusion, which offers possibilities for affective and aesthetic satisfaction almost only through the mechanism

---

64 Amin and Thrift, *Cities*, 46. They refer to bell hooks, *Yearning: Race, Gender, and Cultural Politics* (London: Turnaround, 1991).

of escape within the imagination. My later examples envisage possibilities for such stimulation through various forms of probable or possible action in and interaction with the urban community. Neither model offers an entirely positive vision and both necessitate seeking possibilities by skirting around the monotonous obstructions of everyday life, whether this be in the mode of Sofia's dream or of the fantasy of underground life elaborated by the protagonist of Kubati's *M*. In other words, it is not that texts which (generally) tell of the migration journey and immediate arrival in Italy form a vision of a problem, to which later texts which express what it is to be a non-Italian citizen in Italy form a vision of a solution: engaging with urban space in Italy is problematic, but differently problematic, throughout.

One way of making sense of these differences is to draw upon Edward W. Soja's discussion of space, and specifically, social space. Offering a form of history of responses to space, he outlines two alternatives and points towards a solution:

> The 'illusion of opaqueness' reifies space, inducing a myopia that sees only a superficial materiality, concretized forms susceptible to little else but measurement and phenomenal description: fixed, dead, and undialectical: the Cartesian cartography of spatial science. Alternatively, the 'illusion of transparency' dematerializes space into pure ideation and representation, an intuitive way of thinking that equally prevents us from seeing the social construction of affective geographies, the concretization of social relations embedded in spatiality, an interpretation of space as a 'concrete abstraction', a social hieroglyphic similar to Marx's conceptualization of the commodity form.[65]

The description of the 'illusion of transparency' helps to articulate the ways in which texts by Melliti and Smari engage with space; not, I would stress, because they entertain such an illusion, but precisely because what is easily interpreted in their texts as an almost post-Romantic projection of self onto environment is, in fact, punctuated and punctured by an insistent recognition of the materiality of space, and of the ways in which architectural features or the organization of the urban fabric instate a resistance to

---

65 Edward W. Soja, *Postmodern Geographies: The Reassertion of Space in Critical Social Theory* (London: Verso, 1989), 7.

penetration by those not familiar with the social structures which those material features embody. In other words, whilst 'dematerializ[ing] space' to a significant degree, on the one hand, and specifically as a strategy for overcoming the obstructive hostility of certain enactments by means of urban space of exclusive cultural cohesion, they also draw attention through the very same techniques to 'the concretization of social relations embedded in spatiality'. Lakhous's novels take a different approach which largely accepts 'concretized forms' and takes the organization of urban space in the here and now in Italy as read (though not as 'fixed, dead, and undialectical'), but again, via a different perspective, explores precisely the ways in which the organization of social space works also to organize being in that space: migrants' reorganization of specific spaces of Rome orientates the imagination and the affects of the inhabitants of those spaces in a particular, and largely self-perpetuating, way. Soja states that:

> Social and spatial structures are dialectically intertwined in social life, not just mapped one onto the other as categorical projections. And from this vital connection comes [...] the realization that social life is materially constituted in its historical geography, that spatial structures and relations are the concrete manifestations of social structures and relations evolving over time, whatever the mode of production.[66]

The physical and social difference between the Pantanella complex in 1990 and viale Marconi in the 2000s, as well as the literary and representational shift from *Pantanella* (1993) to *Divorzio all'islamica a viale Marconi* (2010), can, I think, be viewed in terms of the 'concrete manifestations of social structures and relations' which, I would argue, are not 'evolving over time' but shifting in what is probably less a single trajectory forwards (to where or what?) than a capillary network of forces and influences moving in a number of directions. To inject a principle of mobility and ephemerality into the notion of the 'eternal city' and of other historically rooted Italian cities is perhaps the stimulus which migrant writers are best placed to offer to the imaginary of space in (and beyond) Italy.

---

66 Soja, *Postmodern Geographies*, 127. Soja acknowledges his debt here to Lefebvre, *The Production of Space*.

CHAPTER 5

Literature

This chapter exploits the uncertainty of what might be meant by the term 'literature' to fulfil two functions in the overall structure of my enquiry. Firstly, it continues the discussion of figures in Italian migration literature by looking at how writing, reading, and books are imaged in the texts as vital elements in the imaginary of individual writers, and secondly, it moves towards the conclusions of the study by starting to explore the question of 'literature' more widely in the context of migrant culture in Italy and of Italian literature. It asks the question of what it means to write first at the level of the individual consciousness explored in a selection of texts, and then extends this to ask what it means to migrants in Italy to write, and to contribute to a body of texts identifiable – correctly or not – as Italian migration literature. The two sets of questions – related to what literature means in the interior world of the narratives and in the exterior one of the Italian literature and culture industry – clearly must be investigated according to somewhat different parameters, but it is productive to investigate them in parallel in order to discern the specific conditions which have pertained to the growth of this 'new' Italian literature and which have continued to change incrementally.

The chapter begins by analysing the stories told in texts by migrants of reading and writing, expressing the almost totemic quality of the book in certain conditions of estrangement or abjection. Questions of creative and political agency are highlighted, in terms of individual characters' expressed will to write for intellectual or aesthetic fulfilment and/or to write in order to make their story heard, to bear witness, to raise awareness, or to urge for action. The question of language choice, which threads through the entire study, is discussed particularly prominently in this chapter. At this point, questions of literary genres, popular, highbrow, and 'niche' fiction, are addressed, leading into an analysis of the conditions of publication, circulation, and reception for these texts. With these issues in mind, the chapter closes by placing texts by contemporary migrant writers in Italian alongside those by contemporary 'native' Italian writers, in terms of the imaginaries they respectively – or rather, collectively – express (in relation to questions of space, for example, as indicated in Chapter 4), of the imaginaries (of their readers) to which they appeal, and of their place in the culture industry.

As indicated in the introduction to this book, my attention throughout this study is to the sense of 'migrant writers' as migrants who write, but more particularly, as writers who migrate. Viewed from this perspective, it is possible to see the significant place which writing itself often holds in migrant imaginaries, standing as a token or totem of the desire to write which helps to orientate the experience of migration towards a specific goal and to regulate other, and perhaps more negative, responses and affects. The material object of the book itself – often a notebook or diary – holds a particular charge in *Immigrato*, by Mario Fortunato and Salah Methnani, for example, being at once an object within the narrative (the narrator's diary) and a meta-narrative trope, in that it is the raw material from which the novel is elaborated. In this sense, the object itself is invested with the imagination of what the migrating subject hopes to gain from his migration and what he hopes to become in Italy, and as a small, secret possession which he carries with him throughout his journey, amongst a very few personal possessions, it encapsulates the reasons for persisting in the journey. Brought out generally at night and in private, it holds the opportunity for the narrator to reflect and to imagine – and to write – and so to be something other than he is generally perceived as when in public: a writer, rather than a migrant. His writing tends to punctuate the more positive elements of his experience in Italy: when he feels oppressed by his condition, he tends to fall asleep immediately, but when he has been able to realize in his day-to-day experience some element of the identity to which he aspires in Italy, he notes it in his diary at night-time. For example, when the chance of a relationship with a young Italian woman comes to nothing, he states, 'Sul diario, scriverò il nome di Giovanna più volte. Con rabbia.

Con gratitudine'.[1] The close of the novel, as Salah starts his journey back towards Italy after his return visit to Tunisia, brings together the diary of migration in process and the novel of migration recounted in retrospect, underscoring the totemic value of the notebook and confirming the completion of a first phase of migration: 'Cercai nella valigia, allungata sotto il sedile davanti a me, il quaderno giallo. Scrissi poche parole. C'era ancora una pagina poi il quaderno non aveva altri fogli bianchi. Sulla pagina, in diagonale, scrissi in italiano la parola "ciao". Pensai che il viaggio cominciava adesso'.[2]

Creative writing is envisaged as a source of escape from oppressive conditions by means of free self-expression also in Melliti's *Pantanella*. For example, the protagonist, Ahmad, grappling with questions about his status in Italy and with his incomprehension of his marginalized status, identifies the possibility to make a different kind of sense, at least, through alternative modes of expression: 'A volte fuggiva le domande che lo straziavano con alcune risate tristi. Oppure scriveva poesie'.[3] Whilst these examples might suggest a particular currency of the notion of writing in the imaginative economy of earlier, day-to-day narratives of migration, the same figure persists in later texts as well. Younis Tawfik's novel of 2006, *Il profugo*, establishes, through the framework of the eldest brother's first-person account which closes the sixth chapter, that the written narrative has its genesis in the oral account recounted by his younger brother, Firas, which he has transcribed and delivered into the public domain.[4] *Scontro di civiltà per un ascensore a piazza Vittorio*, by Amara Lakhous, posits the diary writings of its protagonist, Ahmed/Amedeo, as the unique location of his own expression of his identity and experience, set against the accounts of him given by others (as transcribed oral statements) which populate the majority of

---

1   Mario Fortunato and Salah Methnani, *Immigrato* (Rome: Theoria, 1990), 98.
2   Fortunato and Methnani, *Immigrato*, 129–30.
3   Mohsen Melliti, *Pantanella: Canto lungo la strada*, trans. by Monica Ruocco (Rome: Edizioni Lavoro, 1992), 19.
4   See Younis Tawfik, *Il profugo* (Milan: Bompiani, 2006), 224.

the text.⁵ Again, these instances of self-expression are private and afford the opportunity not only for the subject to question his experience in the public sphere, but also, ultimately, to articulate a response to the traumatic memory of his past.⁶ Though an imaginary precisely of writing, or being a writer, is not articulated here, the references to Shahrazad and Shahrayar in Amedeo's final 'ululato' create a powerful image of the vital need to tell a story to someone who is willing and culturally equipped to hear it.

This sense of a cultural or acculturated context to writing and reading is important. As suggested by Amedeo's recourse to an Arabic tradition of story-telling – or perhaps, *the* Arabic literary tradition as understood, at least, in Europe – the imaginary of the writers and narrators of narratives of migration is potentially coloured and populated by images and motifs which might have a different currency for the teller than they have for the reader. To posit an essential difference in the literary or creative imagination would clearly be absurd, and in fact, arguably, it might be the possibility of imaginaries to access and to span unfamiliar repertoires of figures which underpins the motivation to tell stories across cultures. However, the recourse to motifs of the desert, for example, as discussed in Chapter 3 (see pages 107–9), draws attention through the very sense of cliché which might trouble a European reader's reception of this motif to the possibility of an imaginary populated differently (where the desert perhaps has the potency of the sea in nineteenth-century English-language novels of adventure). More productive than speculating about defining images for particular cultures is, however, to examine how images posited as different or exotic are deployed in narratives of migration to communicate or even to create an imaginary which crosses cultures, and thus disrupts any sense of cultural sovereignty over particular literary imaginaries or tropes.

Formal features as well as individual metaphors or images perform this function. Tawfik's novel, *La straniera*, echoes the Arabic and Hebrew

---

5   Amara Lakhous, *Scontro di civiltà per un ascensore a piazza Vittorio* (Rome: e/o, 2006).
6   See Chapter 1 of this book, pages 45–6, and Chapter 2, pages 91–4.

form of the *maqama* to combine prose narrative with intervals of poetry.[7] Lyric poems are used within and between chapters of Tawfik's novel to signal transitions, often between present experience and memory of the past. In the terms of my current discussion, these poems, precisely because of their form, have a powerful function in the construction of an imaginary related to the two characters and their experiences, in that they amplify the emotional charge of events described in the prose through the rhetorical escalation of particular images or tropes, such as the moon.[8] Interestingly, given that the *maqama* is related to the *maqam*, a vehicle for assembling different musical forms, songs are used in a similar way in Tawfik's novel, accelerating the transition from one mode of narrative or one location to another through emotional intensification.[9] As my previous chapters have shown, incrementally, it is relatively rare for narratives of migration to be structurally simple, and instead modes of narrating are combined in ways which reflect Tawfik's use of the *maqama* but perform a more fluid assembly. First-person narratives are combined with third-person (Lakhous, Dekhis, Tawfik), or two first persons narrate (Tawfik, Lakhous), dreams or visions break up the narrative and indicate the operation of two forms of consciousness (Smari, Melliti), and in the majority of narratives, two frames of time and place co-exist and overlap, illustrating Mikhail Bakhtin's

---

7   See Jaakko Hämeen-Anttila, *Maqama: A History of a Genre* (Wiesbaden: Harrassowitz, 2002). The use of poems is not unique to *La straniera*: Tawfik's other novels employ similar techniques.

8   The poem which opens the first chapter of the novel includes, for example, the following images: 'Nelle strade delle città, / un uomo / porta la sua luna in mano, / vende parole, / i sorrisi e le lacrime' (Tawfik, *La straniera*, 7).

9   The songs of the highly popular female Egyptian singer of the mid-twentieth century, Umm Kalthum (more widely spelled as Kulthum, and with other variations), figure heavily in this (and other) narratives. The architect's narrative identifies the voices of Umm Kalthum and of Nasser as the two which captivated the Arab world at the time of the Six-Day War (Tawfik, *La straniera*, 117). For a concert performance by Kalthum in 1967 of a song, 'Enta Omri' (You Are My Life), cited in this novel (Tawfik, *La straniera*, 60), see http://www.youtube.com/watch?v=XPGHpBOt5sE (accessed 6 June 2013).

concept of the chronotope.¹⁰ These techniques operate, again, both at the level of the figural and the formal. In relation to the former, they offer the opportunity to propose and explore two or more imaginaries in relation to the narrated events, as evidenced perhaps most strikingly in *I lupi della notte*, by Amor Dekhis,¹¹ or in the visions of elsewheres which offer a parallel consciousness to the daytime narrative of Ahmad's experiences in Rome in Melliti's *Pantanella*. At the formal level, they suggest the possible convergence of multiple narrative traditions and practices of story-telling and expression.

Whilst in some cases, such as Tawfik's *La straniera*, the effect of such mixing may be a somewhat romanticized experience of cultural difference through engagement with an unfamiliar and traditional form, in many cases, the convergence is more abrupt and unsettling. Melliti's *Pantanella*, with its confusion of voices, instances of non-sequential narrative logic, and highly allusive language in places, offers a good example. A particular episode from this novel offers insight into both the explicit exploration of alternative narrative modes and the effect of this on the reader. The protagonist, Ahmad, exploits the imprecision of memory, and the capacity of the past to stand and to signify as a narrative in the absence of facts, dates, and empirically verifiable evidence, as an opportunity to create a particular impact upon the addressee of the account, his partner in Italy, Mary. She proves, in their relationship, insistently keen to know about Ahmad's past – a set of experiences which, the novel takes pains to point out, is unknowable even to Ahmad himself – and Ahmad insists on an indeterminacy in all his answers to her questions, which leaves her increasingly frustrated. Ahmad uses this as a mode of maintaining control in their relationship, parrying her requests for information with responses which encapsulate concepts rather than supplying facts. For instance, she asks where he comes from, and he limits his answer to 'il sud'. He tells her about life in the Pantanella building and about life in his home country in a stylized, allegorical way,

---

10   Mikhail Bakhtin, *The Dialogic Imagination: Four Essays*, ed. by Michael Holquist, trans. by Caryl Emerson and Michael Holquist (Austin, TX: University of Texas Press, 1981).
11   Amor Dekhis, *I lupi della notte* (Naples: L'ancora, 2008).

clearly telling parables rather than recounting lived experiences, relying on the 'logic' of fiction rather than that of reality, and prompting the response: 'Sei ambiguo, non rispondi alla mia domanda'.[12]

The key 'story' which Mary wants to hear and which Ahmad eventually consents to tell is of his partner at home, Suheyr. In order to tell the story of Suheyr, and to satisfy (or reproach) Mary's curiosity, he recounts in some detail Suheyr's imprisonment, torture, and rape at the hands of the ruling military in his country. The details of the delivery are interesting: Ahmad initially uses the conditional tense in his recounting of Suheyr's story, suggesting the hypothetical, as if this were one of his parables of the past, demonstrating not what did happen but what could have happened. At a certain point, however, he shifts to the past historic tense, suggesting a record of past events. However, he is at this point recounting the feelings, physical and emotional, which Suheyr experienced during her torture as a prisoner isolated in a desert detention centre; feelings which he cannot possibly have experienced himself, nor witnessed, nor read in any official record, nor heard directly from Suheyr, since he says that she was ultimately murdered. He is recounting Suheyr's memory, not his own, and it is therefore a projection, a hypothesis, rather than a 'true' record of events. Ahmad thus disrupts the logic of certain grammatical choices and, indeed, disrupts the very relationship between grammar and specific modes of expression. At a different level, but to similar effect, Suheyr is apotheosized in this memoir, using a combination of poetic hyperbole and bald (but necessarily fabricated) fact, for example: 'Ma era forte come il mare, profonda come il mare, bella come il mare, affascinante come il mare. Era una stella marina, una stella che illuminava il mare. La portarono nel deserto, era notte quando l'autista della macchina del carcere si fermò sul ciglio della strada per violentarla con gli altri custodi. Ma lei rideva, rideva forte'.[13]

Ahmad's recollections are marked by emotion in the text: the effect on him of reimagining Suheyr's story is painful. The effect on Mary is one of shock. The effect on the balance of the relationship between the

---

12   Melliti, *Pantanella*, 140.
13   Melliti, *Pantanella*, 145.

two is that Mary is manoeuvred into submission: she accepts the story, 'illogical' to her though it is, and she accepts her position as subordinate to (the memory of) Suheyr. Ahmad exploits the effect of uncertainty again by offering an observation which appears to raise Mary's stature – 'forse sei più bella di lei' – but ultimately belittles her both in its substance and because of the undermining force of the 'forse'. The effect on the reader of this episode is correspondingly disorientating, directed at once towards an imaginary of Suheyr's suffering, towards cognitive doubt about the accuracy of the account given, and towards interpretative uncertainty about the meaning of the story-telling event: put crudely, is it about Suheyr or about Mary? The episode, then, illustrates an alternative mode of expression of the remembrance of the past in the present, and an alternative economy of story-telling, in which fact and fiction may not be balanced in ways familiar to the reader. It draws attention particularly to the risks and possibilities which dog the acts of self-representation and of cultural representation in a situation in which teller and addressee do not share a common cultural (and historical) experience and a mutually recognized set of tools of expression and interpretation.

The possibilities which emerge from a mode of story-telling which challenges dominant narratives are powerfully explored in magical realism, a form or mode strongly associated with the postcolonial.[14] Linda Hutcheon usefully articulates the convergence of postmodernist and postcolonialist priorities in a reconfiguring of realism which expresses the literary *Zeitgeist* of the late twentieth century:

> [Magical realism] becomes part of the dialogue with history that both post-modernism and post-colonialism undertake. After modernism's ahistorical rejection of the burden of the past, postmodern art has sought self-consciously (and often even parodically) to reconstruct its relationship to what came before; similarly, after that imposition of an imperial culture and that truncated indigenous history which colonialism has meant to many nations, post-colonial literatures are also negotiating

---

14 Helen Tiffin, for example, cites magical realism as one of the strategies of 'counter-discourse' deployed by postcolonial writers, in 'Post-colonial Literatures and Counter-discourse', in Bill Ashcroft, Gareth Griffiths and Helen Tiffin, eds, *The Post-Colonial Studies Reader* (London: Routledge, 1995), 95–8.

(often parodically) the once tyrannical weight of colonial history in conjunction with the revalued local past.[15]

It is important to apply here the qualification (established in the introduction to this study) that Italian migration literature is not at all coterminous with postcolonial writing, and is not therefore, in most cases, concerned directly with re-assessing national or local histories following release from the imposition of the history of a dominant power. Indeed, magical realism, strictly speaking, is not a prominent mode of writing amongst the writers whom I have considered in this study, nor more generally in migration literature in Italian. Nevertheless, the uses of realism, or rather, figurations of the real, in the texts which I have explored have clear resonances of magical realism. Melliti's configuration, for example, of the telling of the story of Suheyr is an explicit exploration of challenges to the boundaries of credibility, inserting elements of conjecture and imagination into the account, whilst also stressing the brutal and chilling probability of an underlying course of events which was 'real'. More generally, and in ways more closely comparable with magical realism as used by its most prominent practitioners, such as Salman Rushdie and Gabriel García Márquez, tales of the past attached to specific locations or countries are customarily, in *Pantanella*, revisited in the teller's mind and recounted through the prism of the imaginary, so that the stark and identifiable contours of realistic reproduction are blurred, verifiable fact shifts towards the probable or possible, and representation occurs through imagination.

It is, however, in the gaps where Italian migration literature does not quite fit the model of magical realism that it is possible to identify some salient techniques and tropes which tell quite intensely why the stretching and manipulation of realism might be productive. It is certainly possible to read, for example, Tawfik's account of Iraq in *Il profugo*, or, more directly, Fazel's account of Somalia in both of her novels, as a foregrounding of what Hutcheon terms the 'local past' in order to displace the 'tyrannical weight of colonial history'. More pervasive behind this, though, is the principle

---

15   Linda Hutcheon, 'Circling the Downspout of Empire', in Ashcroft, Griffiths and Tiffin, eds, *The Post-Colonial Studies Reader*, 130–5 (131).

of re-exploring history – a history often figured through personal experience and memory – in such a way as to undermine its status as a universal account, and instead to demonstrate ways in which it can be relativized, localized or personalized.[16] Interestingly, the history thus displaced or re-appropriated may be, in narratives of Italian immigration, the history of Italy, or of (imperial) Europe, or of the 'west', or of migrants' countries of origin. Rather than a specific colonial history, it is a dispersed history of the effects of colonialism and of a related, but much wider, ideology of dominion and control, that these texts counter. The crux of this is perhaps the emphasis on the personal, which persists from early autobiographical accounts to many of the most recent novels which deploy either a first-person narrator or an intense focalization through one particular character. There is an insistence on recording the emotions, ideas, wounds, and impressions (recalling Ahmed) which experience leaves upon the skin, body, and consciousness of individual subjects, both before and during (and after) migration.[17] The tactic of allowing, in the narrative, this record of affects and effects to inflect and inform the ways in which the history is told, producing an imaginary of the real which both, in different instances, expands beyond and shrinks within conventional realism, has the effect of locating the consciousness of the migrant subject as the central and determining factor in the perception of events. This redistribution of focal power from the dominant view of 'history' to the marginalized view of a migrant who, economically, politically and culturally, may have very little purchase on power either in Italy or in her country of departure, enacts an authorizing of the migrant subject which reflects the thrust of magical realism. It also reflects a principle of postcolonial (and feminist) discourse, which is, as Hutcheon points out, that before gaining the privilege of a postmodern challenge to the autonomy of the subject, it 'must work first to assert and affirm a denied or alienated subjectivity'.[18]

---

16   The most potent example of this is perhaps the re-visiting of the history of the Roman Empire by Ahmad, in Melliti's *Pantanella*, which allows him, momentarily, to think and to tell *the* grand narrative of western power in his own terms.
17   Sara Ahmed, *Strange Encounters: Embodied Others in Post-Coloniality* (London: Routledge, 2000).
18   Hutcheon, 'Circling the Downspout of Empire', 131.

Barbara Harlow similarly argues that texts of 'resistance literature' embody or inscribe a political subversion by using the forms of the dominant cultural model and challenging it from within.[19] Narrative, and particularly the novel as a literary form, are so deeply embedded a model for expressing and perpetually re-affirming 'western' global dominance that to use these forms to criticize and challenge that dominance constitutes an acutely direct form of resistance:

> Narrative, unlike poetry perhaps, provides a more developed historical analysis of the circumstances of economic, political, and cultural domination and repression and through that analysis raises a systematic and concerted challenge to the imposed chronology of what Frederic Jameson has called 'master narratives', ideological paradigms which contain within their plots a pre-determined ending. The use by Third World resistance writers of the novel form as it has developed within the western literary tradition both appropriates and challenges the historical and historicizing presuppositions, the narrative conclusions, implicated within the western tradition and its development.[20]

Harlow's argument, almost thirty years on, sounds its age, but the relevance to many examples of Italian migration literature of her notion of 'resistance' remains striking. She draws attention, for example, to the technique of using multiple narrative voices and perspectives to challenge the notions of authority which insist in the tradition of the novel, articulated in the figure of the author and omniscient narrator. The disruption of a central, fixed perspective on the events of the narrative, assumed to 'know best', has its political corollary in the disruption of the hegemonic socio-political ideology, and the textual presence and prominence of diverse perspectives and multiple 'centres' of consciousness privileges instead an attention to minority voices.

---

19 Barbara Harlow, *Resistance Literature* (New York: Methuen, 1987). Interestingly, she notes that she borrows the term of her title from Palestinian literature of the 1960s, indicating a period explicitly remembered in Tawfik's *La straniera* and, by extension, a tradition of modern writing in the Arabic Middle East which plausibly has wider currency (see *Resistance Literature*, 1).
20 Harlow, *Resistance Literature*, 78.

Crucial to the modes of expression of migrant writers, and crucial to the political and creative project of postcolonialism and of 'resistance literature', is also the issue of language. Here again, it is the way in which Italian migration literature both fits and strains against a postcolonial model that illuminates the specific modes of use of Italian by writers whose first language is another. As I have argued elsewhere, the evidence in migration narratives of a 'resistance' to Italian as a dominant language, in terms of disruptive or deliberately inaccurate use of it, is almost entirely absent.[21] Italian appears to be used simply as an instrument for creative expression, rather than as a tool for making dissent or estrangement visible and audible. The narratives themselves often relate an ambition to use Italian like a native speaker and so envisage fluency as an element in the self-definition of a migrant subject as an agent, rather than an object, in Italian social discourse. The anxiety which Salah, as narrator in Fortunato and Methnani's novel, recounts about maintaining control of his diction in Italian, and succeeding in accurately completing the one-to-ten number sequence, bespeaks, as I discussed in Chapter 1 (see page 32), a desire to perform a coherent and autonomous subjecthood in Italian society. In Amor Dekhis's novel, *I lupi della notte*, Salè recalls – again, repeatedly – the refrain of the priest who supported him in his early days in Italy, that 'La conoscenza della lingua è indispensabile se vuoi migliorare le tue condizioni di vita'.[22] He expresses an incomprehension of other migrants who have no interest in acquiring more than a functional knowledge of Italian. Access to Italian society as a whole and active subject again is seen to depend upon full linguistic presence. In short, both in textual and meta-textual terms, migrant narratives in Italian tend to articulate and thereby also to demonstrate a sense of ownership of the Italian language.

To assert that this kind of facility with Italian as a medium of narrative and of creative expression indicates that migrants' use of the language is unpolitical would be, of course, a misrepresentation, as my references

---

21 See Jennifer Burns, 'Language and its Alternatives in Italophone Migrant Writing', in Jacqueline Andall and Derek Duncan, eds, *National Belongings: Hybridity in Italian Colonial and Postcolonial Cultures* (Oxford: Peter Lang, 2010), 127–47.
22 Dekhis, *I lupi della notte*, 129, 136, 142.

to agency, access and ownership indicate. The choice to write in Italian is itself immediately a political decision, but one to which I will return, and the principle established by Deleuze and Guattari that any minority literature carries in itself a political charge, though open to discussion, stands.[23] First of all, it is useful to examine how use of language at the 'micro' level of textual expression points to assertions and conclusions about what it is to adopt the language of others in daily life and in creative writing. Whilst Italian forms the primary means of expression in all texts discussed, it is de-centred by various means. Items of lexis from the author's or narrator's first language create a form of interference to the creation of meaning which forces the reader to take immediate account of another language and another culture insisting behind the Italian text on the page. The interference is often minimized by the use of footnotes or a glossary, or simply by familiarity; for example, words such as *ghurba*, *muezzin*, *burqa* have acquired currency in Italian through journalistic accounts of Islam and through migration literature itself, as well as foreign literatures in translation. This structure of rupture, reference, and realignment within the reading process articulates a combination of 'resistance' and rapprochement which it is possible to extrapolate, I think, to describe a broader process of intercultural accommodation through literary and cultural practice. Predicated upon the degree of 'ownership' of Italian noted above, this use and disruption of Italian stakes its claim to the destination language whilst also offering reminders of linguistic estrangement which draw attention to ownership of another language (or languages) and cultural capital. In effect, the Italian or Italian-native-speaking reader is placed in a position of temporary estrangement which underscores linguistically the thematic and figurative estrangement explored in earlier chapters of this book. However, as the use of explanatory paratext indicates, the ownership which migrant writers claim through their use of Italian is demonstrated, or even promoted, by means of these linguistic strategies, to be an inclusive rather than a 'resistant' one.

---

23 See Chapter 3, 'What is a Minor Literature?', in Gilles Deleuze and Félix Guattari, *Kafka: Toward a Minor Literature*, trans. by Dana Polan (Minneapolis, MN: University of Minnesota Press, 1986), 16–27.

This model of mutual ownership, which seems to operate outside the more politically loaded one of postcolonial discourse, exposes in its fundamental choice of language a resistance to the imperial model and its legacies. Graziella Parati observes that, in the case of most African Italian writers, the deliberate circumvention of the writer's second language – also the colonial language – might be interpreted as itself a gesture of displacement:

> Cultural and linguistic *métissage* is based on the attempt to intertwine traditionally diverse cultures and literatures in order to create a hybrid entity that destroys the separation between the dominant Western literary tradition and the non-Western tradition of, very often, the colonized. [...] In this hybrid context, the French tradition and language become intermediate passages that lead to the acquisition of a third (sometimes a fourth) culture and language. The colonizer's language and literature are therefore displaced from their usual privileged position in order to become secondary to the appropriation and personalization of another culture.[24]

The side-stepping of French thus signals that this group of migrant writers eschew the opportunity of 'writing back' to their colonizers, and, writing three or more decades after the nations of North Africa gained independence from colonial rule, prefer to move beyond the discourses of colonialism and postcolonialism, and to situate their relationship with the countries of Europe within the contemporary global context. It is not unreasonable to consider the choice of Italian as the language of creative writing, rather than French, as a statement on the part of the writer that he is not to be seen as an oppressed or marginalized figure, but rather as some sort of intellectual and social entrepreneur, seizing the opportunity of using a 'new' language, relatively untainted by historical associations, to create a new writing identity. It is impossible to assert, of course, that Italian is somehow washed clean of any colonial associations for any of the writers I am discussing, but it is possible to identify in the inclusive and largely non-resistant use of Italian – even by Somali writers such as Fazel – a strategy to situate the relationships between Africa (or the Middle East) and

---

24 Graziella Parati, 'Strangers in Paradise: Foreigners and Shadows in Italian Literature', in Beverly Allen and Mary Russo, eds, *Revisioning Italy: National Identity and Global Culture* (Minneapolis, MN: University of Minnesota Press, 1997), 169–90 (174).

Europe, and between migrant individuals and their destination country or countries, in a contemporary context. Such a context recognizes that rigid postcolonial arrangements inhere, but do not in themselves determine economies of power, wealth, and cultural agency which are played out in conflicts and co-operations of the present (and future). It is the logic less of colonialism than of the 'clash of civilizations' that they perhaps seek to question through the medium of fluent Italian.[25]

Possible reasons for choosing Italian have thus been sketched; but what further motivations lie behind writing in Italian? The work of Michel de Certeau, primarily in response to the events of May 1968 in Paris, suggests some interpretative strategies transferable to Italian migration literature. Anachronistic though the connection may seem, it is clear that much of de Certeau's reflection relates to the process of French decolonization, taking place in relation to its African colonies in particular between 1956 and 1962, and to consequent questions about the notion of national identity and the accommodation of minority communities. Discussing the 'capture of speech' (*prise de parole*) performed by the May 1968 protesters, de Certeau describes a movement and an articulation of self-assertive rejection which has much in common with Tiffin's 'counter-discourse' and Harlow's 'resistance literature', as discussed above. De Certeau comments: 'The capture of speech clearly has the form of a refusal. It is a protestation. We shall see that its fragility is due to its expression as contestation, to its testimony as negation. Therein, perhaps, lies its greatness. But in reality, it consists in stating, "I am not a thing"'.[26] The language of capture, protestation and contestation is clearly too adversarial to be related directly to most examples of migrant writing in Italian: even those texts which criticize explicitly European economic and cultural hegemony mitigate their protest by underscoring a recognition of their own complicity in pursu-

---

25   See Samuel P. Huntington, *The Clash of Civilizations and the Remaking of World Order* (New York: Samuel and Schuster, 1996). Huntington's thesis is that global conflict in the post-Cold War context will be born of cultural difference.
26   Michel de Certeau, *The Capture of Speech and Other Political Writings*, ed. by Luce Giard, trans. and afterword by Tom Conley (Minneapolis, MN: University of Minnesota Press, 1997), 12.

ing the myth of western affluence. De Certeau proceeds in his discussion, however, to delineate a first, tentative movement of contestation which is highly relevant to my topic here:

> We cannot be satisfied with this initial form that contestation takes when, first of all, it talks about itself. Like the event, it begins by being a narrative, and often an autobiographical, eyewitness account. But such an entry into language remains surreptitious. It is placed under the rubric of the *also*: whoever takes speech is *also* accepted, no doubt, because of the person's modesty, and because for that reason he or she can easily be tolerated by a society strong enough to swallow a foreign element and make use of it.[27]

The capture of political speech in the public arena is, of course, de Certeau's object of analysis here, whereas my discussion focuses on the capture of the literary word in the 'published' arena, but the process described is analogous: the use of narratives of personal experience, 'eyewitness accounts', to establish a foothold in the literature and culture of the nation in which the migrant seeks to establish herself, and the response of a weak or even negative sort of tolerance, based on a confidence that the voice of this element is sufficiently marginal not to unsettle the existing balance of power between centre and margins. De Certeau's stress on the '*also*' suggests the supplementary quality of the 'foreign element', which in turn suggests Derrida's contemporaneous discussion of the 'dangerous supplement' (1967), the element which appears to be merely an adjunct or even surplus, but which has the potential to divert attention from the dominant discourse to the extent that it ultimately subverts the power balance entirely.[28] Following this argument, the 'modest' entry into the Italian literary market of migrant writers in the early 1990s might be seen as a prelude to a significant shift in national literary production from writers of the 'centre', white Italians writing in their first language, to writers from minority cultures. Again, to make such a reference in the early 2000s would have been to overstate massively the impact of migration literature in Italy, but the

---

27 De Certeau, *The Capture of Speech and Other Political Writings*, 19 (italics in original).
28 Jacques Derrida, *Of Grammatology*, trans. by Gayatri Chakravorty Spivak (Baltimore, MD: Johns Hopkins University Press, 1976). The original version in French dates from 1967: *De la grammatologie* (Paris: Éditions de Minuit, 1967).

critical and commerical success in more recent years particularly of African Italian writers, widely labelled as 'second generation', such as Cristina Ali Farah and Igiaba Scego, indicates that such a shift is in progress. A brief reflection on the impact of anglophone writing on English literature and of francophone writing on French literature confirms the 'revolutionary' possibilities, in terms of national canons, offered by migrant, minority, and postcolonial writing.

The relationship between cultural and political presence in the nation is a complex one, particularly in the context of Italy, where the visibility of migrant culture at a national, and particularly, local level, has been significant since the 1990s, in the form of festivals, competitions, theatre productions, readings, initiatives for schools, etc., and yet migrant communities remain relatively unrepresented and visible primarily as a problem in the political arena. De Certeau, discussing – in the terms of the period – *négritude*, asserts very strongly that political representation must precede cultural representation for any minority group: '*Political* autonomy was the basis of a *cultural* identity. Many other examples show how: it is impossible to take speech and to retain it without a taking of power. To want *to be heard* means being committed to *making* history'.[29] Any expression of cultural difference or specificity without this underlying political power is ultimately empty and static, a museum exhibit rather than an intervention in a vital and growing social dialogue. De Certeau, writing in the same period in *Culture in the Plural*, uses the metaphor of spectacle:

> Cultural expression is only the surface of a social unity that has not yet been given its own political and cultural consistency. [...] To hold fast to this cultural presentation means buying into the society that constituted cultural elements as spectacle and as folkloric objects of an expanding economic and political enterprise. From then on, if we identify with a cultural representation, we are caught in a national 'theater' [...]. By seeking to attest to something autonomous, expression is deceived on the very ground on which it is situated.[30]

---

29 De Certeau, *The Capture of Speech and Other Political Writings*, 32 (italics in original).
30 Michel de Certeau, *Culture in the Plural*, introduction by Luce Giard, trans. and afterword by Tom Conley (Minneapolis, MN: University of Minnesota Press, 1997), 69–70.

This assertion raises interesting questions about the status of migrant culture in Italy. Given that, as outlined above, the primary mode of migrants capturing speech, filling cultural space, and communicating their own culture has been, in Italy in recent years, performance. De Certeau's comments prompt a reflection upon the substance of events such as festivals and readings: are they simply 'events', which happen and leave little trace on the local space and culture, or do they produce and mark a permanent, albeit minor, change in that space and culture, so functioning performatively to produce minority culture within Italian culture? De Certeau's conviction that cultural presence can only emerge on the basis of political presence – not precede or collaborate in it – is very much of its time (late 1960s). In the context of Italy in the 2000s (to a lesser extent in the 1990s), where the rise in the use of communications technology and social media has created new channels and modes of organization for social and political movements, for the community-level expression of support and dissent, and for new forms of cultural and social 'presence', to read such 'spectacle' as de Certeau identifies as, in fact, performative, instantiating migrant cultures within Italian public life rather than, ultimately, erasing them, is perhaps sustainable.

I return to de Certeau's statement that 'To want *to be heard* means being committed to *making* history'.[31] This issue of 'making history' is an important textual and political consideration in the discussion of minority writing, and specifically, here, migration literature in Italian. A further 'use' of writing for migrants, a further motivation for writing, perhaps, is that of telling a story which will become or contribute to a history, and of thus inscribing alternative histories within the history of the nation, which is an already multi-centred one, in the case of Italy. These are not only the histories of individual or collective migrations, however; though this is an important component of the history. They are also the 'forgotten' history of Italy's colonialism,[32] and, as repeatedly illustrated in my previous chap-

---

31   De Certeau, *The Capture of Speech and Other Political Writings*, 32 (italics in original).
32   See Jacqueline Andall and Derek Duncan, eds, *National Belongings: Hybridity in Italian Colonial and Postcolonial Cultures* (Oxford: Peter Lang, 2010); Ruth Ben-Ghiat

ters, the histories of other nations and other cultures (Somalia, Algeria, Tunisia, etc.) in their recent and chronologically distant brushings against the history (histories) of Italy or Italy-in-Europe, from imperial Rome to the present. On the levels of both individual and cultural identification, this assertion of a past serves as a vital counterweight to the prevailing sense that, in Italy, immigration is a 'new phenomenon' and that immigrants are bereft of past and of culture, all of which fuels sentiments urging their exclusion from society as strange, unknown and unknowable. The inscription in Italian-language literature of stories of migration and of its contexts, and of stories of other places and other experiences or visions of Italy, has the potential to provide a historical consistency to a 'phenomenon' articulated often as being visited upon Italy from outside national borders, rather than as representing a certain logical continuity with the narrative of the nation.[33]

With regard to 'making history', de Certeau also draws attention to the interdependency between past and future: 'Culture and communication are nourished by stories, not only in order to conserve piously the great moments of a time past, nor in the vain hope of compiling a complete catalog of a sacred patrimony, but in order to engender the future by reinscribing the present within the past'.[34] He describes a conceptual movement between three distinct time periods: the present must be pushed backwards, in effect, to be contextualized within history, and this movement makes possible a trajectory into the future, connecting past, present and future in a logical continuum. What this suggests in terms of immigration in Italy is that only an engagement with the histories of migrants will facilitate social and cultural dialogue and cohesion, which will in turn create the conditions in which an inclusive national (or rather, transnational) culture can

---

and Mia Fuller, eds, *Italian Colonialism* (New York: Palgrave Macmillan, 2005); Cristina Lombardi-Diop and Caterina Romeo, eds, *Postcolonial Italy: Challenging National Homogeneity* (New York: Palgrave Macmillan, 2012).

33 On the construction of narratives of the nation, see Benedict Anderson, *Imagined Communities: Reflections on the Origin and Spread of Nationalisms* (London: Verso, 2006).

34 De Certeau, *The Capture of Speech and Other Political Writings*, 129.

develop. In terms specifically of Italian migration literature, it suggests that only when the stories of migrants have entered into the cultural field in Italy and been read in the context of the histories they bespeak (as described above), can stories of possible futures be elaborated – stories which do not necessarily delineate a future for multicultural Italy, but rather articulate a future for Italian literature which is inclusive of 'minority' or alternative expressions of Italian-ness. This view of a displaced Italian literature inclines towards the principle established by Deleuze and Guattari, studying Kafka, that one of three key elements of a 'minor literature' is the deterritorialization effect enacted by a minor literature written in a major language from a marginalized or minority position.[35] Following this logic of displacing Italian literature from the territorial borders of a nation state, it is perhaps more productive to envisage a transnational Italian literature: a notion to which I return in the Afterword.

Assertions about what Italian migration literature might be or become need to be tested against the conditions of literary and cultural production and circulation in which these texts enter the public domain. The last part of this chapter will therefore consider what insights are offered if this literature is approached through questions of genre, publishers, authorship, and readership.[36] In relation to genre, as noted in the introduction to this book, to trace a progression or evolution from first-person migration narratives of the early 1990s to more complex fictions in the 2000s and 2010s is, in my view, problematic, not least because the evidence of such a direct line is not to be found. In fact, as discussed in this chapter and earlier ones, the consciousness of the individual migrant subject remains central in the majority of texts. Whether or not the narrative itself can be identified as autobiographical, the foregrounding of the individual subject and his histories is a significant discursive and political strategy, as well as a creative one. In the complicating of the notion of autobiography, which

---

35   See Deleuze and Guattari, *Kafka: Toward a Minor Literature*, 16.
36   On these questions, see also Jennifer Burns, 'Outside Voices Within: Immigration Literature in Italian', in Gillian Ania and Ann Hallamore Caesar, eds, *Trends in Contemporary Italian Writing* (Newcastle: Cambridge Scholars Publishing, 2007), 136–54.

occurs in narratives as early as Melliti's *Pantanella*, it is possible to trace a wider strategy which relates closely to my comments above about interrogating and displacing the Italian-ness of this literature. In other words, the mixing of genres – bringing in traditions other than the western novelistic one – or the deployment of established western genres, such as the detective thriller, to tell a story which is also a personal history of transcultural migration, has the effect of displacing definitions of genre and detaching the activity of writing stories from categories which attempt to define the reception as much as the production of the text.

In the narratives analysed throughout this volume, a range of genres and modes can be identified, many of them contested in themselves: autobiography, fairy-tale or folktale, travel writing, war narrative, the adventure novel, historical fiction, journalism, crime fiction, as well as elements of the fantastic. To cross genre borders is a familiar tactic in modern and postmodern literature, and so cannot be identified as only the province of migration literature. However, the example of Amor Dekhis's *I lupi della notte* suggests what specific interpretative charge might be lent to migration literature by the cross-wiring of genres. In constructing the discovery of his personal history in Algeria as the product of an investigation into crime in Italy, he draws on the reader's expectations that crime fiction be violent, 'gritty', and shocking in its uncovering of unpalatable truths about contemporary society, in order to deliver to the reader a history of events which escalates those elements of crime fiction to the level of a national (and international) atrocity. The cover of the novel visualizes and materializes this effect. The cover itself has a small, circular hole, through which can be seen the illustration on the frontispiece of a gun. Seen from the outside, through the hole, the gun looks like the pistol of detective fiction book covers; opening the cover, the gun is seen to exceed the proportions of the hole through which it is viewed from the outside, and is revealed as a Kalashnikov rifle, the weapon of civil war and rebellion. Whilst playing on the notions of civil crime and war crime, this understanding of the narrative is also regulated by privileging the first-person perspective, the history of affects, and the 'modest' perspective of one 'ordinary' citizen. Finally, the novel uses the figures and filters of the fable to narrate the story of the violent abuse of Algyida, framing the story of one victim in thousands within a logic of timelessness which allows the effects of the unspeakable to be expressed in their moral magnitude.[37] In this way, the combination of genres serves particular purpose in the articulation of a transnational imagination.

Genre is, arguably, defined and regulated as much by publishers as by writers and literary traditions, and a further interpretation of Dekhis's use of the framework of crime fiction is that it affords him access to a more mainstream publication and distribution network than a 'migrant writer' might otherwise have. This novel is published, however, by L'ancora, the publishing house formerly known as 'L'ancora del Mediterraneo', and, as this title suggests, privileging texts related to the south of Italy and the Mediterranean. The prevalence of 'niche' publishers in the Italian publishing market is widely remarked, and the constraints, or not, of the association between migrant writers and specialized publishing houses merits consideration. Silvia Camilotti identifies three patterns of publication: publishers, often large, who publish texts by migrant writers sporadically and without any evident policy related to migration literature; publishers who regularly feature migrant writers in their list, but again, eschew dedicated series or other strategic initiatives; publishers established with the express strategy to bring migration literature into circulation.[38] Camilotti's map of the industry seems to me to be accurate and constructive, though I am uncomfortable with her premiss that what is needed is a concerted initiative in the publishing industry to establish 'un discorso interculturale vero e proprio', or 'un vero progetto politico-culturale' in relation to migrant writers.[39] An identifiable outlet – such as Fara, who published the writers successful in the Eks&Tra competitions[40] – through which migrant writers

---

37   For further discussion of this strategy, see Jennifer Burns, '*Lupus in fabula*: The Workings of Fear in Italian Migration Narratives', *Italian Studies*, 68.3 (2013, forthcoming).
38   Silvia Camilotti, 'L'editoria italiana della letteratura della migrazione', in Armando Gnisci (ed.), *Nuovo planetario italiano: Geografia e antologia della letteratura della migrazione in Italia e in Europa* (Troina (EN): Città aperta edizioni, 2006), 383–91.
39   Camilotti, 'L'editoria italiana della letteratura della migrazione', 383.
40   Eks&Tra is an organization supporting migrant writers since the mid-1990s, especially through high-profile competitions (1995–2007) from which the finalists were

might gain access to the publishing industry and to a readership primed to engage with their work is manifestly instrumental simply in increasing the volume of material circulated, and so generating traction in the process of 'deterritorializing' Italian literature. However, the risks of defining immigration or intercultural literature simply in those terms are that reception is similarly defined and self-perpetuating, and that, within the wider space of contemporary Italian literature, migration literature remains in a strictly marked ghetto. Interventions of the kind described above into genres not readily associated with migration literature are also restricted by the perception that such texts are, in the first place, about migration and intercultural exchange. Examples such as the novels of Albanian writer Ornela Vorpsi, published by Einaudi, and Younis Tawfik, published by Bompiani, demonstrate (in very different ways) that commercial and critical appeal can be identified in factors which do not deny or devalue the cultural interest of the experience of migration, but frame those experiences in the context of others which are of interest to a mainstream readership perhaps otherwise not at all concerned with questions of migration and its cultural expression.[41] That Italian migration literature has a presence across the publishing industry, in the lists of publishers whose commercial and cultural capital (though the two do not necessarily go hand-in-hand) is strong, moderate, or weak, is perhaps a more powerful indication that migrant writers have a stake in Italian literature than would be the existence of dedicated intercultural series in the operations of major publishers.

---

published in anthologies, e.g. Alessandro Ramberti and Roberta Sangiorgi, eds, *Le voci dell'arcobaleno* (Santarcangelo di Romagna: Fara, 1995). Many writers, e.g. Dekhis, were first published via this route. Since 2007, the annual competition has become a workshop. See http://www.eksetra.net/online-il-nuovo-sito-ekstra/ (accessed 6 May 2013).

41 Ornela Vorpsi has published a succession of highly acclaimed novels with Einaudi: *Il paese dove non si muore mai* (Turin: Einaudi, 2005), *La mano che non mordi* (Turin: Einaudi, 2007), *Bevete cacao Van Houten!* (Turin: Einaudi, 2010), *Fuorimondo* (Turin: Einaudi, 2012). On Vorpsi's work, see Daniele Comberiati, *Scrivere nella lingua dell'altro: La letteratura degli immigrati in Italia (1989–2007)* (Brussels: Peter Lang, 2010), 215–54.

A separate consideration, which relates to my comments above on the public visibility of migrant cultural production in Italy, is that of 'grass-roots' initiatives to publish, distribute, and more generally publicize migration literature, particularly in the context of the public 'ownership' of the dissemination of cultural information which communications technologies afford. One significant contribution offered by the literary prizes, such as Eks&Tra, and comparable initiatives is simply that they generate a groundswell of interest and activity, and generate an audience or readership. Particularly interesting is the possibility that the very 'event' of a competition or festival might engage in a spectacle viewers who subsequently become readers of texts they might not otherwise have sought out. Visibility thus turns very readily into cultural capital. Similarly, the initiative taken by Edizioni Dell'Arco and other small publishers in the early 2000s of placing migrant booksellers into the streets of major cities to distribute texts related to their home culture directly into public hands is a striking example of locating migration literature in the urban everyday, although its negative effect is perhaps to cement a perception of migrants and their cultural production as marginalized.[42] Nevertheless, this initiative endorses the view that there is cultural and commercial space for migration literature across the strata of Italian cultural life. Tied directly often to cultural associations (such as Eks&Tra) and so to forms of activity which extend well beyond publishing as conventionally conceived, such local and public initiatives create a continuum of cultural activity in which various products and practices co-exist and the published text can acquire a status more flexible than that associated with, for example, the Einaudi novel. Such forms of cultural production and dissemination perhaps achieve significant cultural capital and potential impact in the national public arena by virtue of the ways in which different kinds of cultural associations, cultural and political activists, community groups, and organs of production collaborate or simply

---

42   Edizioni Dell'Arco was the imprint of the Milan-based cultural association, Gruppo Solidarietà Come, and subsequently became Edizioni Dell'Arco-Marna (Ediarco). Examples of texts distributed in this way are Mbacke Gadji, *Numbelan. Il regno degli animali* and *Lo spirito delle sabbie gialle* (Milan: Edizioni dell'arco, 1996 and 1999, respectively). For further comments on this initiative, see Camilotti, 'L'editoria italiana della letteratura della migrazione', 386–9.

co-exist in such a way as to generate a mass of cultural activity. The regional funding and attached notion of a regional identity often associated with such activities may also play an important role, in the context particularly of Italy, in underwriting a principle of social and cultural inclusion for migrants. This pattern of cultural production – which one might define as capillary – characteristically deploys non-conventional modes of production, contact, and dissemination (e.g. communications technology and social networking) alongside more established ones (e.g. the published text), and is pluralistic and often collective in its modes of operation. In the contemporary context, it thus constitutes one potentially very powerful model of cultural production which helps to counter-balance the more conventional agents of cultural production whose activity, nevertheless, maintains its own crucial role in extending and shaping the culture industry.

This role might also be considered in terms of the opening towards migrant and minority cultures offered by publishers, often of the mainstream or 'quality' category. Aside from publishing the works of migrant or postcolonial writers themselves, there is evidence of a turn towards migration cultures and the histories or cultures which they indicate in the work of established writers identified absolutely as Italian. Cristina Mauceri has surveyed quite thoroughly the presence of migrant characters in novels by native Italian writers, but it is also interesting to trace the emergence in their work of figures and modes of expression which, as this volume has argued, have significant currency in the writings of migrants.[43] To quantify this 'influence' – if that is what it is – is not my concern here, but a few examples serve to assemble a perception of how certain thematics and poetics might converge. The aesthetics of walking, for example, animate many narratives of migration (as discussed in my previous chapter), especially those which engage with arrival in Italy and early efforts to find work and accommodation. Whilst a wider context includes a recent upsurge in interest in simple, or 'slow', modes of exploration, and from architecture to literature, there are experiments across cultures in 'vagabond' aesthetics,[44]

---

43 Maria Cristina Mauceri and Maria Grazia Negro, *Nuovo immaginario italiano: italiani e stranieri a confronto nella letteratura italiana contemporanea* (Rome: Sinnos, 2009).
44 The 'slow food' movement began in Italy and has achieved international success, spawning initiatives to promote 'slow travel', etc. See http://www.slowfood.it/

I think it is possible to see in a novel such as Marco Lodoli's *Isole: Guida vagabonda di Roma* a response to the migrant experience of discovering a city from street-level and navigating it along routes determined less by historical or architectural sites than by the needs and opportunities of the everyday.[45] Evidence for this interpretation is also offered by Lodoli's sketches within the narrative of various migrant communities and his expression of somewhat stereotyped and stereotyping responses to them.

More strikingly, Enrico Brizzi has also mobilized various walking initiatives, including walking the length of Italy, and has marked the aesthetic and literary value of walking by launching a series entitled 'A passo d'uomo' with the publisher Ediciclo, to publish narratives of historic journeys by foot.[46] Brizzi is also one of many writers, including Italians, Somali Italians (such as Scego) and migrants, who have brought Italy's colonial histories into the public imagination by means of narratives which include the colonial perspective on or experience of the nation. *L'inattesa piega degli eventi* narrates the journey to east Africa of an Italian sports journalist in 1960 to cover the 'Serie Africa' of the Italian football league, which opens up to him a different view of post-fascist and post-imperial Italy.[47] A collaborator of Brizzi in the 'A passo d'uomo' series is Wu Ming 2, whose novel co-authored with Antar Mohamed, *Timira*, is perhaps the most conspicuous example of a contemporary narrative which implants the experience of Italy from its colonies directly into a national history and into national culture.[48] Telling a story which echoes Fazel's *Nuvole dell'equatore*, it recounts the experiences from childhood to old age, in Italy in two periods and in Somalia, of a mixed-race Somali Italian woman, Isabella Marincola, or

---

(accessed 1 May 2013). For a prominent example of 'vagabond' art, see the designs and architecture of John Hejduk, discussed in Anthony Vidler, *The Architectural Uncanny: Essays in the Modern Unhomely* (Cambridge, MA: MIT Press, 1992), 207–14.

45   Marco Lodoli. *Isole: Guida vagabonda di Roma* (Turin: Einaudi, 2005).
46   See Brizzi's website for details: http://www.enricobrizzi.it/progetti.htm (accessed 24 April 2013).
47   Enrico Brizzi, *L'inattesa piega degli eventi* (Milan: Baldini Castoldi Dalai, 2008).
48   Wu Ming 2 and Antar Mohamed, *Timira* (Turin: Einaudi, 2012).

Timira. Using within the text historical documents and personal records and accounts, and recording in its paratext the archival and other forms of research which contributed to the realization of the novel, it stakes very prominently its claim to be offering an alternative – or, as Fazel phrases it, 'forgotten'[49] – history of Italy and Italians. At the same time, its narrative vitality and its 'epic' scope allow it also to stake a claim to be re-crafting the literary imagination of the nation. In fact, this and other examples suggest very strongly that migration, the postcolonial, and non-European cultures more broadly are an increasingly central, coherent, and historically situated figure of the Italian cultural imagination.

The collaboration of Antar Mohamed with one of the writers central to the 'New Italian Epic' movement and to the prominent Wu Ming collective offers an interesting – and refracted – mirror image of the collaboration between Mario Fortunato and Salah Methnani which was one of the key stimuli to the establishment of immigration literature in Italy. The issue of an imbalance in cultural agency which paved the way for, but also subsequently tripped up,[50] the collaboration between Fortunato and Methnani is tempered by the practice of collaborative writing which defines the Wu Ming collective and thus makes inclusive an operation which otherwise has been perceived as patronizing.[51] A compelling and

---

[49] The first subtitle of Fazel's novel is *Gli italiani dimenticati*.
[50] Disagreement over the 'ownership' of the written and published narrative later disrupted the working relationship between the two authors. Methnani reported to me his disagreement with Fortunato's publishers, Bompiani, over authorship of the novel during an interview (unpublished) in Rome on 13 November 2001. Methnani maintained that he had a written account in notebooks of his experiences, which formed the basis of the novel that the two authors elaborated. Fortunato's preface to the third edition of the novel records that he wrote the text alone after a series of discussions with Methnani about the latter's experiences of migration: Mario Fortunato, 'Introduzione. 16 anni dopo', in Mario Fortunato and Salah Methnani, *Immigrato* (Milan: Bompiani, 2006), I–IX (V–VI).
[51] The risks and responsibilities of co-authorship in these politically sensitive circumstances are discussed in detail in a letter from Wu Ming 2 to Isabella included within *Timira*. See 'Interludio. Lettera intermittente n. 3', in Wu Ming 2 and Mohamed, *Timira*, 342–6.

telling difference (which I am necessarily simplifying, and yet stands) is also that Fortunato and Methnani collaborated to tell a story of Italy, whereas Wu Ming 2 and Mohamed collaborate to tell a story of Somalia in order to establish its insistence in Italy. In this way, they recount not what it is to be in one location and culture or another, but rather what it is to be between them.[52] To present two novels in this way as symbolic of a particular process clearly erases a range of important discontinuities and specificities, but, these doubts notwithstanding, I think it is possible to see in *Immigrato* the beginning of migration literature in Italian, and in *Timira*, the confirmation of an opening out of Italian literature towards the transnational subject and the transnational literary text.

---

52   The cover of the novel announces it, under the title, as a 'romanzo meticcio'.

Afterword

It is not my intention to offer conclusions to this study of migrant imaginaries as expressed through the first twenty or more years of migration literature in Italian. As outlined in the introduction to this book, the purpose of the study has been not to close but to open more widely discussions about the imaginative and affective properties of the texts discussed. My chapters have sought to pose questions, rather than to answer them, about the impact of this literature on cultural imaginaries which might enunciate specific life experiences and connect individuals in ways as influential and arresting as those by which social practice and political policy might aim to encourage community cohesion. With these aims in mind, Chapter 5, 'Literature', drew together both internal and external perspectives on that topic, by analysing expressions in the texts themselves of reading and writing, and then moving outside the texts to consider the forms and possibilities of migration literature within a wider panorama of contemporary Italian literature. In this sense, there is little more to add to the perspectives suggested in individual chapters and consolidated in the latter part of Chapter 5.

One outcome of the enquiries into all of the selected figures in this study merits clearer articulation at this point, however. This is perhaps best described as the expansion not only of the field of Italian migration literature, but more compellingly, of the frame of reference to which these figures afford access. Considering the former, it is reasonable to assert that, twenty or more years on, migration literature itself continues to grow, as demonstrated by the emergence of new writers and the rate of production, and positive reception, of some longer-established writers. The phase of migration literature, understood as the production of those who themselves migrate, is not over, nor is likely to end, as trajectories of migration both consolidate and multiply. In addition, as noted in previous chapters, specifically postcolonial Italian literature is occupying an ever more prominent position in the cultural and historical consciousness of Italians, and both within and alongside this, the emergence of so-called 'second generation' writers is creating a cultural centrality for Italians of mixed ethnicities which, I think, marks a shift in literary imaginaries as well as in broader cultural positions. The field, in other words, is diversifying, productively.

Regarding the second element of expansion noted above – of the frame of reference which literary figures might expose – diversification is again, perhaps, an apt term. A distinction should be drawn in this case, however, between a notion of diversification along multiple, discrete strands, and diversification as incremental diffusion through new and interconnecting channels. What is noticeable in the accumulation of the various textual samples analysed under the umbrella of the selected figures of this study is a steady centrifugal push, which urges a sensitivity not only to imaginaries related to Italy, nor to Italy in relation to another place (of 'origin'), but to other places, or better, to other senses of what it is to occupy and move between plural histories, cultures, languages, and economies of images and affects. This is a literature populated by texts such as Amor Dekhis's *I lupi della notte*, which reads the history of Algeria into the future of Italy, or Shirin Ramzanali Fazel's *Nuvole sull'equatore*, Igiaba Scego's *La mia casa è dove sono*, and Wu Ming 2 and Antar Mohamed's *Timira*, all of which, differently, read the history of Somalia through Italy and the history of Italy through Somalia, or Ornela Vorpsi's novels, which imagine Albania without specifying a position from which to apprehend it. Amongst the authors in this list are migrants, postcolonial subjects, 'second generation' Somali Italians and Italian nationals, some resident in Italy and some elsewhere, and in this inclusion of diverse 'histories' and the cross-wiring of perspectives between them perhaps lies a more productive notion than that of Italian migration literature.[1] It is a notion which might in fact include Antonio Campobasso's work, with which I opened this enquiry.

The label most appropriate to attach to this notion is, arguably, transnational (Italian) literature. It is important to question, though, to what

---

1   For further exploration of this broader perspective on migration literature, cinema and culture more broadly in Italy, see Graziella Parati and Anthony Julian Tamburri, eds, *The Cultures of Italian Migration: Diverse Trajectories and Discrete Perspectives* (Madison, NJ: Fairleigh Dickinson University Press, 2011).

extent the literature outlined above genuinely transgresses the borders of the nation, given that it is a literature published in Italy and in the Italian language, which is one which is itself a 'minor' language in the global context. This said, some of the texts cited above are of those relatively rare ones which have been translated into other languages, and in this sense, they meet one of David Damrosch's definitions of 'world literature', that it passes from one literary system into another.[2] 'World literature' makes somewhat different claims, however, from the notion of the 'transnational', implying a capacity to move and to signify across multiple 'systems' through the globe. Returning to the quotation from Michel de Certeau used at the beginning of this book – 'To speak means to come forward and to locate oneself in one's sphere of existence; it means to claim a modest quantum of agency'[3] – transnational literature makes a perhaps more 'modest' claim to establish a voice between and across nationally defined 'spheres of existence', or indeed, to assert agency in disrupting the notion of 'national' literatures by stretching the borders of one or more languages, cultures, histories, and imaginaries out towards others. It is reasonable to argue, then, that whilst using a 'national' language (though one which is already internally outspread across regions and dialects, as well as extending to emigrant communities across the world), the expanded notion of Italian migration literature which I outline above, and which has emerged from this study, is 'transnational' because its writers move through various, combined trajectories, its readers apprehend multiple histories, cultures, and languages through it, and, perhaps most compellingly, its range of figures have multiple anchoring points by which they provisionally touch ground in and between imaginaries shaped in diverse places and times. This afterword therefore looks forward to the expansion of transnational imaginaries through the medium of Italian literature.

2 '[A] work only has an *effective* life as world literature whenever, and wherever, it is actively present within a literary system beyond that of its original culture'; David Damrosch, *What is World Literature?* (Princeton, NJ: Princeton University Press, 2003), 4 (italics in original).
3 Michel de Certeau, *The Capture of Speech and Other Political Writings*, ed. by Luce Giard, trans. and afterword by Tom Conley (Minneapolis, MN: University of Minnesota Press, 1997), 98.

Bibliography

Primary Texts

Bouchane, Mohamed, *Chiamatemi Alì*, ed. by Carla De Girolamo and Daniele Miccione (Milan: Leonardo, 1990).
Brioni, Simone, ed., *Somalitalia: Quattro vie per Mogadiscio* (Rome: Kimerafilm, 2012).
Brizzi, Enrico, *L'inattesa piega degli eventi* (Milan: Baldini Castoldi Dalai, 2008).
Campobasso, Antonio, *Nero di Puglia* (Milan: Feltrinelli, 1980).
Dekhis, Amor, 'La preghiera degli altri', in Alessandro Ramberti and Roberta Sangiorgi, eds, *Le voci dell'arcobaleno* (Santarcangelo di Romagna: Fara, 1995), 185–97.
——, *I lupi della notte* (Naples: L'ancora, 2008).
Ellis, Bret Easton, *Less Than Zero* (London: Picador, 1986).
Fazel, Shirin Ramzanali, *Lontano da Mogadiscio* (Rome: Datanews, 1994).
——, *Nuvole sull'equatore. Gli italiani dimenticati. Una storia* (Cuneo: Nerosubianco, 2010).
Fortunato, Mario, and Salah Methnani, *Immigrato* (Rome: Theoria, 1990; 3rd edn, Milan: Bompiani, 2006).
Gadji, Mbacke, *Numbelan. Il regno degli animali* (Milan: Edizioni Dell'Arco, 1996).
——, *Lo spirito delle sabbie gialle* (Milan: Edizioni Dell'Arco, 1999).
Khouma, Pap, *Io, venditore di elefanti: Una vita per forza fra Dakar, Parigi e Milano*, ed. by Oreste Pivetta (Milan: Garzanti, 1990).
Kubati, Ron, *M* (Nardò (LE): Besa, 2002).
Kuruvilla, Gabriella, Ingy Mubiayi, Igiaba Scego, and Laila Wadia, *Pecore nere: Racconti*, ed. by Flavia Capitani and Emanuele Coen (Rome: Laterza, 2005).
Lakhous, Amara, *Scontro di civiltà per un ascensore a piazza Vittorio* (Rome: e/o, 2006).
——, *Divorzio all'islamica a viale Marconi* (Rome: e/o, 2010).
Lamri, Tahar, 'Solo allora, sono certo, potrò capire', in Alessandro Ramberti and Roberta Sangiorgi, eds, *Le voci dell'arcobaleno* (Santarcangelo di Romagna: Fara, 1995), 35–53.
Levi, Primo, *Se questo è un uomo* (Turin: Einaudi, 1976).
Makaping, Geneviève, *Traiettorie di sguardi: E se gli altri foste voi?* (Soveria Mannelli: Rubbettino, 2001).

McInerney, Jay, *Bright Lights, Big City* (New York: Vintage Contemporaries, 1984).
Melliti, Mohsen, *Pantanella: Canto lungo la strada*, trans. by Monica Ruocco (Rome: Edizioni Lavoro, 1992).
Orton, Marie, and Graziella Parati, eds, *Multicultural Literature in Contemporary Italy* (Madison, NJ: Fairleigh Dickinson University Press, 2007).
Parati, Graziella, ed., *Mediterranean Crossroads: Migration Literature in Italy* (Cranbury, NJ: Associated University Presses, 1999).
Parenzan, Ramona, ed., *Babel Hotel: Vite migranti nel condominio più controverso d'Italia* (Castel Gandolfo (Rome): Infinito edizioni, 2011).
Ramberti, Alessandro, and Roberta Sangiorgi, eds, *Le voci dell'arcobaleno* (Santarcangelo di Romagna: Fara, 1995).
——, and Roberta Sangiorgi, eds, *Parole oltre i confini* (Santarcangelo di Romagna: Fara, 1999).
Scego, Igiaba, *La mia casa è dove sono* (Milan: Rizzoli, 2010).
Sibhatu, Ribka, *Aulò! Aulò! Aulò! Poesie di nostalgia, d'esilio e d'amore*, ed. by Simone Brioni (Rome: Kimerafilm, 2012).
Smari, Abdel Malek, *Fiamme in paradiso* (Milan: Il Saggiatore, 2000).
Sokeng, Gertrude, 'La storia di Fatima', in Alessandro Ramberti and Roberta Sangiorgi, eds, *Parole oltre i confini* (Santarcangelo di Romagna: Fara, 1999), 157–78.
Tawfik, Younis, *La straniera* (Milan: Bompiani, 1999).
——, *As-Salamu alaikum. Corso di arabo moderno* (Turin: Ananke, 1999).
——, *La città di Iram* (Milan: Bompiani, 2002).
——, *Islam. Dai califfi all'integralismo* (Turin: Ananke, 2004).
——, *Il profugo* (Milan: Bompiani, 2006).
——, *La sposa ripudiata* (Milan: Bompiani, 2011).
——, *La ragazza di piazza Tahrir* (Siena: Barbera, 2012).
Vorpsi, Ornela, *Il paese dove non si muore mai* (Turin: Einaudi, 2005).
——, *La mano che non mordi* (Turin: Einaudi, 2007).
——, *Bevete cacao Van Houten!* (Turin: Einaudi, 2010).
——, *Fuorimondo* (Turin: Einaudi, 2012).
Wu Ming 2 and Antar Mohamed, *Timira* (Turin: Einaudi, 2012).

Secondary Texts

Ahmed, Sara, 'Home and Away: Narratives of Migration and Estrangement', *International Journal of Cultural Studies*, 2.3 (1999), 329–47.
——, *Strange Encounters: Embodied Others in Post-Coloniality* (London: Routledge, 2000).
——, Claudia Castañeda, Anne-Marie Fortier and Mimi Sheller, eds, *Uprootings/Regroundings: Questions of Home and Migration* (Oxford: Berg, 2003).
——, *The Cultural Politics of Emotion* (Edinburgh: Edinburgh University Press, 2004).
Allen, Beverly, and Mary Russo, eds, *Revisioning Italy: National Identity and Global Culture* (Minneapolis, MN: University of Minnesota Press, 1997).
Amin, Ash, and Nigel Thrift, *Cities: Reimagining the Urban* (Cambridge: Polity, 2002).
Andall, Jacqueline, and Derek Duncan, eds, *National Belongings: Hybridity in Italian Colonial and Postcolonial Cultures* (Oxford: Peter Lang, 2010).
Anderson, Benedict, *Imagined Communities: Reflections on the Origin and Spread of Nationalisms* (London: Verso, 2006).
Ashcroft, Bill, Gareth Griffiths, Helen Tiffin, eds, *The Post-Colonial Studies Reader* (London: Routledge, 1995).
Augé, Marc, *Non-places. Introduction to an Anthropology of Supermodernity*, trans. by John Howe (London: Verso, 1995).
Bakhtin, Mikhail, *The Dialogic Imagination: Four Essays*, ed. by Michael Holquist, trans. by Caryl Emerson and Michael Holquist (Austin, TX: University of Texas Press, 1981).
Bal, Mieke, Jonathan Crewe, and Leo Spitzer, eds, *Acts of Memory: Cultural Recall in the Present* (Hanover, NH: Dartmouth College and University Press of New England, 1999).
Bauman, Zygmunt, 'From Pilgrim to Tourist – or a Short History of Identity', in Stuart Hall and Paul du Gay, eds, *Questions of Cultural Identity* (London: Sage, 1996), 18–36.
Ben-Ghiat, Ruth, and Mia Fuller, eds, *Italian Colonialism* (New York: Palgrave Macmillan, 2005).
Benjamin, Walter, *One-Way Street, and Other Writings*, trans. by Edmund Jephcott and Kingsley Shorter (London: Verso, 1997).
——, *The Arcades Project*, translated by Howard Eiland and Kevin McLaughlin (Cambridge, MA: Belknap Press, 2002).

—— , *The Writer of Modern Life: Essays on Charles Baudelaire*, ed. by Michael W. Jennings, trans. by Howard Eiland, Edmund Jephcott, Rodney Livingston and Harry Zohn (Cambridge, MA: Belknap Press, 2006).

Bhabha, Homi K., *The Location of Culture* (London: Routledge, 1994).

Booth, Wayne, *The Company We Keep: An Ethics of Fiction* (Berkeley, CA: University of California Press, 1988).

Braidotti, Rosi, *Nomadic Subjects: Embodiment and Sexual Difference in Contemporary Feminist Theory* (New York: Columbia University Press, 1994).

Brison, Susan J., 'Trauma Narratives and the Remaking of the Self', in Mieke Bal, Jonathan Crewe, and Leo Spitzer, eds, *Acts of Memory: Cultural Recall in the Present* (Hanover, NH: Dartmouth College and University Press of New England, 1999), 39–54.

Burns, Jennifer, 'Recent Immigrant Writing in Italian: A Fragile Enterprise', *The Italianist*, 18 (1998), 213–44.

—— , *Fragments of impegno: Interpretations of Commitment in Contemporary Italian Narrative, 1980–2000* (Leeds: Northern Universities Press, 2001).

—— , 'Exile Within Italy: Interactions between Past and Present "homes" in Texts in Italian by Migrant Writers', *Annali d'Italianistica*, 20 (2002), 369–83.

—— , 'Borders Within the Text: Authorship, Collaboration and Mediation in Writing in Italian by Immigrants', in Jennifer Burns and Loredana Polezzi, eds, *Borderlines: Migrant Writing and Italian Identities (1870–2000) / Borderlines: Migrazioni e identità nel Novecento* (Isernia: Iannone, 2003), 387–94.

—— , 'Provisional Constructions of the Eternal City: Figurations of Rome in Recent Italophone Writing', in Christian Emden, Catherine Keen and David Midgley, eds, *Imagining the City*, 2 vols (Oxford: Peter Lang, 2006), II, 357–73.

—— , 'Outside Voices Within: Immigration Literature in Italian', in Gillian Ania and Ann Hallamore Caesar, eds, *Trends in Contemporary Italian Writing* (Newcastle: Cambridge Scholars Publishing, 2007), 136–54.

—— , 'Language and its Alternatives in Italophone Migrant Writing', in Jacqueline Andall and Derek Duncan, eds, *National Belongings: Hybridity in Italian Colonial and Postcolonial Cultures* (Oxford: Peter Lang, 2010), 127–47.

—— , '*Lupus in fabula*: The Workings of Fear in Italian Migration Narratives', *Italian Studies*, 68.3 (2013), forthcoming.

Butler, Judith, *Gender Trouble: Feminism and the Subversion of Identity* (London: Routledge, 1990).

—— , *Bodies That Matter: On the Discursive Limits of 'Sex'* (London: Routledge, 1993).

—— , *Giving an Account of Oneself* (New York: Fordham University Press, 2005).

Camilotti, Silvia, 'L'editoria italiana della letteratura della migrazione', in Armando Gnisci, ed., *Nuovo planetario italiano: Geografia e antologia della letteratura della migrazione in Italia e in Europa* (Troina (EN): Città aperta edizioni, 2006).

Caruth, Cathy, ed., *Trauma: Explorations in Memory* (Baltimore, MD: Johns Hopkins University Press, 1995).

Cavarero, Adriana, *Tu che mi guardi, tu che mi racconti: Filosofia della narrazione* (Milan: Feltrinelli, 1997).

Chambers, Iain, *Migrancy, Culture, Identity* (London: Routledge, 1994).

Cixous, Hélène, and Catherine Clément, *The Newly Born Woman*, trans. by Betsy Wing, introduction by Sandra M. Gilbert (Manchester: Manchester University Press, 1986).

Comberiati, Daniele, *La quarta sponda: Scrittrici in viaggio dall'Africa coloniale all'Italia di oggi* (Rome: Edizioni Pigreco, 2007).

——, *Scrivere nella lingua dell'altro: La letteratura degli immigrati in Italia (1989–2007)* (Brussels: Peter Lang, 2010).

Connerton, Paul, *How Modernity Forgets* (Cambridge: Cambridge University Press, 2009).

Damrosch, David, *What is World Literature?* (Princeton, NJ: Princeton University Press, 2003).

de Certeau, Michel, *The Practice of Everyday Life*, trans. by Steven Rendall (Berkeley, CA: University of California Press, 1984).

——, *The Capture of Speech and Other Political Writings*, ed. by Luce Giard, trans. and afterword by Tom Conley (Minneapolis, MN: University of Minnesota Press, 1997).

——, *Culture in the Plural*, introduction by Luce Giard, trans. and afterword by Tom Conley (Minneapolis, MN: University of Minnesota Press, 1997).

Deleuze, Gilles, and Félix Guattari, *Kafka: Toward a Minor Literature*, trans. by Dana Polan (Minneapolis, MN: University of Minnesota Press, 1986).

Derobertis, Roberto, 'Insorgenze letterarie nella disseminazione delle migrazioni. Contesti, definizioni e politiche culturali delle scritture migranti', in *Scritture migranti*, 1 (2007), 27–52.

Derrida, Jacques, *Of Grammatology*, trans. by Gayatri Chakravorty Spivak (Baltimore, MD: Johns Hopkins University Press, 1976).

Duncan, Derek, 'Cultural Assimilation and Heterosexual Entitlement in Fortunato and Methnani's *Immigrato*', in Jennifer Burns and Loredana Polezzi, eds, *Borderlines: Migrant Writing and Italian Identities (1870–2000) / Borderlines: Migrazioni e identità nel Novecento* (Isernia: Iannone, 2003), 379–85.

Eco, Umberto, *Opera aperta* (Milan: Bompiani, 1962).

Fischer, Michael M.J., 'Ethnicity and the Post-Modern Arts of Memory', in James Clifford and George E. Marcus, eds, *Writing Culture: The Poetics and Politics of Ethnography* (Berkeley, CA: University of California Press, 1986), 194–233.

Fortier, Anne-Marie, *Migrant Belongings: Memory, Space, Identity* (Oxford: Berg, 2000).

Gedalof, Irene, 'Taking (a) Place: Female Embodiment and the Re-grounding of Community', in Sara Ahmed, Claudia Castañeda, Anne-Marie Fortier and Mimi Sheller, eds, *Uprootings/Regroundings: Questions of Home and Migration* (Oxford: Berg, 2003), 91–112.

Ginzburg, Carlo, 'Spie. Radici di un paradigma indiziario', in *Miti emblemi spie. Morfologia e storia* (Turin: Einaudi, 2000), 158–209.

Gnisci, Armando, *Il rovescio del gioco* (Rome: Sovera, 1993).

——, *Una storia diversa* (Rome: Meltemi, 2001).

——, ed., *Nuovo planetario italiano: Geografia e antologia della letteratura della migrazione in Italia e in Europa* (Troina (EN): Città aperta edizioni, 2006).

Hall, Stuart, 'Cultural Identity and Diaspora', in Jonathan Rutherford, ed., *Identity, Community, Culture, Difference* (London: Lawrence and Wishart, 1990), 222–37.

——, and Paul du Gay, eds, *Questions of Cultural Identity* (London: Sage, 1996).

Hämeen-Anttila, Jaakko, *Maqama: A History of a Genre* (Wiesbaden: Harrassowitz, 2002).

Harlow, Barbara, *Resistance Literature* (New York: Methuen, 1987).

hooks, bell, *Yearning: Race, Gender, and Cultural Politics* (London: Turnaround, 1991).

Huntington, Samuel P., *The Clash of Civilizations and the Remaking of World Order* (New York: Samuel and Schuster, 1996).

Hutcheon, Linda, 'Circling the Downspout of Empire', in Bill Ashcroft, Gareth Griffiths, Helen Tiffin, eds, *The Post-Colonial Studies Reader* (London and New York: Routledge, 1995), 130–5.

Iser, Wolfgang, *The Act of Reading: A Theory of Aesthetic Response* (London: Routledge & Kegan Paul, 1978).

Laub, Dori, 'Truth and Testimony: The Process and the Struggle', in Cathy Caruth, ed., *Trauma: Explorations in Memory* (Baltimore, MD: Johns Hopkins University Press, 1995), 61–75.

Lefebvre, Henri, *The Production of Space*, trans. by Donald Nicholson-Smith (Oxford: Blackwell, 1991).

——, *Writings on Cities*, trans. and ed. by Eleonore Kofman and Elizabeth Lebas (Oxford: Blackwell, 1996).

——, *Critique of Everyday Life*, trans. by John Moore (London: Verso, 2008).

Lombardi-Diop, Cristina, and Caterina Romeo, eds, *Postcolonial Italy: Challenging National Homogeneity* (New York: Palgrave Macmillan, 2012).

Mauceri, Maria Cristina, 'Andare e non tornare: I finali in alcuni romanzi della letteratura della migrazione in Italia', in Franca Sinopoli and Silvia Tatti, eds, *I confini della scrittura. Il dispatrio nei testi letterari* (Isernia: Iannone, 2005), 89–99.

——, and Maria Grazia Negro, *Nuovo immaginario italiano: italiani e stranieri a confronto nella letteratura italiana contemporanea* (Rome: Sinnos, 2009).

Morone, Antonio Maria, *L'ultima colonia: come l'Italia è ritornata in Somalia, 1950–1960* (Rome: Laterza, 2011).

Parati, Graziella, 'Strangers in Paradise: Foreigners and Shadows in Italian Literature', in Beverly Allen and Mary Russo, eds, *Revisioning Italy: National Identity and Global Culture* (Minneapolis, MN: University of Minnesota Press, 1997), 169–90.

——, *Migration Italy: The Art of Talking Back in a Destination Culture* (Toronto: University of Toronto Press, 2005).

——, and Anthony Julian Tamburri, eds, *The Cultures of Italian Migration: Diverse Trajectories and Discrete Perspectives* (Madison, NJ: Fairleigh Dickinson University Press, 2011).

Pezzarossa, Fulvio, and Ilaria Rossini, *Leggere il testo e il mondo: Vent'anni di scritture della migrazione in Italia* (Bologna: CLUEB, 2011).

Ponzanesi, Sandra, 'Imaginary Cities: Space and Identity in Italian Literature of Immigration', in *Italian Cityscapes: Culture and Urban Change in Contemporary Italy*, ed. by Robert Lumley and John Foot (Exeter: University of Exeter Press, 2004), 156–65.

——, *Paradoxes of Postcolonial Culture: Contemporary Women Writers of the Indian and Afro-Italian Diaspora* (Albany, NY: State University of New York Press, 2004).

——, and Daniela Merolla, eds, *Migrant Cartographies: New Cultural and Literary Spaces in Post-Colonial Europe* (Oxford: Lexington Books, 2005).

Said, Edward, *Orientalism* (London: Routledge & Kegan Paul, 1978).

——, *Reflections on Exile and Other Essays* (Cambridge, MA: Harvard University Press, 2000).

Sheringham, Michael, *Everyday Life: Theories and Practices from Surrealism to the Present* (Oxford: Oxford University Press, 2006).

Sinopoli, Franca, 'Poetiche della migrazione nella letteratura italiana contemporanea: il discorso autobiografico', in Armando Gnisci, ed., *Miscellanea comparatistica*; *Studi (e testi) italiani: Semestrale del Dipartimento di italianistica e spettacolo dell'Università di Roma 'La Sapienza'*, 7 (2001), 189–206.

——, and Silvia Tatti, eds, *I confini della scrittura. Il dispatrio nei testi letterari* (Isernia: Iannone, 2005).

Soja, Edward W., *Postmodern Geographies: The Reassertion of Space in Critical Social Theory* (London: Verso, 1989).

Thrift, Nigel, *Non-Representational Theory: Space, Politics, Affect* (London: Routledge, 2007).
Tiffin, Helen, 'Post-Colonial Literatures and Counter-Discourse', in Bill Ashcroft, Gareth Griffiths and Helen Tiffin, eds, *The Post-Colonial Studies Reader* (London: Routledge, 1995), 95–8.
van der Kolk, Bessel A., and Onno van der Hart, 'The Intrusive Past: The Flexibility of Memory and the Engraving of Trauma', in Cathy Caruth, ed., *Trauma: Explorations in Memory* (Baltimore, MD: Johns Hopkins University Press, 1995), 158–82.
Vidler, Anthony, *The Architectural Uncanny: Essays in the Modern Unhomely* (Cambridge, MA: MIT Press, 1992).

Filmography

Il divo, dir. Paolo Sorrentino (2008).
La dolce vita, dir. Federico Fellini (1960).
Romanzo criminale, dir. Michele Placido (2005).

Websites

Acqua Marcia, http://www.acquamarcia.it/website/projects.aspx?pid=45&sid=2&cid=1&lid=1 (accessed 6 December 2012).
Albanese, Carmelo, 'Via Casilina n.0 – storia del Pantanella, nel 1990', http://www.youtube.com/watch?v=aR62UXhhyRU (accessed 6 December 2012).
BASILI (Banca Dati sugli Scrittori Immigrati in Lingua Italiana), http://www.disp.let.uniroma1.it/basili2001/ (accessed 1 May 2013).
Biblioteca Salaborsa, http://www.bibliotecasalaborsa.it/content/percorsi/scrittorimigrantifilm.html (accessed 30 April 2013).
Brizzi, Enrico, http://www.enricobrizzi.it/progetti.htm (accessed 24 April 2013).
Corriere della Sera, http://archiviostorico.corriere.it/1993/luglio/29 (accessed 6 December 2012).

Corriere della Sera, http://archiviostorico.corriere.it/1993/luglio/29/svolta_Formentini_appello_all_unita_co_0_9307296791.shtml (accessed 6 December 2012).
Eks&Tra, http://www.eksetra.net/online-il-nuovo-sito-ekstra/ (accessed 6 May 2013).
Kulthum, Umm, 'Enta Omri' (You Are My Life), Théâtre Olympia, Paris, November 1967, http://www.youtube.com/watch?v=XPGHpBOt5sE (accessed 6 June 2013).
Roma sparita, http://www.romasparita.eu/foto-roma-sparita/tag/via-casilina/page/1/ (accessed 6 December 2012).
Slow food, http://www.slowfood.it/ (accessed 1 May 2013).

Interview

Methnani, Salah, interviewed by Jennifer Burns (unpublished), Rome, 13 November 2001.

Index

Ahmed, Sara 14–15, 19, 21, 25, 30, 33, 34, 48, 54, 103–4, 112, 116, 118, 120, 125, 126, 129, 130 n, 186
Albania 17, 82, 199, 206
Algeria 6, 9, 13, 24, 41, 69, 84–91, 94–5, 96, 97, 110, 127, 129–30, 158, 160, 166, 168, 195, 197, 206
autobiography 15, 16, 26, 186, 192, 196, 197
 see also genre

bodies 13–14, 24, 34, 53, 56, 59–60, 62, 74–5, 79, 81, 83, 105, 106 n, 107, 112, 116–19, 127, 129, 165, 170, 186
Bouchane, Mohamed 23
Brizzi, Enrico 202

Campobasso, Antonio 1–3, 9, 13, 206
colonialism, Italian 2–3, 20, 55, 126–7, 168, 190, 194, 202
 see also postcolonial literature and theory

de Certeau, Michel 1, 4, 6, 12, 20, 23, 99, 102–3, 104, 106, 119, 122, 130, 134–5, 136, 141, 144, 164–5, 191–5, 207
Dekhis, Amor 18, 69, 84–90, 91, 92–8, 109 n, 112, 127, 181, 182, 188, 197, 198, 206
desert 74, 97, 107–9, 143–4, 180, 183

Egypt 47, 54, 119, 121, 169, 171, 181
Eks&Tra 198, 200

Fazel, Shirin Ramzanali 18, 185, 190
 Lontano da Mogadiscio 105, 122–6
 Nuvole sull'equatore. Gli italiani dimenticati. Una storia 26, 55–64, 126–8, 202, 203, 206
Fortunato, Mario
 see Methnani, Salah

Gadji, Mbacke 200
genre 9, 95, 177, 180, 196–8, 199
 crime fiction and thriller 95, 197, 198
 fable, fairy-tale, folk-tale 98, 122, 123, 180, 197
 magical realism 184–6
 maqama 181
 see also autobiography; New Italian Epic

Iraq 13, 50, 75–82, 113, 122, 151, 185
Islam 12, 17, 23, 24, 47–54, 76, 97, 106, 112, 114, 116, 119, 121, 169, 189
 Islamic extremism 50, 86–9, 91, 94–5, 98, 171

Khouma, Pap 10, 15
Kubati, Ron 163–6, 171, 174

Lakhous, Amara 18, 26, 40, 166, 175
 Scontro di civiltà per un ascensore a piazza Vittorio 41–6, 70, 91–3, 166–8, 179, 181
 Divorzio all'islamica a viale Marconi 46–55, 61, 105, 111–12, 115–16 n, 119–21, 125, 168–73, 181

Lamri, Tahar 129–30
language, use of 4, 8, 18–19, 26, 27, 33, 37, 47, 74, 99, 168, 177, 188–91, 192, 195, 196, 207

Melliti, Mohsen 9, 18, 69–75, 98, 139–50, 160, 162, 169, 174, 179, 181, 182–4, 185, 186 n, 197
Methnani, Salah 10, 203 n
   Fortunato, Mario and Salah Methnani 10, 15, 18, 26–35, 40, 70, 144 n, 178–9, 188, 203–4
Milan 1, 24, 126, 133, 136, 138, 158–62, 200 n
Mohamed, Antar
   see Wu Ming 2 and Antar Mohamed
Morocco 30, 36, 114, 152, 161 n

New Italian Epic 203
nomadism 8, 63–4, 103 n, 120

postcolonial literature and theory 7, 13, 16, 38, 125, 126–7, 168, 184–8, 190–1, 193, 201, 203, 205, 206
   see also colonialism, Italian

Rome 32, 40, 42–5, 47, 48, 52, 54, 59, 63, 70, 72, 91, 92, 94, 111–12, 119–21, 126, 127 n, 128, 133, 136, 138, 139–51, 155, 166–73, 175, 182, 186 n, 195, 202
   Stazione Termini 63, 128, 144

Scego, Igiaba 16 n, 127, 193, 202, 206
sexualities 24, 27–8, 31–4, 36–7, 49, 62, 76 n, 106, 115–19
Smari, Abdel Malek 18, 24, 110–11, 112, 135, 158–62, 174, 181
Somalia 6, 13, 16, 55–64, 122–7, 128, 185, 190, 195, 202, 204, 206

Tawfik, Younis 18, 76 n, 199
   La straniera 26, 35–40, 41, 46, 49, 105–10, 112–19, 151–8, 162, 169, 180–1, 182
   Il profugo 69, 75–83, 84, 98, 122, 179, 185
transnational literature 20, 90, 91, 195, 196, 198, 204, 206–7
trauma 67, 69–70, 82–96, 103, 125, 140, 180
Tunisia 6, 22, 26, 27, 29, 31, 33, 34, 46–7, 69, 121, 169, 179, 195
Turin 35, 37, 39, 78, 105, 108, 133, 136, 138, 151–8

Vorpsi, Ornela 199, 206

wolves 98, 168
women, representations of 26, 36, 47–64, 112–13, 114–21, 148, 155–7, 169–71
Wu Ming 2 and Antar Mohamed 203–4, 206
   Wu Ming, Wu Ming 2 202, 203

ITALIAN MODERNITIES

Edited by
Pierpaolo Antonello and Robert Gordon,
University of Cambridge

The series aims to publish innovative research on the written, material and visual cultures and intellectual history of modern Italy, from the 19th century to the present day. It is open to a wide variety of different approaches and methodologies, disciplines and interdisciplinary fields: from literary criticism and comparative literature to archival history, from cultural studies to material culture, from film and media studies to art history. It is especially interested in work which articulates aspects of Italy's particular, and in many respects, peculiar, interactions with notions of modernity and postmodernity, broadly understood. It also aims to encourage critical dialogue between new developments in scholarship in Italy and in the English-speaking world.
Proposals are welcome for either single-author monographs or edited collections (in English and/or Italian). Please provide a detailed outline, a sample chapter, and a CV. For further information, contact the series editors, Pierpaolo Antonello (paa25@cam.ac.uk) and Robert Gordon (rscg1@cam.ac.uk).

Vol. 1 Olivia Santovetti: *Digression: A Narrative Strategy in the Italian Novel*. 260 pages, 2007.
ISBN 978-3-03910-550-2

Vol. 2 Julie Dashwood and Margherita Ganeri (eds):
The Risorgimento of Federico De Roberto. 339 pages, 2009.
ISBN 978-3-03911-858-8

Vol. 3 Pierluigi Barrotta and Laura Lepschy with Emma Bond (eds):
Freud and Italian Culture. 252 pages, 2009.
ISBN 978-3-03911-847-2

Vol. 4 Pierpaolo Antonello and Florian Mussgnug (eds):
*Postmodern Impegno: Ethics and Commitment in
Contemporary Italian Culture.* 354 pages, 2009.
ISBN 978-3-0343-0125-1

Vol. 5 Florian Mussgnug: *The Eloquence of Ghosts:
Giorgio Manganelli and the Afterlife of the Avant-Garde.*
257 pages, 2010.
ISBN 978-3-03911-835-9

Vol. 6 Christopher Rundle: *Publishing Translations in Fascist Italy.*
268 pages, 2010.
ISBN 978-3-03911-831-1

Vol. 7 Jacqueline Andall and Derek Duncan (eds): *National Belongings:
Hybridity in Italian Colonial and Postcolonial Cultures.*
251 pages, 2010.
ISBN 978-3-03911-965-3

Vol. 8 Emiliano Perra: *Conflicts of Memory: The Reception of
Holocaust Films and TV Programmes in Italy, 1945 to the
Present.* 299 pages, 2010.
ISBN 978-3-03911-880-9

Vol. 9 Alan O'Leary: *Tragedia all'italiana: Italian Cinema and Italian
Terrorisms, 1970–2010.* 300 pages, 2011.
ISBN 978-3-03911-574-7

Vol. 10 Robert Lumley: *Entering the Frame: Cinema and History in
the Films of Yervant Gianikian and Angela Ricci Lucchi.*
228 pages. 2011.
ISBN 978-3-0343-0113-8

Vol. 11 Enrica Maria Ferrara: *Calvino e il teatro: storia di una
passione rimossa.* 284 pages, 2011.
ISBN 978-3-0343-0176-3

Vol. 12 Niamh Cullen: *Piero Gobetti's Turin: Modernity, Myth and
Memory.* 343 pages, 2011.
ISBN 978-3-0343-0262-3

Vol. 13 Jeffrey T. Schnapp: *Modernitalia*. 338 pages, 2012.
ISBN 978-3-0343-0762-8

Vol. 14 Eleanor Canright Chiari: *Undoing Time: The Cultural Memory of an Italian Prison*. 275 pages, 2012.
ISBN 978-3-0343-0256-2

Vol. 15 Alvise Sforza Tarabochia: *Psychiatry, Subjectivity, Community: Franco Basaglia and Biopolitics*. 226 pages, 2013.
ISBN 978-3-0343-0893-9

Vol. 16 Katharine Mitchell and Helena Sanson (eds): *Women and Gender in Post-Unification Italy: Between Private and Public Spheres*. 282 pages, 2013.
ISBN 978-3-0343-0996-7

Vol. 17 Enrico Cesaretti: *Fictions of Appetite: Alimentary Discourses in Italian Modernist Literature*. 280 pages, 2013.
ISBN 978-30343-0971-4

Vol. 18 Jennifer Burns: *Migrant Imaginaries: Figures in Italian Migration Literature*. 228 pages, 2013.
ISBN 978-3-0343-0986-8

www.ingramcontent.com/pod-product-compliance
Lightning Source LLC
LaVergne TN
LVHW012014060526
838201LV00061B/4309